Schools for the shires

The reform of middle-class education in mid-Victorian England

DAVID IAN ALLSOBROOK

Schools for the shires

The reform of
middle-class education in
mid-Victorian England

MANCHESTER UNIVERSITY PRESS

Copyright © David Ian Allsobrook 1986

Published by Manchester University Press,
Oxford Road, Manchester, M13 9PL, UK

British Library cataloguing in publication data
Allsobrook, David Ian
    Schools for the shires: the reform of middle-class
    education in mid-Victorian England.
    1. Middle classes – Education – England – History
    – 19th century
    I. Title
    371.96   LC4975.G7

ISBN 0–7190–1972–9

Photoset in Linotron Sabon by
Northern Phototypesetting Co., Bolton
Printed and bound in Great Britain by
Biddles Ltd, Guildford and King's Lynn

Contents

Preface and acknowledgements

I heartily thank the Keepers of Records, Librarians, and the multitude of their assistants for so much invaluable help in the long trawl of research which was the central activity in this project: the staff at the Public Record Office, at Chancery Lane and in Kew, and of the Guildhall Record Office in London; the local archivists in the old County of Glamorgan and the new County of Gwent, in Leicester, Hampshire, Worcester and Devon; at the Royal College of Agriculture, Cirencester, at the Universities of Bath (Bath and West Collection) and Bristol, and especially at University College, Cardiff.

Above all I am most grateful to the Archivist of the Northants County Record Office whose staff, in 1969, were worried into finding the Minute Books of the Northants Education Society without which this study would have lacked any sense of direction.

With more than customary candour I claim the errors in this book as wholly my own. But without the initial interest shown by Professor Brian Simon of Leicester University, I should never have begun; and if I had ever lacked his encouragement, the project would never have been completed. My colleagues at University College, Cardiff, by sometimes easing my considerable teaching load in past years, have contributed more significantly than perhaps they appreciate. At various times I have discussed the main thesis of the book with Professor John Roach of Sheffield University, Dr David Reeder of Leicester University, and Mr William Bailey of Garnett College, Roehampton. I know that they will generously forgive my expression of gratitude to each of them in this place.

Finally I need only say that I owe almost everything to my wife, Marian, and to two very tolerant people, Daniel and Gudrun.

CHAPTER I

Prologue and Recommendations

. . . You are likely to take a farm in hand, but will probably continue to let the whole as your great-grandfather, grandfather, and father did before you. . . . Then there are the various local functions which a country gentleman may perform. He may be a Poor Law Guardian and attend their meetings at Petty Sessions once a month, and at Quarter Sessions four times a year; a manager of Lunatic Asylums and similar institutions; a trustee of public endowments. . . . I have long thought there is no more useful or noble life than one spent in honest and zealous devotion to those things. The men who will do it are very rare, for to do it well requires a great deal of attention to minute details, and much patience, good sense, tact and temper besides, while the work brings in no money, and no reputation beyond the society affected by it. But such men are the very cement of society . . . and they find their reward in seeing things go right instead of wrong, in their own self-respect, and in the respect of those about them.

Letter of Arthur Hobhouse (Endowed Schools Commissioners, 1869–72) to a nephew, c. 1874. Quoted in L. T. Hobhouse and J. L. Hammond, Lord Hobhouse: A Memoir, London, 1905, 2.

It may happen that, by the end of this century, everyone will be living in towns. This probability is shaping our images of the past. The Victorian city has begun to dominate our perception of the whole canvas of nineteenth-century society, in much the same way as the metropolis has increasingly eaten up the countryside in the twentieth century. This preoccupation with the evolution of urban communities has tended to efface the effects of the historic survival of ideas and systems which had their origins in rural, agricultural society.

Education as a social function lies at the core of the history of British society in the last two hundred years. Educational history, particularly the history of administrative systems, has in recent times been treated largely as contemporary history; that is, as the tracking of issues and institutions of current significance back to their early origins. This has led to a heavy concentration upon the evolution of educational institutions in an urban context: our recent anxieties about problems of inner-city schooling have determined the ways in which we begin to perceive past developments. This is nowhere more true than in secondary schooling where, it has been consistently implied, the energy which impelled administrative, institutional and curricular change was generated in the Radical–Utilitarian setting of the growing nineteenth-century towns and cities of England. The argument here advanced is that while such urban energy did exist, it was comparatively diffuse; a more coherent reform movement emerged from the agrarian context of traditional society in the countryside. It was not until the last two decades of the Victorian era that a strong initiative for changes in secondary schooling began to reveal itself in the industrial and commercial centres of population. Furthermore, the pre-eminence of a Georgic model for middle-class education has continued to shape the national system of secondary schooling and its curricula into our own times.

The period between 1850 and 1872 in England and Wales contained a series of investigations which comprehensively anatomised the condition of the nation's educational institutions and made proposals for their reform. In the middle of this period Palmerston's Government initiated the largest and most searching educational investigation of the Victorian era, which culminated in the publication of the Report of the Schools Inquiry, or Taunton, Commission in 1867 (with twenty later volumes appearing in sequence up to 1870). The monumental Taunton Report on middle-class education has subsequently provided a substantial quarry for English social historians and for the authors of hundreds of school histories. As a means of delineating that ambivalent chimera, the Victorian middle class, it will continue to attract cautious and casual inquirers. Yet, despite its singular academic usefulness, and although it has served as a basis for several reputable studies of educational development, it has never been explored as a document of itself, and no attempts have been made to trace the roots of the recommendations it proposed and more specifically to relate the formulation of those recommendations to localities where new experiments in middle-class schooling were being tried.

The purpose of this study is twofold: to reveal how one group of Victorian education commissioners went about their tasks of inquiry and recommendation; and to associate their findings and proposals with particular counties. The Schools Inquiry Commission's Report became the basis of Forster's Endowed Schools Act of 1869 by which

Gladstone's Government hoped to improve considerably educational provision for the middle classes – in our terms, to reform and organise secondary schooling. In this task the Act must be considered a failure in the important sense that it did not succeed in establishing either a curricular or administrative pattern for English education. But, given this species of failure, it is necessary to get behind interpretations of general reasons for the subsequent emasculation of the 1869 Act. It is indisputable that there was increasing opposition to the Act's intentions. But, concurrent with this opposition there were local attempts to make its provisions work in a number of English counties and to co-operate with the Commissioners appointed under the Act. These attempts have been largely ignored by education historians, but they reveal clearly not only inherent weaknesses in the S.I.C. Report and the 1869 Act, but also the firm roots of the development of secondary education in England after 1902. They also demonstrate what may seem to be a surprising feature of nineteenth-century history: that a much more immediate general response to the need for educational improvement emerged in the countryside around 1870 than in the reputedly more dynamic urban industrial communities.

The deficiencies of English secondary education in the nineteenth century are so well known as not to need a detailed summary in a work of this kind. A copse of seven or eight hundred endowed grammar schools was accompanied by a dense and ever-changing thicket of private schools, and a staid and limited plantation of more promising proprietary schools. The ancient endowments were scattered arbitrarily across the country, the location of each determined in most cases by the birthplace of the founder. They varied considerably in size, wealth and efficiency, and were devoted almost exclusively to classical studies in an age when that kind of curriculum was increasingly thought to be inappropriate. It is impossible to make a general judgement on the private schools: a few were excellent, with modern curricula, while thousands must have been quite awful. The proprietary boarding and day schools, gradually establishing themselves from the 1820s onwards, usually set out to serve the needs of educated, ambitious middle-class families. Each of these schools, in each category, was autonomous. The endowed schools were subject only to the autocratic control of the master, the whims of the trustees, and, theoretically, the jurisdiction of the Equity courts. Each private school set its own standards and responded only to market forces, with a few notable exceptions like the schools of the Hill family in Birmingham and Tottenham. The proprietary schools, like Cheltenham and Malvern, Radley and Clifton, Marlborough and Wellington, were a cut above even the best of the endowed grammar schools, and since they were run on joint-stock principles, their headmasters generally acceded to the demands of the stock-holders. Apart from the legal guardianship of the Equity courts over endowments, none of these institutions was subject to the supervision of a central authority. There was no 'system'.

This was the chaos of secondary schooling which confronted the Schools Inquiry Commission in 1864. W. L. Burn has called the Report produced by the Commission 'a remarkably radical–collectivist document', and concluded that what the Commissioners proposed 'was infinitely more radical than anything that has come to pass . . . (in secondary education) since their report was published.'[1] It cannot be denied that their proposals were radical; but it is remarkable that, when it was issued, the Report encountered little immediate criticism. Its 'radicalism' had extensive roots in the past: in a traditional critique of equity jurisdiction as it affected educational endowments; in a practical tradition of attempts to reform those endowments, in Ireland as well as in England; in an ideological tradition of middle-class education which began with Thomas Arnold and was related to a wider pattern of attempts at political and social reform, and to specific anxieties about the rôle of the rural lower-middle class. The roots of the Commissioners' recommendations were set in a pattern of rural, county-based initiative and practice which drew the members of the Commission closer to the rural county than to the municipality when they came to select knowledgeable witnesses, to examine their own presuppositions, and to draw conclusions.

In the triptych of Royal Commissions investigating aspects of schooling in the mid-Victorian era, the S.I.C. has seemed to justify its place in an inexorable way: in 1861 the Newcastle Commission reported upon the condition of popular education; in 1864 the Clarendon Commissioners completed their inquiry into nine great public schools. The S.I.C., instituted in 1864, has therefore been seen as filling a gap: the hierarchy of investigations was being completed by an examination of the educational middle ground in society. Yet there was no logical inevitability about the appointment of the Taunton Commission. It was gazetted in December, 1864, because particular pressure had been brought to bear on **Palmerston's** admin-istration. Furthermore, the S.I.C. was the consummation of a long period of concern for the condition of middle-class schooling, and its recommendations were the result of a gestation whose beginnings can be traced back to the beginning of the century in England and Ireland. The appointment of the S.I.C. was not simply the expression of a desire to complete tidily the investigative map of English schooling.

The leading members of the S.I.C. were Lord Taunton, formerly a Whig minister; Lord Stanley, a liberal Tory and later to become Lord Derby; Lord Lyttelton, Gladstone's brother-in-law, and the leading aristocratic scholar of the age; Dean Hook of Chichester, sometime educational reformer as Vicar of Leeds; Sir Stafford Northcote, later a Conservative Chancellor of the Exchequer and formerly secretary to Gladstone; Edward Baines, the statutory Dissenter on the Com-mission; W. E. Forster; Frederick Temple, then Headmaster of Rugby and much later to become Archbishop of Canterbury; and T. D. Acland, scholar, agriculturist and co-founder, with Temple, of the Universities' Local Examinations for middle-class schools.

The Commission compiled detailed reports on nearly one thousand endowed grammar schools, in the process providing a group of brilliant young assistant commissioners with, in most cases, their first acquaintanceship with the beehive of lower-middle-class life in London and the provinces. The Commissioners took oral evidence from nearly 150 witnesses and sent questionnaires to every school which might have a middle-class clientèle. This intensive activity was their energetic response to the terms of reference handed down to them in December 1864: 'to inquire into the education given in schools not comprised within Her Majesty's two former Commissions (Newcastle and Clarendon) . . . and also to consider and report what measures (if any) are required for the improvement of such education, having special regard to all the endowments applicable, or which can rightly be made applicable, thereto'.[2]

Their complete findings were published between 1867 and 1870. The Report itself, stating recommendations, was the first in a sequence of twenty-one volumes. The remaining ones were a massive collection of reports on each of the endowed grammar schools and proprietary schools, general surveys of selected areas undertaken by the assistant commissioners, and written and oral evidence of witnesses. The recommendations were drafted in three sections, the first dealing with measures suggested for the improvement of the schools; the second, which came within the second part of the terms of reference, with the machinery for carrying these suggestions into effect; and the third, which, strictly speaking, stood outside the terms of reference, with the methods for providing schools where there were insufficient or no endowments.

In dealing with the first category the Commissioners saw the existing curriculum as generally too narrow: 'The country is in some places thickly dotted with grammar schools which have fallen into decay because they give undue predominance to what no parents within their reach desire their child to learn.' As a framework for reform in this respect they recommended a three-tiered grading of endowed schools: a first grade, with pupils staying until eighteen or nineteen, in which Latin and Greek would be taught; a second grade, in which pupils stayed till sixteen, with no Greek but with the possibility of two modern languages; and a third grade, where pupils staying until fourteen learnt the elements of Latin and a modern language. The fees charged in the schools would be appropriate to each grade, but the headmaster would be left to determine the detailed structure of the curriculum, in consultation with the governors, in each case. Except in strictly denominational schools, a conscience clause ought to be incorporated in the regulations; and it should no longer be necessary for masters to be in holy orders.

Gratuitous entry to endowed schools ought to be abolished: there should be competitive examinations for boys at about thirteen years of age. This would be to the advantage of poorer pupils. 'It is certainly not for the interest of the poor that they should be marked as such within the school to which they are admitted . . .' Competition would raise academic standards. The master's traditional freehold should be abolished, and a small official salary would ensure continued exertion by the teaching staff. Clothing and feeding of pupils should not be the functions of an endowment, even where the founder had emphasised such features: 'It is rarely a good thing to relieve the parents so entirely of the burden of maintaining their children: to aid them in bearing it is a real charity; to bear it for them is generally a blunder.' However, girls' education, where possible, should be made the object of local charity. So that school fees should not become excessively high, their regulation ought to be in the hands of the trustees, rather than of the master. Nothing would be more likely to improve the standard of the profession of schoolmaster than 'a well-devised system of certification' administered by examination. There should be annual inspection of school buildings and annual examination of the pupils.

In suggesting machinery for reform the Commissioners noted that 'vigour, tact, patience and readiness of adaptation' were required; that there were 'deep-rooted prejudices to be met', as well as the possibility of failure. The means had to be seen to be well adapted to the aims. First, they proposed a Central Authority, based upon a reconstituted Charity Commission, for dealing with endowments in an educationally as well as a legally well-informed way. Referring to evidence given to them by Earl Fortescue, they suggested that local authorities would be an essential part of their overall scheme, since by these means 'much local bitterness' would be avoided. The composition of a county authority posed considerable problems since the Commissioners thought that there was as yet too little general interest in this kind of education to make elected bodies viable. Therefore, the Registrar–General's districts should at first be the bases for Provincial Authorities. To each of these the Central Authority would appoint an Official District Commissioner who would be an *ex officio* member of all boards of trustees in the locality and act as local Inspector. Between six and eight further unpaid District Commissioners, appointed by the Crown, would 'represent the feelings of the district.' These Commissioners together, after surveying local endowments and canvassing opinions, would prepare schemes of reform for groups of schools. Towns with populations over 100,000 might have Boards of their own. At the lowest level the S.I.C. criticised the conduct of governors and suggested that the principle of general co-optation should be abandoned, since it encouraged unnecessary adherence to ancient traditions. City Companies and College Fellows were identified as being amongst the worst sorts of existing trustees and embodied the general fault of being at a distance from their schools. Local experience should be enlisted wherever possible, and co-optation used to a limited extent. To improve the quality of local trusteeship, education trusts in towns should be amalgamated for administrative purposes. The most novel proposal of all was the Council of Examinations. This would draw up general rules for the examinations of teachers for certificates and of pupils, and would appoint examiners who might be paid for by a tax on endowments. The Council would produce an annual report.

The endowed schools were to make up the core of the S.I.C.'s recommended 'system'; but private schools of proven efficiency might be added to them. Where no suitable endowments existed, new schools might be created, financed initially by a levy on the local rates. 'But the real force whereby the work is done must come from the people. And every arrangement which fosters the interests of the people in the schools, which teaches the people to look on the schools as their own . . . will do as much service as the widest advice and the most skilful administration.'[3]

The Commissioners presented the needs of the parent in tripartite form, and it is their model of the class structure which will form the basis of the discussion which follows here.[4] If the tripartite assumption of the Commissioners was incorrect, then that was never a point of argument at the time; and as a rough working model of a portion of Victorian society, it has never been abandoned by social analysts.

The S.I.C. related the needs of the parents to each of the three grades of schools they had recommended. The first grade of education was required by 'men with considerable incomes independent of their own exertions, professional men and men in business' who appeared to have 'no wish to displace the classics from their present position in the forefront of English education.'[5] The second-grade parent was described even more vaguely: he was often from among 'the larger shopkeepers, rising men of business, and the larger tenant farmers.'[6] The third grade, as will become more apparent later, was really the central issue confronting the Commissioners, and was hardly more precisely defined as 'the smaller tenant farmers, the small tradesmen, the superior artisans.' It was true, they said, 'that the number concerned is larger than that of any except the lowest', and 'that the wealth and prosperity of the country depend to so great a degree on the industry, and that industry on the intelligence, of those who are left thus uneducated.'[7] Of all the groups within this third grade of parents, special and significant attention in the Report was given to the needs of 'the smaller tenant farmer' who, it was feared, did not aim very high and, 'if it were not for fear of being outdone by the class below them, would probably not care much for education at all.'[8] This preoccupation with the tenant farmers as a group points to the bearing which experience of educational and social needs within their own rural communities had upon the leading members of the Commission who were themselves the natural leaders of county society.

The Commissioners were also favoured, by Dr Farr of the Regis-trar-General's Office, with a paper on the number of pupils coming within the scope of their inquiry.[9] He defined the lower limit of the middle class by two methods: firstly, by measuring the proportion of the population living in houses of assessed value of £20 and upwards, thus providing 3,172,064 as the number of the upper and middle classes in 1864–5; secondly, by deducing a figure from the number of marriages by licence, as distinct from marriages by banns, which were a feature of lower-class life, thus producing a middle- and upper-class population figure of 3,060,080. Farr said, 'It is difficult to draw the line between what are called the working classes and the middle classes, requiring such an education as the Commis-sioners are inquiring into; but here we have broad lines drawn by the people themselves, and recognised for practical purposes by the Chancellor of the Exchequer. From one class he collects the house tax, and he does not venture to go lower.'' He further recommended the Commission to employ someone to go over the occupation return of the Census. It seems that this was never done; but one of the Com-missioners, T. D. Acland, in Exeter, and an assistant commissioner, D. C. Richmond, in the Eastern Counties, undertook limited popu-lation surveys.[10] The final conclusions deduced from these coarse estimates were that, in order to bring education within reach of parents who required it, there should ultimately be school provision in the towns for not less than sixteen boys per thousand of the population; that in every town large enough to maintain a day school there should be immediate provision for ten boys per thousand of the population, with a power of extension; and that of the whole of the present demand one half at least should be assigned to the requirements of the third-grade scholars. No attempt was made to arrive at a statistically accurate estimate of the proportion of places needed by each of the three grades.

By 1832 the term 'middle class' had come of age. Asa Briggs has outlined the early history of 'middle class', suggesting that the inven-tion of the term was the result of conscious pride in their economic achievements on the part of the manufacturing interests in the 1780s and 1790s.[11] The problem of the education of the new order was pointed out in the *Westminster Review* in 1824:

Of the political and moral importance of this class there can be but one opinion. It is the strength of the community. It contains, beyond all compari-son, the greatest proportion of the intelligence, industry, and wealth of the state. In it are the heads that invent, and the hands that execute; the enterprise that projects, and the capital by which these projects are carried into operation. The merchant, the manufacturer, the mechanist, the chemist, the artist, those who discover new arts . . . the men in fact who think for the rest of the world, are the men of this class. . . . The proper education of this portion of the people is therefore of the greatest possible importance to the well-being of the state.[12]

The repeal of religious tests in 1828 freed a large proportion of this broad class from irritating social and political restraints, and the passing of the great Reform Act completed the formal process of liberation. It is interesting to consider the terms in which the politicians of the old order viewed and rationalised these changes. Macaulay declared that the principle of the 1832 Bill was 'to admit the middle classes to a large and direct share in the representation, without any shock to the institutions of our country.'[13] The Reform Act certainly seemed to have been a capitulation, but its passage was not a headlong flight into the abyss of democracy; rather was it among the first of those moments when the aristocratic political leadership of the country gave ground while maintaining its firm control over the constitutional machinery.

In one sense the accession of the middle classes to a share in political power in 1832 was a victory over the masses, achieved by the aristocracy through its new alliance with the commercial and industrial classes. The real motive for aristocratic good will in the early 1830s was disclosed in the Scottish Memorandum on Reform delivered to Lord John Russell in November 1830:

. . . any plan must be objectionable which, by keeping the franchise very high and exclusive, fails to give satisfaction to the middle and respectable ranks of society, and drives them to a union, founded on dissatisfaction, with the lower orders. It is of the utmost importance to associate the middle with the higher orders of society in the love and support of the institutions and government of the country.[14]

Thomas Attwood, addressing a meeting of the Birmingham Political Union at this time, said,

The interests of masters and men are, in fact, one. If the masters flourish, the men are certain to flourish with them; and if the masters suffer difficulties, their difficulties must shortly affect the workmen in a three-fold degree. The masters, therefore, ought not to say to the workmen, 'Give us your wages', but take their workmen by the hand, and knock at the gates of the Government and demand the redress of their common grievances. In this way the Government is made answerable for its own acts at its own doors;

and in this way only can the rights and interests of the middle and lower classes be supported.[15]

Fear of this kind of sentiment permeated the political climate of the period between the first two Reform Acts. Those who watched the ebb and flow of revolution and reaction in contemporary Europe perceived gradual constitutional and educational change in England as guarantees of the enduring stability of English society and its institutions. As a consequence of Grey's capitulation in 1832 a repetition of an alliance between the middle and lower classes during the period of Chartist activity was largely forestalled. The aristocracy retained its political supremacy under the constitution despite the attachment of middle-class numbers; aristocratic control in politics continued until the economic crises and redistributions of Parliamentary seats in the 1880s began to cause the landed interest to crumble. This control was guaranteed by a series of discreet withdrawals from direct confrontation with middle-class interests. Bernard Cracroft wrote, in 1866, of the aristocracy:

. . . So vast is their traditional power, so deep and ancient are its roots, so multiplied and ramified everywhere are its tendrils and creepers, that the danger is never lest they should have too little but always lest they should have too much power, and so, even involuntarily, choke down the possibilities of life from below. . . . The Parliamentary frame is kneaded together almost out of one class; it has the strength of a giant and the compactness of a dwarf.[16]

The most famous of the aristocracy's withdrawals permitted the repeal of the Corn Laws. One historian has written, 'the repeal . . . is now more generally regarded not as a victory for the 'Middle Classes', whoever they were, but as a skilful and successful holding operation by the governing class, the landowners.'[17] The corollary of the aristocrats' policy of discreet withdrawal was their tendency to flatter the middle classes publicly. Lord Derby, in a speech at the Liverpool Collegiate Institution in 1863, said,

. . . Suppose there were excluded, as higher classes, all those who, because of inherited fortune, have had a liberal education, and are independent of the necessity of applying to any provision (of education); suppose, on the other hand, we exclude as belonging to the lowest class of all those whose daily subsistence is dependent upon their daily manual labour – I ask you to look what a vast amount, what an immense social range . . . are left between these two extremes, all of which gradations and ranks constitute what we mean by the middle classes of society of this country. It would be very easy to say, of this or that person, 'he belongs to the higher classes, this one to the lower class', but for one whose position you could distinctly, accurately define, there are hundreds of whom it would not be possible to say, and with regard to whom two people could not agree, whether they belonged to the higher, or the higher-middle, to the lower-middle, or to the lower classes. Such is the happy fusion by which one rank and one gradation melts into and is absorbed by another, forming the harmonious chain by which the whole of society is bound together in this happy country. (Loud cheers.)[18]

In his windy apostrophe he took care to associate the artisan and the clerk with two marginally more successful men of the middle class – Gladstone and Peel.

Subtle strategy did not smother criticism of aristocratic government entirely. Momentarily, in 1855, largely because of what was seen as mismanagement of the Crimean War by aristocratic politicians and military men, criticism of upper-class domination became strident, and then, just as quickly, died down. This short-lived movement expressed itself through the Administrative Reform Association,[19] which was supported chiefly by the wealthy commercial and professional classes. Radical feeling also infused the deliberations of other organisations which discussed social problems in the 1850s and 1860s – notably the British Association and the National Association for the Promotion of Social Science.

So far an attempt has been made to depict the character of the middle class as it may have appeared to the men who mattered in England in the first six decades of the nineteenth century, and in particular as it appeared to the members of the Taunton Commission. But there was a further group in society, coming from a variety of social levels, which to some extent stood apart from the three conventional categories of upper, middle and lower classes, and whose members possessed the common characteristic of being men of ideas who often occupied professional positions. The careers of some of these men – like Brougham, Nassau Senior and Edwin Chadwick – spanned at least the period from the first Reform Act to the 1860s. But in the years immediately before 1864 the figure most characteristic of the group was Matthew Arnold who, from the aloofness of his position as an apparently objective observer, could inveigh against the failings of the three main social classes. Arnold addressed his remarks to the 'middle classes', as well as to contemporary politicians, through periodicals; but these were not the only forum for the dissemination of critical ideas: the Societies of the 1820s and 1830s, the Conferences and Associations of the 1850s and 1860s, provided further outlets through which professional men, or men of ideas, could reach a wide public among the middle classes. In addition, by a process which S. E. Finer has called 'suscitation'[20], they reached and influenced even aristocratic and gentry politicians.

The crystalising effect of the transmission of ideas relating to middle-class education in the mid-1850s is a subject which will be developed later.[21] Here it is necessary to consider the remarks of one who not only inspired the educational work of his most famous son, but fathered and drew together the movement of ideas which found its most substantial exposition in the Report of the S.I.C. Thomas Arnold, after the failure of his own journal in July 1831, published a series of letters in the radical *Sheffield Courant* which were on the subject of improving the condition of the lower classes. The same newspaper, in April 1832, printed a letter of his on 'The Education of the Middle Classes'.

He began by saying, 'We are all aware of the growing power of the middling classes of society, and we know that the Reform Bill will at once increase this power and consolidate it.'[22] He continued, 'It seems, then, that the education of the middling classes at this time is a question of the greatest national importance.'[23] In this, and in a further letter in May, Arnold outlined a set of proposals which became the blue-print for the continuing debate about middle-class education until 1867. His statement of ideals was quoted repeatedly, his ideas borrowed, trimmed and modified, by men of a variety of political and religious complexions. It is one of the main contentions of this study that he was the chief fountainhead of the notions which comprised the leading points of discussion of middle-class schooling. In this respect a very important factor in the assessment of him as a powerful and influential educational figure has been overlooked by his biographers. His ideas on this subject therefore deserve description.

He drew attention to a dilemma which was to become more marked as English education developed in the second quarter of the century. The schools for the richer classes were conducted generally by the clergy; the parish clergy superintended parochial schools for the lower orders. 'But between these two extremes there is a great multitude of what are called English or commercial schools at which a large proportion of the sons of farmers and tradesmen receive their education.'[24] He included in this category, rather indiscriminately, the endowed schools; but even so, he was thus anticipating the similarly broad scope of the Taunton inquiry. In the following year, 1833, he might have added the more telling social distinction which resulted from the Government grant to the voluntary societies. The creation of the Committee of Council on Education in 1839, and the subsequent growth of an educational bureaucracy controlling much of the education of the poor, highlighted still more dramatically the plight of the middle classes. Nevertheless, as early as 1832 Arnold began a train of complaint about the 'injustice' of subsiding popular education while neglecting middle-class schooling.

His next concern also foreshadowed the problem which the Taunton Commissioners thirty years later invited their first group of witnesses to help them solve:[25] the registration and certification of schoolmasters for middle-class schools. 'There is now no restriction', said Arnold, 'upon the exercise of the business of a schoolmaster and no inquiry made as to his qualifications.' The practice of issuing the Bishop's Licence had fallen into disuse: 'and as the government for the last century has thought it right to leave the moral and religious interests of the people pretty nearly to themselves, an impracticable restriction was suffered to become obsolete, but nothing was done to substitute in its place one that should be at once practical and beneficial.'[26] This aspect of Arnold's thinking anticipated the experiments of the 1850s in the form of the Local Examinations of Oxford and Cambridge Universities and the certificate of the College of Preceptors.

'It has long been the reproach of our law, that it has no efficient secondary punishments: it is no less true that we have no regular system of secondary education.' The classical schools had the Universities above them to provide standards of attainment. 'But anything like local universities, – any so much as local distinction or advancement held out to encourage exertion at a commercial school, it is as yet vain to look for.'[27] The concept of the local or county college, as part of a federal university, was to be taken up later, again in the 1850s, by Earl Fortescue and his colleague, an Old Rugbeian of Arnold's time, the Revd. J. L. Brereton, in Devonshire.[28]

Arnold also pointed to the weakness inherent in the dependence of the private schoolmaster upon the whims of middle-class clients: '. . . if he offends them then he is ruined.' In the 1860s the S.I.C. claimed that 'many parents need education themselves in order to appreciate education for their children, and their present opinion cannot be considered final or supreme.'[29] He concluded his first letter by suggesting that the dubious status of school-masters would be improved, not only by developing their personal qualities, but by raising their position in society. 'For this the *interference of the government* seems to me indispensable, in order to create a *national and systematic course of proceeding*, instead of the mere feeble efforts of individuals; to provide for the middling classes something analogous to the advantages offered to the richer classes by our great public schools and universities.'[30] In this Arnold was departing from the pattern suggested by his Utilitarian contemporaries while it is inconceivable that he would have had any truck with the subsequently fashionable 'supply and demand' principles of Robert Lowe, which Matthew Arnold treated so roughly in 'A French Eton'.[31] Thus, in 1832, Thomas Arnold was anticipating the more drastic action by the State which the S.I.C. was to propose unreservedly over thirty years later.

In his second letter he set out to examine critically the curriculum common to most commercial schools. In the first place, because of the educational inadequacy of many pupils' homes, he said, some of them had to be taught to read when they first entered a commercial school.[32] In most schools the rudiments of arithmetic, history and geography were taught; there was some physical science; 'and with a view to his particular business in life, he learns land surveying, if he is to be brought up in agricultural pursuits; or book-keeping if he is intended for trade.' Incidentally he was revealing in his own approach to middle-class schooling a feature which was to characterise what might be called the mainstream of thinking about the subject in the period before the Taunton inquiry: industrial England, save for the descriptions he may have read in periodicals and newspapers, his meeting with Stephenson's railway navvies, and occasional glimpses on his way north to Fox How, was *terra incognita* to Arnold. His images of education were drawn from the county, from the rural community and its needs. His experience in this respect was shared generally by the men who read what he had written, and who were themselves to carry the debate to its interim conclusion in 1867. It will be suggested later that the models for reform produced by the S.I.C. were rooted in the countryside, rather than in the urban industrial centres where the numerical bulk of the middle class flourished.

Arnold's criticisms of the commercial-school curriculum did not so much deal with the subjects taught as with the unsuccessful way in which boys were prepared for the business of life. Or rather, he said that every man had two businesses: the one his own calling, his career or profession; the other his general calling, the calling of a citizen and a man. 'The education which fits him for the first is called professional; that which fits him for the second, is called liberal.'[33] Commercial schools prepared boys for the first, but not, usually, for the second. Nevertheless, and unfortunately, everyone was willing to put forward an opinion on the business of being a citizen: '. . . false notions are entertained and acted upon; prejudices and passions multiply; abuses are manifold; difficulty and distress at last press upon the whole community . . .' He attributed this ignorance of the business of the citizen to the tendency, 'at least in the agricultural districts', to take the boy away from school before the age of fourteen.

It is significant that the next letter in the Sheffield series was entitled 'Reform and Its Future Consequences'. Arnold was perhaps more honest than some of his political successors in the middle-class debate: he said, 'I have much to lose by revolution: I have nothing to dread from reform.'[34] He showed a willingness to relate his anxieties about the condition of society as he saw it to his own condition, and this characteristic was shared by few of the protagonists of educational reform in the next generation. Yet his espousal of the cause of reform, as an antidote to the possibility of revolution, was a principle for action taken up by the men of the 1850s and 1860s. It lay firmly at the centre of the deliberations of the Administrative Reform Association and the Social Science Association; and it formed the framework for the gradual amelioration of social and industrial conditions by legislative and voluntary effort from 1832 to 1884. Arnold qualified his fear of revolution by admitting that it had its roots, not in pure love of property, but in his affection for 'the habits and feelings and society of English gentlemen'.[35] He looked, therefore, to moderate government, in sympathy with the wishes of the people; government which would turn its back upon the narrow principles of Toryism, while 'manfully and honestly' eschewing the excesses of a minority of 'Revolutionists'.

He wished to put down the party of Godless men who were trying to turn Dissenters into Jacobins by inflaming their hatred of Church rates, of the tithe, and of Tory bishops. Property, too, was exposed to attack by those who wished to make a more equal division of it.

'When a man has property of his own, although it may be very small in comparison with his neighbour's, he prefers holding what he has got on the old tenure to the risk of gaining somewhat more by breaking society to pieces.'[36]

Arnold perceived very clearly the main lines along which the discussion of middle-class education was to run. He isolated the schooling of the middle classes from the public schools above, and from the voluntary schools below; he challenged what he saw as the meretricious aims of the commercial and private schools, and lumped in with them most of the endowed schools; he posed the question of how to set a standard for these schools, which ultimately and logically produced an answer according with his proposal in the form of University Local Examinations in the 1850s; he preached the making of a teaching profession; he determined the path along which Broad Churchmen were to march towards a generous compromise with the demands of Dissent, in the interest of social and political harmony; he suggested, albeit obliquely, that classical subjects need not be the 'core' of secondary education for all middle-class pupils; and he warned against tolerating a school system which had at its heart a moral vacuum, the political consequence of which would be oblivion. At the same time he anticipated and codified the rural, not to say 'Georgic', metaphors and models which were to form the frame in which the Taunton Commissioners built up their picture of a system of middle-class education.

There is little need to draw a line of succession between the principles thus expounded by a Broad Churchman in the early 1830s and the policies discussed by the S.I.C. in the 1860s. And it would be unrealistic to make faint criticism of Arnold for his failure to prophesy the subtle changes of social emphasis which were to develop in the intervening period. He anticipated government intervention, without considering the uproar it might cause later; and, by implication, he foresaw that change, when it was attempted, would be engineered mainly within the framework of aristocratic and county politics. In Thomas Arnold the principles of reform and guardianship of an aristocratic, gentlemanly tradition lived side by side. And, in a modified form – a desire to see the State 'organise' its secondary education, and in a wry affection for the 'Barbarians' of the aristocracy – these elements were kept alive by his son, Matthew, by Frederick Temple, and by numerous faithful pupils and disciples.

On the mere evidence of this description of Arnold's ideas it is

clear that discussion of national education in the nineteenth century,
and consideration of religious controversy, are inseparable. Denominational groups had begun to establish schools for their own children before repeal of the Test Acts, and they continued to do so
throughout the whole of the period covered by this study. But
Dissenting protest was mingled with other radical and anti-Esta-
blishment voices: as Professor Chadwick has said, in the early Victorian period 'the claims of dissenters were spun into webs of acri-
mony, fabricated not only from the ills of dissenters, but from the
farmers' vexation against the tithe, or radical abuse of aristocratic
corruption . . . the war of conservative and radical became identified
with a war of Churchman versus dissenter'.[37]

It is difficult to generalise about Dissent in relation to educational
issues. Even over a crucial problem like Disestablishment, Dissenters
never really presented a united front to Anglicanis ': in the 1830s
Wesleyans and Congregationalists were opposed to concerted
action. But a number of factors contributed to an increasing unanimity of approach: the formation of the Free Church of Scotland in
1843; the dispute over the education clauses of Graham's Factory
Bill of 1843, which for a time seemed to be welding Dissent into a
major political force; the rise of Tractarianism in the Church of
England; and the Maynooth Grant – all these events encouraged a
common suspicion of the motives and policies of the leaders of the
Established Church and of lay Anglicans in government.

But Dissent never developed as a coherent political force in the
nation as a whole. Perhaps the most interesting phase in the history
of the dissenting party coincided with the period of the Newcastle
and Taunton Commissions, on which official bodies Dissent was
represented by Miall and Baines respectively. There can be little
doubt but that, as Matthew Arnold suggested, the more primitively
militant attitudes and prejudices of the older generation of Dissenters were softening by the 1860s; he expected that, in middle-class
education, Dissent and Anglicanism were about to resolve their
ancient differences.

In the 1840s, for men like Edward Baines, Russell had seemed a
possible helpmeet, if not a champion. But Russell had disappointed
in office after 1846. Palmerston's Broad Church attitudes smacked
more of complacency than of genuine tolerance, and the Liberation
Society had failed in its aim of providing a steady flow of M.P.s
sympathetic to the cause of Dissent. So in the early 1860s there grew

up an astonishing alliance between the High Church Gladstone, M.P. for Oxford University, and the Dissenting interest in the Commons. A revival of nonconformist morale was needed. Miall, the only Dissenter with a broadly based national reputation, was out of Parliament between 1857 and 1869. Bright had become unpopular because of his repeated refusals to lead the Liberation Society after 1854.

Gladstone's new motives were clear: on his route to the leadership of the Liberal party he had to conciliate the great mass of Dissenting supporters. In accepting after 1860 nonconformist political aims for which he had previously expressed revulsion, he believed that some concessions to Dissent would not destroy the Church, but rather strengthen it by removing some of the bases for hostility between Dissenters and Anglicans. He thought that the process of conciliation should be gradual. His new attitude, particularly after his support for Peto's Burials Bill in 1862, provoked comment from Pusey: 'What the Dissenters really want, as you know, is not that they should be buried in churchyards, but that everything which the Church has should be divided with them'.[38] Gladstone suggested to Samuel Wilberforce in 1862 that the time had come for the adoption of a more liberal tone by the Bishops;[39] and in this he was anticipating his appointment of Temple to Exeter in 1869.

For the moment the only apparent connection between Gladstone's new position and the problem of middle-class education lay in his supporting the last of Lewis Dillwyn's Bills to allow Dissenters to become trustees of 'Anglican' endowed schools. The Bill failed in 1863, but Gladstone's attitude provoked from the Vice-Chancellor of Oxford University a tart note in which he informed the Chancellor of the Exchequer that the University's petition against the Bill had been sent for presentation to the other Oxford M.P., Heathcote: 'You will at once understand why I have forwarded it to him instead of to you'.[40] This did not, however, prevent Gladstone from developing his contacts with Dissent: he began to mix socially, though privately, with prominent Congregational leaders, like Hall and Allon.[41]

The significance of these developments lies chiefly in the fact that the Government which set out, as part of its announced programme in 1868, to act upon the recommendations of the S.I.C., was founded partly upon the political alliance of its leader with the main body of Dissent, an alliance fashioned largely during the period when the

S.I.C. was at work. More than any previous administration, the Liberals of 1868 seemed well placed to deal with middle-class education against a background of religious controversy which was sure to be provoked by legislation which interfered with the Church's privileges in education. In this respect the central issues were the need to promote conscience clauses; to make governing bodies more representative of local religious interests; and the possibility of throwing open headships to laymen in endowed schools.

The removal of Anglican features which so irritated Dissenters is connected with another issue which was at the core of the work of the S.I.C. This was the continuing process of attempting to reform the management of endowed charities in the first seven decades of the century. The resistance of the City of London Corporation to the work of the Endowed Schools Commission after 1869 marked an important stage in an intensifying campaign of criticism which originated in the reports of the Commissioners between 1818 and 1837, the establishing of the permanent executive Charity Commission in the 1850s, and the efforts to neutralise the power and patronage of the City Corporation and the great City Companies.[42]

A further feature of the period under consideration has been touched upon at various points already. This is the separation of two clearly defined interests in society: Land, on one side; Commerce and Industry, on the other. The Industrial Revolution had sharpened the differences between these two interests, and the 1832 Reform Act had attached not only a new class, but a new species of property, to the constitution. The next hundred years was to see the struggle, first for parity, then for final superiority, between these interests; though it must be admitted that at certain points the two sides seemed to coincide. The banker – like Samuel Loyd Jones – and the industrialist – like John Josiah Guest of Merthyr – often become men of landed property when they reached the peaks of their commercial prosperity.[43] Landed aristocrats, like Earl Granville in Staffordshire, became involved in the industrial capitalist activity of their localities.[44] The chief concern here is with the landed interest, since it will be argued that from this 'declining' sector came the most far-reaching attempts to create on a national scale an education system for the middle classes such as Thomas Arnold had suggested; and that the county as a unit possessed, and its proponents tried to use, a hierarchical structure which enabled its leading members to propose reforms which were more sweeping than any of the piecemeal plans which were propounded and practised in the larger towns and cities.

The 1851 Census marks a turning point in the history of English society: the beginning of a preponderance, in terms of numbers, of the industrial urban interest. But in 1851, though there had been a rapid increase in the size of London, most towns were still small by modern standards: only eleven towns had populations over 100,000; only five of these were over 200,000; and only twenty towns had populations more than 50,000. It is worth recalling here that the S.I.C. reckoned that only towns with populations over 100,000 should possess their own local education 'authority'.[45] G. D. H. Cole said that only in 1851 was 'the great age of one-class urban and suburban areas beginning, with important effects on social relations and the development of local government'.[46] Until well into the 1860s, then, the landed interest, in terms of control of established institutions, could ensure that its imprint remained deeply engraved on most of the country, outside the growing conurbations of the North and the Midlands; though even in these territories, magnates like Lord Derby in Lancashire, Earl Fitzwilliam in south Yorkshire, and the Calthorpes in Birmingham, could still wield great influence.[47]

The landed interest not only controlled the established institutions of central and local government; it also had great and historic cohesiveness, and this was to be an important factor in attempts to solve the problem of educational provision for the children of the middle classes. Disraeli, speaking at Shrewsbury in May 1843, described the landed interest in almost romantic terms:

> When I talk of the landed interest, do not for a moment suppose that I merely mean the preponderance of the 'Squires of high degree'. . . . I do not undervalue the mere superiority of the landed classes; on the contrary I think it is a most necessary element of political power and national civilisation; but I am looking to the population of our innumerable villages, the crowds in our rural towns; aye, and I mean something more than that by the landed interest – I mean the estate of the poor, the great estate of the Church. . . . I mean also . . . that great judicial fabric, that great building up of our laws and manners which is, in fact, the ancient polity of our realm.[48]

This kind of summary statement shares, in its apparent simplicity, the flavour of Lord Derby's flattering address to the middle classes of Liverpool in 1863.[49] It must be admitted that landed proprietors like Derby may have wished to project on the confusion of industrial society the apparently simple harmony of the rural county community. But Disraeli was, by contrast with Derby, expressing an essential truth about the nature of rural society: it was cohesive and relatively harmonious, and its cohesiveness enabled it to survive 'Captain Swing' and the mid-century crisis which followed Repeal, and to maintain its influence upon the work of the legislature.

Lewis Namier denied the validity of the view that the English have little respect for mental achievement; and his interest in the eighteenth-century constitution led him to dispute, by implication, Cobden's poor view of the English aristocracy. Namier contrasted English experience with that of the Continent: in Germany, he said, scholarships were traditionally seen as a form of poor relief; in England the scholar held a much more privileged position:

English civilisation is essentially the work of the leisured class. . . . More intellectual work is done by aristocrats in England than anywhere else, and, in turn, scientists, doctors, historians and poets have been made peers – to say nothing of the discipline most closely connected with the State, the law, where peerages have for centuries been the regular and almost unavoidable prizes for the leaders of the profession.[50]

This combination of the aristocracy and the law has an interesting bearing upon the progress of reform in middle-class education: it is possible to see the concerted attempts to bring about change in the 1850s and 1860s as the joint efforts of a 'country party', based in rural society, and a significant group among the practitioners and officials of the Equity courts.[51] The aristocratic element, as it was represented on the Taunton Commission, fitted nicely Namier's depiction of the aristocracy as a dynamic group in English intellectual life: Lords Lyttelton and Stanley, and to some extent the newly ennobled Taunton, exemplified the interest and expertise in public affairs of the élite of county society. Howard Staunton, England's greatest chess player (an interest he shared with Lyttelton, who was President of the British Chess Association) and the illegitimate son of a peer, pointed in 1869 to the immense influence of the aristocracy in English education. But he said that the aristocracy 'does not exist for its own sake; does not exist merely to monopolise certain privileges: it exists that it may crown the social hierarchy, which should symbolise the hierarchy of nature'.[52] He went on, '. . . the English aristocracy is the only aristocracy in Europe which is still powerful, and even the progress of democracy adds seemingly to its strength. The aspiration of the English aristocracy is to be, not the best educated, but for practical purposes the most cultivated'.

One must consider the continuing control and influence of the aristocracy, in alliance with the intellectual–professional elements in the community, exercised through the annual meetings of the Social Science Association from 1857 onwards.[53] Here the traditional leaders of society lectured to, led, and sought to educate, or in Staunton's case, 'cultivate', audiences of middle-class men. There was also, running parallel to the coalition of Liberalism and Dissent, the feature of the development of an equally remarkable alliance between aristocratic Liberals and Radicals of various kinds. This alliance was capped by Gladstone's first administration which was an uneven blend of upper-class Whigs and Liberals, Radical Dissenters and former Peelites.[54] It was this unnatural coalition which piloted the 1869 Endowed Schools Bill through Parliament. At this time Gladstone had by no means abandoned the principles which had caused him to write to Russell thus, in 1854, on the subject of Civil Service competitive examinations:

. . . the great recommendation of this change to my eyes would be its tendency to strengthen and multiply the ties between the higher classes and the possession of administrative power. . . . I have a strong impression that the aristocracy of this country are even superior in natural gifts, on the average, to the mass: but it is plain that, with their acquired advantages, their insensible education, irrespective of book-learning, they have immense superiority.[55]

In this remark he seems to be bridging the gap between the apparently antipathetic concepts of continued leadership by a traditional aristocracy, and of rational reform of the public service with the abolition of patronage which that implied.

In fact the policies of the Liberal Government of 1868 can be seen as representing an attempt by aristocratic leadership to harmonise the needs and demands of many elements in society; and it will be shown that the Endowed Schools Act foundered in the wide strait which separated the comprehensive, aristocratic schemes of a Liberal Government, and the conservative defensiveness of privileged urban groups. It will be demonstrated that the counties, in a number of cases, under gentry and aristocratic leadership, had the will and the organisation appropriate to assisting the central government in its attempt to implement a large plan for secondary education.

This county organisation rested firmly on principles of aristocratic government. Lord Willoughby de Broke, writing of his mid-Victorian youth in Warwickshire, constructed a table representing the social hierarchy of the landed interest within county society:

The Lord Lieutenant;
the Master of Foxhounds;
the Agricultural landlords;
the Bishop;
the Chairman of Quarter Sessions;
the Colonel of the Yeomanry;
the Members of Parliament;
the Dean and Archdeacons;
the Justices of the Peace;
the lesser Gentry;
the larger Farmers.[56]

The power of the landed interest in county local government in this period is central to the discussion of the attempts by the S.I.C. to make local arrangements for the reform of educational endowments. These attempts must be seen against the background of the sequence of nine Bills, introduced between 1836 and 1868, each of which had the object of substituting elected or partly elected County Boards to take over the powers of Quarter Sessions. J. S. Mill described Quarter Sessions in 1861 as the most aristocratic institution in principle still remaining in England: '. . . far more so than the House of Lords, but it grants public money and disposes of important public interests, not in conjunction with a popular assembly, but alone'.[57]

The aristocrats in the counties were generally willing to assist in the local execution of the 1869 Act, by breathing new life into the old institutions and relationships of county society. But the fears of the middle-class trustees – the leaders of small urban communities in many cases – were aroused and united around the standard of resistance to State interference and of the organisational expertise of the City of London Corporation.

The failure to implement fully the terms of the Endowed Schools Act, and the decision of the Liberals to omit some of the proposals of the S.I.C. from the 1869 Bill, constitute together one of the riddles of mid-Victorian politics. The Bill was a measure promoted by the heterogeneous coalition described earlier; it has been called an attempt to freeze upward mobility in a society where most citizens were conscious of its hierarchical pattern; it tried to enact a whole series of reforms – relating to obsolete or inefficient charities, mismanagement, patronage, the government and curricula of schools, the implementation of conscience clauses, and the geographical redistribution of secondary schools – all of which seemed to have been agreed upon as necessary in principle by intelligent men of all parties in the late 1860s. But in these attempts it touched upon many nerves which lay just beneath the skin thinly covering the excited body politic in the period immediately after the 1867 Reform Act. The Endowed Schools Act was embedded, almost ignored, amid a series of seemingly more important and controversial measures which initially drew the fire of opposition to Gladstone's Government: the 1870 Elementary Education Act, Disestablishment in Ireland with the accompanying anxiety about the future of the Church in England; the Irish Land Act, which seemed to foreshadow a similarly radical reform of property arrangements in other parts of Britain; and the Universities Tests Act. But unlike these measures, with each of which it shared at least one feature, the Endowed Schools Act was painfully slow in operation and therefore subject to mounting opposition. It suffered the full concentration of opposition to the other main pieces of legislation passed by Gladstone's Government.

The answer to the twin riddles of the Taunton Commission and the 1869 Act – the failure to implement some of the most interesting recommendations of the one, and the terms of the other – must be related to the fundamental incongruity of the task laid before the Commission in 1864: a group of interested men, only one of whom could himself be certainly called 'middle-class', set about determining the educational needs of that class, without detailed reference to their demands; and they produced a massive series of proposals which, while meeting the requirements of a widely held desire for particular reforms, seem collectively to have been calculated to arouse profound hostility based upon historic prejudices. The Commission stands at the heart of the most significant period of social and political transition in the Victorian period.

Notes

1 W. L. Burn, *The Age of Equipoise*, London, 1968, pp. 200–1.
2 *Schools Inquiry Commission*, Report, I, p. 1.
3 Ibid, 571–661.

4   So the grosser sociological models of Victorian society have been ignored: e.g., R. S. Neale, 'Class consciousness in early nineteenth-century England: three classes or five?', *Victorian Studies*, XII, No. 1, September 1968, 1 5–32; also, J. H. Vincent's more historically pleasing analysis in *The Formation of the Liberal Party, 1857–1868*, London, 1972, p. 24 onwards.

5   *S.I.C.*, I, p. 16.

6   Ibid, p. 20.

7   Ibid, loc. cit.

8   Ibid, loc. cit.

9   Ibid, Appendix II, pp. 6–10.

10   Ibid, Appendix II, pp. 10–15; pp. 15–27.

11   Asa Briggs, (i) 'Middle-class consciousness in English politics, 1780–1846', *Past and Present*, April 1956; (ii) 'Language and class', A. Briggs and J. Saville (eds.), *Essays in Labour History*, London, 1960.

12   *Westminster Review*, I, No. I, 1824, pp. 68–9.

13   Quoted in O. F. Christie, *The Transition from Aristocracy, 1832–67*, London, 1927, p. 67.

14   Quoted in N. Gash, *The Age of Peel: a Study in the Techniques of Parliamentary Representation*, London, 1953, p. 15.

15   Quoted in A. Briggs, 'Thomas Attwood and the economic background to the Birmingham Political Union', *Cambridge Historical Journal*, IX, p. 2.

16   B. Cracroft, 'The analysis of the House of Commons', reprinted in W. L. Guttsman (ed.), *A Plea for Democracy, an Edited Selection from the 1867 Essays on Reform and Questions for a Reformed Parliament*, London, 1967, p. 118.

17   G. Kitson Clark, 'The electorate and the repeal of the Corn Laws', *Transactions of the Royal Historical Society*, 1951.

18   *Times*, 12 October 1863.

19   See (i) R. Lewis, 'Edwin Chadwick and the Administrative Reform Movement, 1854–6', *University of Birmingham Historical Journal*, II, 1949–50, pp. 178–200; (ii) O. Anderson, *A Liberal State at War*, London, 1967, 114ff.

20   S. E. Finer, 'The transmission of Benthamite ideas', in G. Sutherland (ed.), *Studies in the Growth of Nineteenth-century Government*, London, 1972, p. 13.

21   See below, chapter VI.

22   A. P. Stanley, Thomas Arnold: *Miscellaneous Works, Collected and Published*, London, 1845, p. 226.

23   Ibid, p. 227.

24   Ibid, loc. cit.

25   See below, chapter VIII, p. 190.

26   Stanley, op. cit., p. 228.

27   Ibid, p. 229.

28   For Fortescue's proposals, see below, chapter III, 73.

29   *S.I.C.*, I, p. 15.

30   Stanley, op. cit., p. 230.

31 See below, chapter VI, 134.
32 Stanley, p. 231.
33 Ibid, p. 232.
34 Ibid, p. 235–6.
35 Ibid, p. 236.
36 Ibid, p. 238.
37 O. Chadwick, *The Victorian Church*, I, London, 1966, p. 61.
38 G. I. T. Machin, 'Gladstone and nonconformity in the 1860s: the formation of an alliance', *The Historical Journal*, XVII, p. 2, 1974, 350–1.
39 Ibid, p. 352.
40 Ibid, pp. 351–2.
41 Ibid, pp. 354–5.
42 See below, chapter V.
43 F. M. L. Thompson, *English Landed Society in the Nineteenth Century*, London, 1971, pp. 34–6.
44 Ibid, p. 174.
45 S.I.C., I, pp. 643–4.
46 G. D. H. Cole, *Studies in Class Structure*, London, 1955, pp. 49–51.
47 See below, chapter VII, p. 174 for a discussion of landed proprietors' continuing influence on the development of urban areas.
48 Quoted in Q. Hogg, *The Case for Conservatism*, London, 1947, p. 124.
49 See above, this chapter, p. 12.
50 L. Namier, *England on the Eve of the American Revolution*, London, 1930, pp. 16–17.
51 See below, chapter V, for the evidence of Equity lawyers and officials to the S.I.C.
52 H. Staunton, *The Great Schools of England*, London, 1869, p. xvi.
53 See below, chapter VI.
54 S. Maccoby, *English Radicalism*, London, 1938, p. 163.
55 J. Morley, *The Life of William Ewart Gladstone*, I, London, 1905: the exchange with Russell is discussed at p. 511 and printed as an appendix to II, pp. 807–8.
56 H. J. Hanham, *Elections and Party Management: politics in the time of Disraeli and Gladstone*, London, 1959, p. 35.
57 J. S. Mill, *Representative Government*, Everyman edition, London, 1910, p. 349.

CHAPTER II

The Georgic model of middle-class education

. . . To education in its widest sense we look as the most powerful aid in the further progress of British agriculture. Knowledge – of his business, and true interest to the landlord and the tenant – and of the best mode of promoting his own welfare to the labourer – is the first requisite to obtain an improvement of their condition. A wise pursuit of individual interest will . . . be most conducive to their own and the general welfare. It is by individual energy that this is to be developed. . . . All the evidence we have collected tends to show, that in the districts where the increase of manufacturing and commercial enterprise and wealth has been greatest, there the rent of the landlord, the profit of the tenant and the wages of the labourer have increased.

James Caird, English Agriculture in 1850–1, London, 1852, p. 526.

It has been customary to associate the increasing demand for both the reform and the organisation of middle-class education in the first half of the nineteenth century with the rapid growth of industrial towns and the consequent rise to political consciousness of a new urban middle class. There were direct links between these phenomena. But too little has been said hitherto about the development of clearly defined models for middle-class education which had originated in the gradualist, even conservative, tradition of the rural agrarian counties. In spite of the revolution which occurred in the countryside in the eighteenth century, rural England has nevertheless been characterised as representing political and economic decadence; while the *laissez-faire* energy of manufacturing and commercial England is seen as having supplied the dynamic element in movements of nineteenth-century social, political and economic change.[1]

This kind of comparison was made by Baldwin Francis Duppa in 1839:

In the business of the farmer, the degrees of being wrong are infinite; . . . In Manufactures the relative advantages of different processes are soon known

from the circumstances of the manufacturers living in large towns. . . .
Farmers have none of these advantages; in the first place, they cannot so
associate together as to know the results of all the successful experiments
which concern them; and in the second, as not only the soil and other
physical characteristics of large tracts of our country differ from each other,
but that of every farm also, the practice of each individual farmer must
consequently be a modification of the general practice to suit his own local
circumstances. The results, moreover, of any new experiment on agriculture
.are more widely worked out. . . . Can anything be done to better his position,
and what . . .?[2]

Duppa believed that the general transmission of new ideas and
techniques in agriculture presupposed the creation of novel institutions of education in the countryside. But this notion was not original or new in 1839. Not only was Duppa armed with a wide range of
foreign and British models and experiments; he followed a broad
tradition of agrarian writing and practice which had roots probing
beyond the farming revolution of the eighteenth century. His ideas
rested on a concept of agricultural education which took its tone
from the classical agrarian writers, through the sixteenth-century
doggerel pamphleteers, to John Milton. They followed in a century-
old tradition of enlightened aristocratic and gentry patronage of
agricultural experiment; in central and local interest in agricultural
innovation in Britain – notably the Board of Agriculture, the work of
Arthur Young and his contemporaries, and the energetic activities of
numerous agricultural societies throughout Britain. Also, in his rôle
as de Fellenberg's English amanuensis, he drew upon foreign sources
for his ideas;[3] and here again he trod in Young's footsteps. Duppa
could move in the universal sphere of European agriculture, using its
common currency, in a way which suggests a possible modification
of his own point about the isolation and uniqueness of the farmer;
and his work, and the work of his predecessors and successors,
derived much of its nourishment from the true 'Augustan
honeycombs of Science'[4] – in particular the writings and experiments of agricultural chemists – which flourished across Northern
Europe. In a very real sense, it can be argued, the world of the
agriculturist in the early nineteenth century was wider and more
coherent than the insularly competitive sphere of the manufacturer;
it transcended national frontiers in its search for aphorisms, new
ideas and techniques.

The problem confronting Duppa's agricultural contemporaries
was not shortage of ideas, but rather how the wealth of existing and

proliferating ideas might be more widely transmitted. His solution lay in ensuring the progress of rural education. While the pattern of agricultural revolution in the eighteenth century had been char-acterised largely by innovation on the part of enlightened proprie-tors, the problem of passing their ideas on to the ruck of tenant-farm-ers in the middle ground of rural society became an important issue in the early nineteenth century. An international, aristocratic enve-lope of shared experience existed at the uppermost level: yet the rural middle class had still to be converted to new agrarian ideologies.

G. E. Mingay, writing in 1963, pointed to a select group of great landowners in England who had been agrarian improvers on a considerable scale during the eighteenth century. From Lord Ernle he took the well-known figures of Townshend and Coke, with others less familiar, like Earl Ducie in Gloucestershire, the Dukes of Bedford, and Sir John Sinclair. Mingay quoted Harte, in 1764, as saying that the tenant-farmer, 'poor and uninstructed', plodded on heavily in the beaten track of his ancestors and neighbours, 'like a beast of burden, overladen and disconsolate'.[5] According to Mingay, when eighteenth-century landlords spoke of 'improve-ment', 'it was usually an "improved rental" that they had in mind'.[6]

More positively influential than the great landlords were the shows and agricultural societies which began to flourish in the second half of the eighteenth century. By 1800 most English counties had some kind of organisation for agricultural improvement.[7] The Royal Dublin Society, founded in 1731, was the first of all, and it was the model for the Bath and West of England Society of 1777. Increas-ingly, the communication of new techniques and ideas was seen as the main rôle of these county societies. They became taken for granted as necessities in the search for improvement.

In 1780 the Bath and West Society published in its *Letters and Papers on Agriculture* an article by the Revd William Lamport entitled, 'Proposal for the Further Improvement of Agriculture'.[8] He expressed his anxiety about the progress of the science in England, but set his remarks in the long context of the development of English agricultural theory and practice during the previous three centuries. In this country, he said, even after the Reformation, the discovery of the New World had deflected the attention of energetic men away from agriculture at home into the channels of trade and commerce. Milton had tried to revive general interest, by recommending the establishment of a school in which rural economics should be a principal subject. His pupils would read the works of Cato, Varro and Columnella, the ancient classical authorities.[9] Evelyn had carried Milton's ideas forward in the Preface to his *Sylva*.[10]

Under the Commonwealth, Mr Cowley had recommended the founding of a college at each university, and the appointment of professors for instructing young men in the principles and practice of agriculture. But his plans were ignored and farming had languished during the reign of Charles II.[11] A contemporary of Milton and Evelyn wrote, in 1669: 'Until our Philosophers and Heroes of Science and Art handle the Plough and Spade, and undertake the plenary discovery and description of these Rustic operations. . . . I hope this indigested Piece may find a place in our Rural Libraries, and then I shall willingly be the first that shall commit this to the Flames to give way for a better.'[12] In the early eighteenth century Lord Molesworth sought to generate interest with his *Considerations for Promoting Agriculture, and Employing the Poor*,[13] in which he had written: '. . . I would humbly propose that a school for husbandry be established in every county, wherein a master well skilled in agriculture should teach at a fixed yearly salary: and that Tusser's old book of husbandry be taught the boys to read, to copy, and to get by heart, for which purpose it might be reprinted'. Like Duppa later, Lamport was concerned to secure universal transmission of experience and knowledge, without the anxiety attendant upon unilateral experiment. 'Were schools established in different parts of the Kingdom for the education of farmers' sons who might be but in low circumstances, gentlemen would never want sensible and rational improvers of their estates, who would likewise be the most proper persons to instruct parish apprentices and inferior servants'. In support of this Lamport quoted 'old-experienced Varro', who had written, 'the bailiffs should be men of some erudition and some degree of refinement'. But a bailiff, thought Lamport, ought to be skilled especially in rural economics; he should not only give orders but also work himself, so that the labourers might imitate him and respect him for his excellence in practical as well as scientific things. In the same way the sons of farmers would be listened to more favourably by inferior servants than would persons of higher rank.

Lamport would have instituted the kind of 'literary workhouses' recommended by Sir William Petty in 1648, 'where children may be taught as well to do something towards their living as to read and write . . . that all children, above seven years old, may be presented to this kind of education: none being excluded by reason of poverty or inability of their parents; for hereby it hath come to pass that many are now holding the plough, who might be made fit to steer the state'.[14]

This Bath and West article is significant for a number of reasons. Firstly it presumably enjoyed wide circulation among members of the Society, and may be considered one of the main sources of later propositions relating to the foundation of institutions devoted to agricultural education in the West Country. In addition, his plan encompassed almost all the elements which later came together to provide a model for schools for the rural middle classes in the mid-nineteenth century: the traditional classical element in the curriculum, with 'old-experienced Varro' and Milton as justifications; the clear stratification of pupils by social class, leading to a concentration upon the needs of the tenant-farmer class particularly, and the complementary but distinct institution of the elementary industrial school – on Petty's pattern; the need to train for moral excellence as well as for technical superiority, in the bailiff class – in other words, the need to educate the tenant-farmer above the level of the peasantry; the implied necessity for boarding education; the emphasis upon the economic profit to be gained by the landowning class from their promotion of education for the tenant-farmers' sons; and finally, a recommendation that the Anglican clergy should take an interest in the business of farming. In fact, Lamport's essay forms a matrix for the three-class model of schooling which was to become one of the conventions of nineteenth-century thinking about education in England; and, as will be made clear later, the pattern here put forward was taken up by the Bath and West of England Society and by other exponents.

Lamport, as early as 1785, was not alone in making such proposals. In the same year, Arthur Young presented an article in *Annals of Agriculture* whose author proposed that in every county 'a professor of agriculture' should be appointed, who could explain agricultural theory and direct the work of a 'county farm', the expense being defrayed by a levy on the rates.[15] A correspondent writing to the *Commercial and Agricultural Magazine* in 1801 complained of the Government's continuing neglect of agriculture, and especially of the failure to form 'one particular system of education for those who are intended to follow it as a science, or as a means of livelihood'.[16] Agricultural societies would labour in vain, thought the author of the letter, 'X. D.', until they found the means of making farmers less than total strangers to the principles and language of mineralogy, botany, zoology, natural history, 'and even Chymistry'. The education of youths intending to become farmers ought to be based on the study of those sciences, so that they might be freed from 'the prejudices and ignorance of custom'. At a meeting of the Board of Agriculture in April 1806, Sir John Sinclair, speaking from the chair, made some remarks on the subject of 'Agricultural Education and Experimental Farming'.[17] He suggested the establishment of one or more experimental farms, 'instituting at each a sort of Academy or College, where youth might be instructed in the theory, as well as trained in the practice, of Agriculture'. He merely touched upon the subject, he said, at a time when the circumstances of war precluded the immediate prosecution of the project.

The most interesting proposal of this kind in the early nineteenth century was again associated with the Bath and West Society. In 1808 the Committee discussed, in favourable terms, the proposition of Captain Williamson, who had travelled widely in Europe in pursuit of agricultural ideas, that a farm and school should be established near Bath.[18] Williamson, rather typically, was here taking up an idea originally proposed by the late Secretary, William Matthews. The 'College' was to consist of three classes: one for gentleman's sons or relations, who should board with the Professor on liberal terms, 'each to have a separate chamber, furnished according to the regulations prevailing at Oxford'. The Second Class was to be received at a lower rate, and to board under the control of an assistant. As the First Class would be considered rather as "Supervisors", the Second class would be expected to labour on the farm; it would, however, be a fixed principle that all should acquire practical experience in husbandry. The Third Class would consist of youths taken, perhaps, from a charitable institution, or from parishes, to serve for a certain number of years. These would commence as drivers, and would gradually perform the more labourious duties, as their strength might permit. This was not the first time that the Society had discussed such a proposal: Matthews's scheme had been put forward in 1805, a year before Sinclair had uttered his. Little is known of Captain Williamson, though the eclectic nature of his writings on agriculture was submitted to some rather wry comment in a journal of 1810.[19] Apart from Matthews's otherwise unrecorded plan, the model for Williamson's proposal may well have been the school system of de Fellenberg at Hofwyl, about which two articles by Charles Pictet and others were published in England in 1808.[20]

The uncertainties of the rural economy in the immediate post-war years were reviewed by two Parliamentary Select Committees in 1821 and 1833. The latter Committee, comprising Althorp, Peel, Russell and Graham, among others, reinforced many of the conclusions of the earlier one. As might have been expected, the tone of their recommendations was cautious. They agreed with Burke 'that it is a perilous thing to try Experiments on the Farmer', since the farmer's capital was more limited than was generally supposed; and 'although it is in the power of the Legislature to do much evil, yet it can do little positive good by frequent interference with the agricultural industry'.[21] The debate on the state of agriculture, therefore, was conducted according to the principle that shocks which affected farming were felt at all levels of the landed interest, and that, consequently, remedies, such as they were, should be conceived in relation to the whole of landed society, rather than to separate sectors of it.

Though the debate was couched in these traditional terms, the realities behind the expressions of anxiety were rather different. The most significant changes in rural society between 1750 and 1850 were the increasing 'proletarianisation' and pauperisation of the peasantry. The peasant was weakened first by loss of land, and then by his lack of collective self-defence which his counterpart in the town was developing during the same period.[22] There had been disturbances among the peasantry in the mid-1790s, in the eastern counties in 1816 and 1822, all over southern England in 1830, with a scattering, mainly in the eastern counties again, in 1834–5 and 1843–4. The 'farmer' witnesses to the 1833 Select Committee argued that their own dilemma was due to their having to pay artificially high wages and employ excessive numbers of labourers so that they might avoid being afflicted with outbreaks of rick-burning.[23] Rudé and Hobsbawm conclude, however, that the solidarity of rural society as represented in the Select Committees was an illusion. The rioters may have had the sympathy of 'the bulk of the counties' rulers'; but the central government, 'full of ideology and the fear of revolution', took rather a different view.[24]

The evolving triple division of landed society in the early nineteenth century had an important bearing upon the demand, from above, for the provision of kinds of education appropriate to the lower divisions of society. For the landlord, economic common sense dictated that he should attempt to get the maximum rent from the most businesslike farmers, by organising tenancies so as to encourage the most profitable production. For the largest estate-owners such considerations may not have mattered; but for the ruck of gentry who controlled county society, there was the need to produce greater efficiency among their farmers. And it was this need which accounted for the continuing desire to provide a species of middle-class education appropriate for improving the quality of the farmer-class. This problem was intensified by the pauperisation of the peasant, and his transformation into a hired labourer: potentially successful tenant-farmers were not easy to find among a depressed peasantry. Education was seen, by a number of those who mattered, as a means of stabilising and reinforcing the fabric of rural society during a difficult period. A writer in the *Westminster Review* said in 1833, 'In the catalogue of mischiefs which beset the condition of the landed interest . . . their system of education is not the least prominent'.[25]

The general problems of English agriculture in the period immediately after the era of 'Swing' – the need to support tenant-improvements and to provide a more equitable system of leases; above all, the need to respond to growing economic demand by introducing technical innovations on a large scale – received an interim solution with the founding of the Royal Agricultural Society in 1839. Its first members declared the urgency of their economic and social intents by prohibiting the discussion of political matters, like agitation for repeal, at its meetings, thus expressing the hope that it might be possible for Whig and Tory magnates to work together for common ends in reasonable harmony.[26]

The obvious failings of rural society, and the model rural schools of de Fellenberg in Switzerland were the chief inspirations for Duppa's proposal of a system of county colleges of agriculture in 1839.[27] He suggested that the colleges should be founded upon the joint-stock principle, with moderate fees, to provide a measure of practical farming education for boarders. A peasant school might be attached to each institution, as at Hofwyl. Duppa openly expressed his debt to de Fellenberg, but did not indulge in an excessive optimism about his own proposals:

. . . de Fellenberg is a man of an age; we must not wait until his like arises in this country. He has shown us what to do; and if we do it, and do it upon such a scale, and so generally throughout the country, as to be of material service, we must do it by such means as will not call for more than moderate sacrifices from any person . . . and even those who are called upon to make a small sacrifice should have a prospect of such eventual advantages, either in the education of their children or in the improvement of their estates, as would operate forcibly upon the minds of all intelligent and reflecting persons.[28]

Significantly, Duppa's essay ended with a long quotation from the report of the Irish Board of Education, for 1838, on the agricultural schools at Templemoyle.[29] Two years before, he had submitted evidence to Thomas Wyse's Select Committee on Irish Endowed Schools, and again, in that place, he had emphasised the importance of de Fellenberg's example.[30] Duppa concluded, 'Let me therefore interest all those who inhabit the halls of their ancestors throughout this beautiful country, to reflect upon what I have said, and act – follow the example of the illustrious de Fellenberg – and hand down their possessions to posterity, with a title doubly secure'.[31]

Both de Fellenberg and Duppa (along with Thomas Arnold and the proponents of the public boarding schools idea) were in the mainstream of a tradition of rural education for all – that is, even for those who had been born in industrial cities – which may now seem archaic and misdirected, but which continued to exercise its influence well into the present century.[32] Certainly in de Fellenberg's work there is a clear anticipation of the kind of social engineering, rooted in the county community, which achieved its classic fulfilment in the recommendations of the Taunton Commission in the 1860s. And Duppa could at least point to one area of the United Kingdom where the kinds of experiments he was suggesting were already working successfully: this was in Ireland. The *Journal* of the Royal Agricultural Society in 1842 contained an article suggesting that the experiments in agricultural education of the Dublin Agricultural Improvement Society might be transplanted to England.[33] The author noted that some 'patriotic individuals', notably Earl Ducie in Gloucestershire, 'have founded what are called model-farms, with the view of pointing out to the neighbouring agriculturists the most approved methods of culture at present recognised'.[34]

The 1842 article came in the midst of the evangelising work of the Anti-Corn-Law League; and sympathy for the social and economic plight of the tenant-farmer in the years immediately before Repeal was reflected in H.M.I. the Revd John Allen's General Report to the

Committee of Council on Education in 1842. The chief part of Allen's inspection had been undertaken in rural counties. He wrote:

> ... but there are other inhabitants of our agricultural districts who are often worse taught than the labourer's child, I mean the children of our farmers; and unless they are properly educated very little is done. The character of the farm servant depends in a great degree upon that of his master; and if a lasting and salutary effect is to be produced upon the lower classes of society, attention must be paid to the establishment and superintendence of good middle schools.[35]

It seems likely that, in this instance, Allen was partaking of the kind of anxiety about the rural economy and country society which was common to many of his colleagues in the parochial clergy, who were amongst the most enthusiastic supporters of agricultural societies and farmers' clubs.

The experiments in Ireland and the pressure upon the farming community associated with Repeal agitation were factors which had some bearing upon the only major experiment in agricultural education undertaken in England in the 1840s. This was the founding, under Royal Charter, of the Agricultural College at Cirencester. The *Gardener's Chronicle* noted, in February 1846, that, of late, local farmers' clubs had been in the forefront of those proposing to diffuse an interest in the cause of agricultural improvement.[36] 'We have lately asked, WHERE ARE THE SCHOOLS FOR FARMERS' SONS?' The question had, apparently, remained unanswered, except for the evidence of the founding of a Chair of Agriculture at Edinburgh and 'the many agricultural schools in Ireland', until it was taken up by the Fairford and Cirencester Farmers' Club, or rather by Mr Brown, a leading member of that Society, a local businessman, not a farmer.

In November 1842, Brown had read a paper to the Club on the advantages of a specific education for agricultural pursuits in which he hoped that soon every district of England would have its own special agricultural college. These colleges would serve, not the 'finical gentleman, afraid of soiling his hands', but 'intelligent, active, hardy young men who will maintain the substantial, honest character of the English yeoman', combined with learning based upon the latest scientific advances, careful training in 'moral and religious culture'; so that they might be elevated to 'the station in the country that they ought to fill'. The Club enthusiastically endorsed his idea; but the direction of subsequent events passed into the hands of Earl

Ducie, Lord Bathurst, and others of the county élite, who were more experienced in the manipulation of affairs on a grand scale. 'A committee of gentlemen', therefore, was constituted, to carry the plan into effect. It was at this stage, too, in the following year, that it was decided to put the plan forward as a unilateral scheme for the Cotswolds area alone, and to obtain a Royal Charter.[37] Earl Ducie acted as chief publicist for the venture, and a long list of subscribers from all over England was compiled in 1845. Ducie's motion, at the great meeting of 1844, was: 'That it is expedient to provide an Institution in which the rising generation of farmers may receive instruction, at a moderate expense, in those sciences, a knowledge of which is essential to successful cultivation; and that a Farm form part of such Institution'. Some of the subsequent subscribers were the descendants of famous eighteenth-century improvers: Ducie himself, the Dukes of Bedford and Grafton, Prince Albert, the Marquis of Lansdowne (then President of the Council), the radical Earl of Radnor, Earls Fortescue, Granville and Harrowby, Lord John Russell, Lords Ebrington, Lyttelton and Redesdale, Hicks Beach, a local M.P., T. D. Acland, Henry Labouchere, M.P. (later, as Lord Taunton, to preside over the S.I.C.), and Philip Pusey, friend of Acland and Editor of the Royal Agricultural Society's *Journal*.[38]

The Royal Charter was granted in March 1845, but it did not guarantee an untroubled sequence of development and expansion for the College during the next three decades. The Royal College was inevitably one of the first institutions to engage the attention of the S.I.C. early in 1865. The Commissioners interviewed Augustus Voelcker, Professor of Chemistry at the College, who told Lord Taunton that 'all who devote themselves in any way to agriculture as a class, are deficient in their education; no matter whether they are tenant-farmers' sons or the grade above'. He said that he preferred a system of county schools and public schools, as a means of educating tenant-farmers' sons, to 'miserable' private schools. But Cirencester had failed to attract boys from the tenant-farmer class. 'What I should like to see is a good plain English education, given in county schools, with a higher department on the plan of Cirencester'.[39]

Repeal put pressure on the landowning class to treat its tenants with more equitable consideration. As a landowner himself in Staffordshire, Peel showed material concern for his tenants. James Caird, his bailiff, writing in 1851, recorded how, two years before, faced with the results of his own policy, Peel offered his tenants an investment, equal to one-fifth of current rent, in such immediate improvements on each farm as might reduce costs or increase output.[40] Of Devonshire – the county of Acland, Fortescue and Stafford Northcote – Caird said, 'we found among farmers a unanimous expression of opinion that prices must rise or rents be reduced'.[41] Lord Lyttelton, in 1851, wrote to the tenants on his estates in Worcestershire guaranteeing a stop in rents for the current year.[42] And in 1850, on the advice of Pusey, T. D. Acland, currently out of Parliament after supporting Repeal, submitted an article to the R.A.S. *Journal* on farming in Somerset. He stressed the need for 'fuller security for the farmer. . . . Let it only be remembered that no man can farm well unless he can look with confidence beyond Michaelmas'.[43] The year before, Acland had written to his wife that he was alarmed by the price of American corn: 'I begin to think that a serious fall of rents is inevitable, in which case we must come down considerably, and I hope it may lead to fresh arrangements in which my farming knowledge may be of service, and help us all to live'.[44]

The economic challenge of the post-Repeal era in agriculture led directly to a revival of the publishing activities of the Bath and West Society. A new *Journal* was founded in 1853, edited by Acland; and alongside learned articles on agricultural science and practice by Pusey, H. S. Thompson, and Professor Voelcker,[45] there were considerable contributions on the farm labourer, but more particularly on farmers' sons, by Acland himself, Brereton and Richard Dawes,[46] by the Revd H. J. Barton, Secretary of the Northants Education Society,[47] and by Lord Ebrington, later Earl Fortescue.[48]

In the pages of the Bath and West *Journal* were recorded the origins of the prize scheme for the sons of farmers which developed into the Oxford and Cambridge 'Locals'.[49] More especially there were extracts from the Minute of the Council of the Society pledging support for Ebrington's proposals in October 1855.[50] Lord Ebrington's memorandum on middle-class education, which he submitted to the Society in 1856, contained several points which were significant indicators of future developments. For instance, he said that his object in offering the prize was 'not merely to give young farmers an incentive to exertion, but also to endeavour to ascertain (with a view to amendment, if necessary) the means of education at present practically available for that class in Devonshire. I mean of general education, as distinguished from business training'.[51] He went on to say, developing a theme which had been part of Arnold's initial analysis,[52] that more accurate knowledge was essential for the middle class, because he believed 'that more has latterly been done for improving the education of the classes above and below the farmers than for them'.[53]

His preference at this stage was for the Society of Arts as the examining authority for middle-class schools. The universities, he thought, were still necessarily preoccupied with their internal affairs, and could not yet take on the work of supervision. This may have reflected his earlier truncated university career: a fellow-student of Lyttelton at Trinity, he had been taken away from Cambridge by his father, Earl Fortescue, so that he could serve as one of his secretaries during his Lord Lieutenancy in Ireland. Acland, on the other hand, who favoured Oxford as an examining body for schools, had taken a Double First and had a Regius Professor brother.[54]

In two other ways Ebrington's ideas shared common features with Thomas Arnold's. He thought that the £50 franchise would best indicate the minimum qualification for candidates for his Devon prizes, 'since it is with their educational qualifications for their position as Englishmen of the middle class, and for their duties as citizens of a free country, that we are here concerned, rather than with their technical or professional knowledge as persons engaged in the business of farming'.[5] Also, he took up directly another point first raised by Arnold: in order to deal with the fast-growing problem of Dissent, he suggested refounding the order of deacons, in a subordinate position to the formally ordained clergy of the Church of England. An efficient system of middle-class education would provide a source of recruitment for such offices: 'I believe, with the wise and good Dr. Arnold, that the want of such a body . . . is one of the greatest causes of Dissent in the middle and lower classes. . . . God forbid that in the hierarchy of the Church alone, of all our institutions in England, an impassable line should be drawn between the higher, middle and lower ranks'.[56]

Thus far, two distinct, yet interrelated, currents have been distinguished in the mainstream of writing upon the subject of rural middle-class education: they are, the need to promote greater technical expertise among the tenant-farmers, with resultant benefits for the landowning class; and the necessity of using a distinctive kind of schooling to reinforce and enhance the social position of the middle-class in relation to those below them. In the writings of Duppa these two themes were equally balanced. For Ebrington, the social theme took precedence over the technical: social engineering, it seems, was of paramount importance in the 1850s in rural society, to be reinforced only incidentally by practical training. This new emphasis was developed by Ebrington's ally, J. L. Brereton, in two papers he published in the Royal Agricultural Society's *Journal* in 1863 and 1864.[57] But the balance was never completely upset, since Ebrington confined his notion of examinations to the farming class, saying that he set the age-limit for the candidates in his prize-scheme relatively high 'simply to ensure that all having fairly committed themselves to the pursuit of agriculture'. And in 1864, almost at the very moment when the members of the S.I.C. were gazetted, Ebrington (now Fortescue) remarked, at the Devon County School prize day, upon the 'necessity of farmers' sons being so trained as to avoid the two extremes – sticking too fast to what is old, and rushing too quickly to what is new'. Earlier in this speech he had reflected upon Arnold's remarks, made thirty years before, on the subject of middle-class education.[58]

In the Bath and West *Journal* for 1857, Acland's editorial was partly devoted to a discourse on Brereton's further development of Ebrington's plans in the same issue. Brereton was suggesting that in the county of Devon about twenty farm-schools, for the lower classes, and a farm-college, should be established, with fees for tuition, and labour employed to maintain the farms. The basic elements were, 'a system of self-supporting public education, starting with parish schools and ending in a county degree'; and 'a classification of ages, the limits of each class being the time at which education of a large class of society would naturally cease'. The efficiency of each subordinate school would be secured by the immediate demand created by a school or examination on the same system. To his summary of Brereton's proposals Acland appended two-and-a-half pages of quotation from Arnold's 1832 letters, which, he said, 'cannot be too often quoted'.[59]

Acland's own pamphlet, *The Education of the Farmer*, was printed as part of the 1857 Bath and West *Journal*.[60] The Arnoldian influences are again very apparent, extending to another appendix of quotations from the Sheffield letters. Acland developed the opinions of Arnold in a way very similar to Ebrington's, and provided the basis for a prescription for middle-class education which was to dominate practice until well into the twentieth century. He wrote:

Although addressing farmers, I have treated middle-class education in

general. I have endeavoured to describe a really useful 'Middle-class Education', and yet I doubt not it will appear to some that I have passed too
lightly over commercial and technical requirements, and have under-stated
the value of particular sciences; but my object has been not so much to lay a
system for a particular class, as to awaken attention to the spirit and aim of
all education that can fairly claim to be called 'practical'. Feeling as I do great
respect for the manly virtues and practical habits of Englishmen in the
middle ranks, I believe that they are not far wrong in preferring their own
common sense as a guide in business to what they call theory. But it may be
confidently asserted that their habits and business need not suffer, and that
new sources of enjoyment and usefulness will be a warm interest in the
mental cultivation which is going on in other classes of society . . . success in
the efforts made for national education by religious bodies and by the State
will to a great extent depend on the interest which the middle classes may be
induced to take in it, and it imports much to the welfare of the nation
that the practical activity called forth in agriculture, manufactures, and the
arts, should be guided not only by sound teaching of science, but by moral
and humanising influences.

He claimed to have established two main points: first, that a special
agricultural education was not necessary for young boys; and,
second, that the middle-class education of farmers' sons should be
complete in itself, 'and not a truncated portion of a loftier edifice –
not the first stage of a journey broken off in the middle'.[61] His
concern was chiefly for the education of the sons of the 'small
farmer', the man with £100 a year profit, who was 'in reality little
above' . . . the superior town mechanic or small tradesman'.

In connection with that particular group, he confessed that he
could not understand the antipathy of the rural middle class to the
country elementary schools. He quoted at length from Richard
Dawes's *Suggestive Hints on Secular Instruction*; and he insisted that
the mingling of the children of the middling and the poorer classes in
village and town schools would be qualified by a process of economic
selection: '. . . the advantage of both parties would be very great, and
by proper management, no confusion of ranks need ensue; the
labourer's child, alas! is sure to be driven out to work at an early age,
and the boys in the first class will generally be drawn from a higher
grade in society owing to their staying longer at school'. The poor
need not suffer, since this is 'the old-fashioned English arrangement
under which a great man has arisen from the Village School through
the University to high places in Church and State. The country
schools in England will never be what they might be until the middle
classes take more interest in them'.

Acland put his trust in a liberal system of education conducted in existing schools, including the National schools, the high quality of whose teaching would be stimulated and maintained by 'Local' examinations associated with Oxford and Cambridge. He acknowledged, but otherwise ignored, the proposals of Fortescue and Brereton for establishing a system of county schools and colleges. Brereton's detailed scheme, which he published in 1858, owed its inspiration, if not its specific proposals, to Thomas Arnold who was the first Englishman to utter the concept of a 'county' university; though, as is shown in the discussion of Ireland, below,[62] the idea of a county college had been suggested for Ireland some time before Arnold took it up. In *Principles and Plan of a County School*, Brereton said that his main proposition was that of 'public schools for the Middle Classes'; with the important qualification that 'the old organisation of our Counties' would afford the best basis for organising such schools.[63] A system of interrelated public schools would serve to overcome the indifference of parents; and for no class was such a stimulus more required than for farmers and their sons, 'who necessarily live in detached houses and pass a more isolated life than other people, and who are not influenced by general public opinion, unless it reaches them through an organisation with which they are specially connected'.

In preparing to establish farm-schools, Brereton was assuming that the practice of agriculture in England had become sufficiently well formulated to comprise a distinct branch of education, in combination with other necessary studies. On this point he was strangely at odds with Acland who, from his own experience, and by his own enterprise, had come to know more about agricultural chemistry than Brereton, and yet seems to have been more sceptical about its usefulness in the early training of farmers' sons. In his memoir of his father, A. H. D. Acland recorded that as soon as T. D. entered the political wilderness, in 1847, after his support of Repeal, 'he was hard at work learning chemistry in the laboratory of King's College (London) . . . he felt himself to be particularly bound, after his vote for the abolition of the Corn Laws, to do what he could to show the farmers a better method of improving their position than was to be found in any reliance upon protection'.[64]

Brereton's general plan as summarised by Acland in the Bath and West *Journal*, included the establishment, in each registration division, of a public school with a farm attached; and in each county a college with a larger farm and complete equipment for advanced studies. There would also be an annual examination leading to a degree and honours. The initial step would be the creation of a single middle-class school. For this experiment 'I have the offer from Earl Fortescue . . . of premises and land, rent free, and I am prepared for appointment of both master and bailiff'. But he needed assistance in the form of contributions from his neighbours before he could actually start the school, and he appealed for this support. He solicited the attention, 'not only of farmers but of the landlords and clergy, to the expedience of establishing some independent public system of education, which shall affect, in a measure, all classes, but dealing principally and directly with the great middle class, shall, by elevating them, lift with them those who are and must be dependent upon them'. Despite his insistence upon an element of practice and scientific training, he could not ultimately diguise the basic social purpose of the experiment.

The school which Brereton and Fortescue set up at West Buckland, originally called the Devon County School, began inauspiciously in a farmhouse. The first headmaster was engaged on the recommendation of Canon H. G. Robinson, the Principal of the York Training College, later to become an Endowed Schools Commissioner.[65] The title, 'Devon County School Association', was adopted at the suggestion of the Duke of Bedford, and the limited liability principle became the basis of operations; Earl Fortescue and the Duke presented their shareholdings to the Association which held in trust £1,000 of the £5,825 capital. The shareholders in 1865 included thirteen landlords, eleven farmers, eight clergy, and twenty-two others. Before the S.I.C., Brereton was confident that such schools would be widely supported, though, because of the low fees, a large dividend could never be expected.[66]

Brereton's general principles underwent a change at this time; the farm part of the new school was soon abandoned. In April 1863, a paper by Brereton was taken as the ground for discussion of middle-class education by the Weekly Council of the R.A.S. Other contributors on that occasion were leading members of the Society's Education Committee, like Sir E. C. Kerrison, one of the leading promoters of the Suffolk County School; H. S. Thompson, a proponent of agricultural progress and railways in Yorkshire, who took a prominent part in the Social Science Association's discussions of middle-class education in 1864, and who gave important evidence to the S.I.C.; the Earl of Powis, who was to head a commission examining Irish intermediate education in 1870, and Professor Voelcker. In his paper, Brereton, like Duppa before him, had emphasised the educational isolation of the farmer, by comparison with the landlord and the labourer, whose children were instructed at the expense of various kinds of public funds, either in the endowed public schools or in the public elementary schools. The new concept which Brereton introduced was that the social and civilising part of the middle-class education was more important than the acquisition of special knowledge:

> Public proprietary schools, distributed through the various counties of England, and associated as much as possible with all the honourable and influential names and personages of these counties, are, I have long ventured to think, the first requisite towards improved agricultural education. Such schools will supply, not only to the future farmer, but to all the farmers' sons, that general groundwork of education which should precede and be the foundation of all sound knowledge and special practice.[67]

He supported this broad notion of middle-class education by pointing out that 'not all farmers are farmers' sons, nor all farmers' sons destined to be farmers'. He also mentioned 'the ancient organisation of the English counties', which were sufficiently connected with all the best associations in Church and State, while being characterised by freedom and religious toleration, 'to offer a common name and many local centres round which the public education of the middle classes may be safely and honourably grouped'. At this meeting, support for Brereton's opinions was provided by quotations from the report of the Revd Bellairs, H.M.I., who had said of the farmers of the West Midlands that there was no other class of society 'as imperfectly educated, or whose opinions are so crudely formed'.[68] Voelcker thought that the practical part of farming education was best achieved at home; the 'farm' was an expense which fell very heavily upon agricultural schools.[69]

The proprietary-school part of Brereton's plan found immediate and widespread responses. A later chapter will show that the idea of a county school or 'academy' had been part of the debate about middle-class education in Ireland also for almost a century before the founding of West Buckland.[70] In one of his letters of advice to Granville, while the S.I.C. was being put under way in 1864, Frederick Temple, admitting that his list of suggested members of the Commission had a West-Country bias, excused this characteristic by saying that West Countrymen had been more active than others in the promotion of ideas and schemes in the field of middle-class education.[71] Letter VII in Caird's *English Agriculture* provides some clues about the economic background to schemes hatched in the West of England. There were, according to Caird, two classes of tenant-farmer in Devon: 'men with small holdings, little elevated above the condition of the labourer'; and 'educated agriculturists', holding large farms into which they had introduced improved methods of husbandry. The latter group had been responsible for the main improvements in drainage, irrigation and enclosure, and stock-breeding. In general, however, tenant-farms were of moderate, even small, size – fifty to 200 acres – though there were a few farms of 600 to 700 acres. The arable land, 'where the tenants have sufficient capital', was managed wisely, the small farmers profiting by the example set by richer and more far-sighted neighbours.[72] He said, 'We found among the farmers an unanimous expression of opinion that prices must rise or rents be reduced. . . . A general reduction in rents is the great object which they are all driving now to accomplish. Reduced rents are widely requested.'[73]

It is not difficult to relate this evidence of economic pressure upon tenants to the desire among enlightened West-Country landlords for a measure of distinctively middle-class education as a means of developing greater flexibility of agricultural practice – and, thereby, increased profits and rents – among the tenant-farmer class. Caird pointed to the example of Gloucestershire where the experimental farms at Whitfield-in-the-Wolds and Cirencester had provided a strong stimulus for local tenants: '. . . by degrees many hints will be taken by the surrounding farmers, whose prejudices will yield to the satisfactory evidence of success'.[74] In Kerrison's county of Suffolk, the farmers complained that, 'until within the last two or three years', their landlords were little concerned about the welfare of tenants, or the management of their estates. There had been no 'leading man' in the county for a long time: '. . . the repeal of the Corn Laws and the fall in prices have at least compelled attention to a business which has been far too long neglected'.[75]

From the late eighteenth century until the 1850s the agricultural community was subject to a series of crises and depressions, which partially explains the desire of some notable landlords to promote both greater social stability and a higher degree of technical expertise among their tenants. But equally there can be little doubt but that this desire was heightened by the effects of Repeal upon the county communities in the late 1840s and the 1850s. In the period 1837 to 1842 the farmers were able to profit while the manufacturing communities suffered severe depression. But thereafter, until the 1880s,

> ... the current flowed strongly in favour of large additions to land-lords' capital with the express purpose of attracting and encouraging substantial and liberal-handed farming. Particularly in bad years, but also in good times, landlords' outlays were generally diminished.... Behind the façade of the 'Golden Age of English Agriculture', which is said to have lasted for the twenty years after the outbreak of the Crimean War, a distinct weakening in the economic position of agricultural landowners can be detected.[76]

The crisis of 1850–2 was probably the most substantial for thirty years, and although landlords' reactions to it seem to have varied considerably, abatements of rent of ten per cent were common; and as one great landowner set the pace for such abatements his lesser neighbours tended to follow suit, in order to avoid the charge of injustice. F. M. L. Thompson has written, 'with the great landowners the mid-century age of improvement was a matter of pouring money into their estates for very meagre rewards, a far cry indeed from the age of enclosure'.[77]

The main conclusion to be drawn from this depiction of the landed interest defending the established order of rural society is that major contributions were made to the mainstream of S.I.C. ideas by a powerful élite group, most of whom had their roots in the West Country. These members of a traditional ruling class, despite differences of party allegiance, co-operated and interacted with one another in promoting schemes for middle-class education. They associated together as M.P.s, as magistrates, even as Lords Lieutenant; they were in most cases prominent members of the Bath and West Society; a number of them were founding members of the Devon County School Association, and a significant sub-group of them helped to create the Oxford and Cambridge Local Examinations. Their wider influence was exerted through national agencies and associations: as members of the Central Society for Education, the Social Science Association and the Royal Agricultural Society. One common component of their thinking was the concept of the county as the main cell around which future developments in

middle-class education should occur; another was their liberal
Anglicanism, which distinguished them from supporters of the High-
Church ritualism of Woodard's institutions in Sussex. This was the
most distinctive and powerful group to feed evidence and ideas into
the deliberations of the Schools Inquiry Commission.

But the most important feature was their common emphasis upon
the educational needs of the tenant-farmers' sons. This was based
upon two impulses. Firstly, there was a desire to strengthen the
agricultural community economically after the shock of Repeal and
the earlier rent crises; more efficient middle-class schooling was seen
as a long-term, relatively cheap means of avoiding damagingly large
increases in capital investment by the landowning class. Secondly,
there was a clear commitment to social engineering: the need to
preserve the tripartite organisation of the landed interest. By the
1850s owners of land were prepared to patronise the process of
schooling on three distinct levels: they supported, in some cases,
industrial schools to deal with extreme instances of deprivation;[78]
they subscribed for the maintenance of voluntary schools;[79] and they
promoted the educational interests of tenant-farmers' sons by spon-
soring middle-class schools and providing ancillary encouragement.

The ideas of this rural group do not fit neatly into the later pattern
of S.I.C. recommendations: their influence was less precise than that,
and more pervasive. They provided, not a complete, unitary solution
to the problem of middle-class education, but rather a range of
important presuppositions which formed a framework into which
other necessary considerations might be fitted. Up to 1864 the West-
Country group had avoided trying to deal with legal complexities
associated with the reform of endowed schools. But the 'insiders'
among that group – those who sat on the S.I.C.[80] – were forced to
come to terms with endowments as one of the resources available for
the construction of a middle-class school system.

The Report of the S.I.C. said, in 1867, 'Lord Fortescue has pointed
out that local opposition to many changes would probably be much
diminished and perhaps disappear if a considerable district, for
instance, as a county, were handled by itself, and the endowments
were administered for the benefit of that county'.[81] They accepted
that a local board had several advantages over a central authority: it
could act from personal knowledge of the district, consulting the
feelings of the people: it could inquire into important endowments
on the spot, and give every person interested an opportunity of being

thoroughly heard. But the Commissioners finally decided that, for the time being, it would be extremely difficult to devise a board for each county which would gain general acceptance.[82]

The Taunton idea of local control was not based exclusively upon evidence from and about Devonshire. Canon H. G. Robinson, whose connections with West Buckland have been mentioned earlier, said in his evidence that there should be an elaborate arrangement of local boards. After suggesting the amalgamation of endowments for the purpose of providing a good middle school for a neighbourhood, Robinson proposed his scheme for a county board, 'chosen from the persons most competent to decide in their respective districts. I should expect that the county would get for that service the men of the highest position in the county'.[83] Replying to Lord Lyttelton, he said he would certainly not restrict membership to Anglicans, and would insist upon conscience clauses in county schools. He wanted the country to be divided into educational districts. The members of the district or county boards should be partly nominated, partly elected. The nominated members would be provided by different bodies of local trustees; 'and certain leading county officials might be *ex officio* members', for example, the Bishop and the Lord Lieutenant. He admitted that the elected element would be more difficult to provide for, 'because there seems to be no constituency necessarily available for electing them'. However, such a constituency might be formed, he thought, in the case of the county proprietary schools, from among the financial contributors; various religious denominations might elect representatives, and all subscribers to education in a district might choose members. Such a system for the management of middle-class education over a district might be extended to cover elementary education as well, 'and thus a complete national system would be developed'.[84]

Lord Harrowby was the last of those witnesses to the S.I.C. who were in favour of some sort of local association, making his famous assertion, 'I should like to club the grammar schools with some relation to locality, and I should like to say, *You* shall be a lower middle-class school; *you* shall be a middle middle-class school; and *you* shall be a higher middle-class school, that which is now called a grammar school'.[85] Questioned by Acland about local arrangements for effecting changes among the schools, he replied that it was an extremely difficult matter, 'because . . . you are brought into contact with very tender feelings in different localities and with a rather jealous feeling as to the interference of the State'.[86]

Despite the lack of detailed knowledge about the course of their deliberations, it must be presumed that the discussion of the notion of local agencies for reform and control must have long engaged the attention of the S.I.C. in its later stages, for in May 1866, before they received the evidence of their last oral witnesses, they decided to canvass opinions of further leading figures, by means of a four-point circular, one of whose propositions was:

> To improve the machinery for the management of endowments, it has been suggested that the endowed schools should be grouped together in districts, and that a local board should be formed to manage the endowments in each district, subject to a central authority in London. It is important to decide whether this is the best machinery for the purpose; and if so, how the boards should be formed, and with what powers they should be entrusted.[87]

Replies were requested from forty-four persons, thirty of whom sent answers.[88] Tantalisingly, neither Charles Vaughan, formerly headmaster of Harrow and a disciple of Arnold, nor H. A. Bruce, vice-president of the Committee of Council for Education, replied. J. T. Coleridge, one of Acland's West-Country associates and a supporter of West Buckland School, wrote, 'The small local boards of trustees must be put an end to, and a board for the county created, in whom should vest the powers of appointing and removing the master and inspectors'. The headmaster of Hereford Cathedral School, replying for Dean Dawes, who was unwell, said that 'a local board for the management of the examination of the schools of the district might with advantage be established'. Such a system, in embryo, he said, already operated in connection with Hereford Cathedral School and Ludlow Grammar School.[89] John Jackson, Bishop of Lincoln, the teacher of Brereton at his first school in Islington,[90] said that a county board would be more useful in connecting the work of the various grades of schools he was proposing for the middle classes. But he thought that 'in a district containing few resident gentry it would be very difficult to form an efficient board', which would have to be composed of a few official persons such as the Lord Lieutenant, the Chairman of Quarter Sessions, and the Bishop and Archdeacons. A larger number of persons, each closely interested in the immediate neighbourhood, would be 'perhaps not so well qualified to administer a whole district judicously and harmoniously'.[91]

Edward Miall, representing the views of broad dissent, in a lengthy and diffuse reply, suggested that, 'until public opinion on the subject (of endowments) shall become enlightened and energetic, vested interests are too many, and touch society at too many points, to admit of their being dealt with by Parliament as reason would prescribe'. 'Ecclesiastical exclusiveness', he thought, prevented an arrangement of local boards.[92]

The balance between the 'pros' and 'cons' in this survey was weighted towards those who were sceptical about the possibility of creating local boards. Yet a long recommendation concerning provincial boards – with a qualifying admission of the difficulties which would be involved – was included in the Summary chapter of the final Report.[93] This was, of course, omitted from the 1869 Endowed Schools Bill. But in 1872 the Endowed Schools Commissioners appointed under the 1869 Act, in their Report to the Privy Council, complained particularly about the difficulty attending their work which resulted largely, they claimed, from the absence of local machinery for operating the Act.[94] And when, in the following year, Lyttelton made a more elaborate oral complaint before the Select Committee on the 1869 Act, Forster, as chairman, had to remind him of their discussions before the drafting of the Bill, which had caused the omission of the provincial board proposal.[95]

The sensitivity shown by the draftsmen of the 1869 Bill to the difficulties which would attend the establishment of provincial or county boards is remarkable in a special way. The classic attack upon the management of county government through quarter sessions had been mounted by J. S. Mill in his *Representative Government* in 1861. He wrote that the institution of quarter sessions 'is the most aristocratic in principle which now remains in England', far more so than the House of Lords, since quarter sessions granted public money and disposed of a wide range of public interests without reference to a representative body.[96] A recent commentator on English local government in the nineteenth century has said that Mill's principle, in this connection, 'passed into the perceived wisdom' almost without being questioned.[97] Municipal government had been reformed in 1835, and thereafter radical politicians like Joseph Hume continued to peck at the parallel, but less susceptible, problem of county government. The failure of these attempts has been interpreted as a consequence of 'the reluctance of M.P.s to sanction an assault on their own class'; the lines were marked out in the 1830s: the 'new middle class' was allowed to dominate the represented and self-governing towns, while 'the traditional landed class continued pre-eminent in both county government and national politics' for fifty years.[98] J. L. Hammond, commenting upon the relatively unruffled progress of local government, noted 'it has no pitched battles leaving behind them heroic echoes. It has no Midlothian campaigns'.[99]

It is quite clear that Forster, as draftsman of the 1869 Bill and spokesman for the strong Radical wing of a heterogeneous Liberal administration, avoided the S.I.C.'s tactic of proposing a local authority for middle-class education based on the old model of county government. In the absence of detailed evidence of discussions within the S.I.C., it is necessary to look for traces of other elements which may have shaped decisions. Between the publication of the Taunton Report and the beginning of Gladstone's first administration a Select Committee was appointed on 29 April 1869, 'to inquire into the present mode of conducting the Financial Arrangements of the Counties in England and Wales', and 'whether any alterations ought to be made either in the persons by whom, or the manner in which, such arrangements are now conducted'.[100] Among other members of the Committee were Lord Henley and H. A. Bruce. On the same day in April, James Wyld, Liberal M.P. for Bodmin,[101] had introduced the second reading of his County Financial Boards Bill.[102] In the debate on Wyld's Bill, Forster said that he was M.P. for a borough, Bradford, which was rated by the county. The time had come, he said, for the application of the elective principle to county government. He trusted that 'the result of this debate would be, not only to refer this Bill to a Select Committee, but that various other questions in connection with it would receive full consideration'.[103] He did not specify what these 'other questions' were; but it would seem likely that, having been a member of the S.I.C. until a year before, the question of 'county government' for middle-class (and perhaps other) schooling was one of them.

In the report of the 1869 Select Committee on county government it was noted that 'a desire prevails on the part of the county rate-payers to place the County Finance more directly under their own control, by means of elected representatives to be associated with the magistrates in the expenditures of the rates'.[104] Wyld's Bill, with the corroborating evidence of the Select Committee, probably supplied the main reason for the Gladstone administration's decision to abandon the Taunton idea of provincial or county boards. The Liberals were generally sympathetic to the notion of reforming county government according to the representative principle; but such a policy was not part of their official programme. The problem which would have resulted from the creation of provincial boards under a Bill dealing with the endowed schools would have inhibited any possible progress towards the general reform of county government.

Just as the concerns of the leaders of rural county communities provided a simple framework for the discussion of middle-class education by the S.I.C. after 1864, so the Commissioners persisted in their desire to balance the creation of a central authority for middle-class education with the formation of provincial or county bodies which, though containing a selective element, would represent the interests of the traditional leaders of county communities – the diocesan officials, landowners and magistrates. In this sense, some of the S.I.C. proposals can be seen as the last fling of the landed interest; though this assertive action was qualified by the incorporation of liberal ideas for a measure of representation and religious toleration. The ways in which the middle classes at first failed to produce an alternative model or scheme of their own before 1869, and later combatted this attempt at continued autocratic control, are considered in greater detail in later chapters. Here it has been thought necessary to say only that the rural community produced a multifarious body of ideas which on their own were seen to be sufficient for providing the basis for what was essentially an internal discussion among upper-class persons who dominated the S.I.C. in the middle of the 1860s.

Notes

1   See E. J. Hobsbawn, *Industry and Empire*, London, 1969, pp. 97–9; A. Briggs, *The Age of Improvement*, London, 1960, pp. 42–3; A. Cheesborough, 'A Short History of Agricultural Education up to 1939', *The Vocational Aspect of Secondary and Further Education*, No. 41, Autumn, 1966, XVIII, pp. 182–3. Briggs says, 'The slow movement of ideas, the lack of basic techniques and the often unsatisfactory system of leases and tenures held back "revolutionary advances". . . . The new "improved agriculture" stopped short in most places at the point where mechanisation began, and it continued to demand large numbers of agricultural workers. There were still powerful barriers to long-distance movement'.

2   *Central Society of Education*, 3rd publication, London, 1839, reprinted 1968, B. F. Duppa, 'County Colleges of Agriculture', pp. 49–50.

3   See H. Pollard, Pioneers of Popular Education in England, London, 1956, pp. 42–9; also, the article by E. de Fellenberg in *Central Society of Education*, 2nd publication, 1838, p. 273; and Duppa's evidence to the Select Committee on Irish Education, 1838 (see below, chapter II).

4   W. H. G. Armytage, 'Augustan Honeycombs', in M. Seaborne, *The Changing Curriculum*, London, 1971, pp. 37–50.

5   G. E. Mingay, *Landed Society in the Eighteenth Century*, London, 1963, p. 167.

6   Ibid, p. 170.

7   K. Hudson, *Patriotism with Profit: British Agricultural Societies in the 18th and 19th centuries*, London, 1972, p. ix.

8   *Letters and Papers on Agriculture selected from the correspondence of the Bath and West of England Society for the Encouragement of Agriculture, Arts, Manufactures and Commerce*, I, 4th edition, Bath, 1802 (first printed 1785), pp. 11–19.

9   K. M. Burton, *Milton's Prose Writings*, London, 1958, p. 324.

10 *Letters and Papers . . .*, I, 17. Evelyn's *Sylva* was published in London, 1664.

11 Cowley's *Prose Works* were published in 1689, and reprinted in 1887.

12 J. Worlidge, preface to *Systema Agriculturae*, 1669, quoted in E. L. Jones, *Agriculture and the Industrial Revolution*, Oxford, 1974, p. I.

13 *Letters and Papers . . .*, I, pp. 20–1.

14 Ibid, p. 49. Petty's pamphlet, published in 1647, was entitled, 'The Advice of W. P. to Mr. Samuel Hartlib for the advancement of some particular parts of learning.' Milton's essay was also addressed to Hartlib.

15 *Annals of Agriculture and Other Useful Arts . . .*, IV, London, 1785, p. 109.

16 *Commercial and Agricultural Magazine*, V, June–December 1801, p. 386, Letter entitled, 'On agricultural education'.

17 *Agricultural Magazine*, XIV, January–July 1806, p. 332.

18 Bath and West of England Society, *Prospectus for an agricultural college and experimental farm*, 1811. (Manuscript document in City of Bath Reference Library, listed there under Bath and West Society materials as B. 630).

19 See *Agricultural Magazine*, VII, July–December, 1810, pp. 396–404, a review of 'Agricultural Mechanization' by Captain Williamson: 'We leave it to our readers to determine by the present performance, and indeed by the tenor of Captain Williamson's other publications, as to the justice of his pretensions in future to such as high tone of originality'.

20 *Edinburgh Review*, XXI, 1819, p. 150, review article on publications relating to the work of de Fellenberg. These included (i) M. Gautheron on de Fellenberg, 'Tirée de la bibliotheque britannique, No. 292, de la partie agriculture', 1795, and (ii) de Fellenberg, 'Vues relatives a l'agriculture de la Suisse . . . traduit de l'allemand par Chas. Pictet', Mêmes libraires, 1808.

21 Report from the Select Committee on Agriculture, with minutes of evidence, London, 1833, p. iii.

22 E. J. Hobsbawm and G. Rudé, *Captain Swing*, London, 1969, pp. 16–17.

23 Ibid, loc. cit.

24 Ibid, p. 31.

25 'Causes of the Distress of the Landed Interest', *Westminster Review*, XVIII, No. XXV, January, 1833, p. 126.

26 C. S. Orwin and E. H. Whetham, History of British Agriculture, 1846–1914, London, 1964, p. 49.

27 See above, note 2.

28 Duppa, *Central Society*, p. 32.

29 Ibid, pp. 76–82.

30 See also, *Central Society*, 3rd Publication, 1839.

31 B. F. Duppa, *The Education of the Peasantry*, . . . London, 1834, p. 102.

32 See, e.g., James Mortimer (headmaster of the Grammar School and County School of Agriculture, Ashburton, Devon), 'A plan for a great agricultural school', *Board of Education Special Reports on Educational Subjects*, VIII, 1902, pp. 637–44. It is only fair to say, however, that Mortimer's model was derived from Goethe, not de Fellenberg.

33 C. Daubeny, MD, FRS (professor of Rural Economy at the University of Oxford), 'on the public institutions for the advancement of agricultural science which exist in other countries. . . .', *Transactions of the Royal Agricultural Society*, III, 1842, pp. 364–386.

34 Ibid, p. 376.

35 Minutes of the Committee of Council for Education, 1841–2, Revd J. Allen's report on certain schools in Kent, Sussex, . . . etc., p. 191.

36 *Gardener's Chronicle and Agricultural Gazette*, 1846, London, 21 February 1846, p. 121.

37 For details of this scheme, and of the acquisition of the Royal Charter, see Anon., *History of the Royal Agricultural College, Cirencester, with a description* . . ., Cirencester, no date. (From evidence of the Librarian of the Royal College, Mr. Hetherington, it might have been published in 1860.)

38 Ibid, p. 14.

39 S.I.C., IV, Minutes of Evidence, Part I, 29 March 1865, p. 226.

40 J. Caird, *English Agriculture in 1850–1*, London, 1852, p. 55.

41 Ibid, p. 56.

42 Lord Lyttelton, *Ephemera*, London, 1865, p. 94–9.

43 A. H. D. Acland, *Memoirs and Letters of the Rt. Hon. Sir Thomas Dyke Acland*, privately printed, London, 1902, p. 142.

44 Ibid, letter dated 4 December 1849, p. 160.

45 *Journal of the Bath and West Society* . . ., IV, 1856, p. 176ff; p. 287ff.

46 Ibid, VII, 1859, p. 261ff; X, 1857, p. 237ff; IV, 1857, p. 340ff.

47 Ibid, V, 1858, p. 308ff.

48 Ibid, IV, 1856, p. 343ff.

49 See below, chapter VI, p. 145.

40 *Bath and West Journal*, IV, 1856, p. 342.

51 Ibid, p. 344. See also another version of the same article in *The*

Farmers' Magazine, VIII, 3rd Series, July–September 1855, p. 525–7.
52 See above chapter 1, p. 13.
53 *Bath and West Journal*, IV, 1856, p. 344.
54 See below, chapter VIII. Also, Earl Fortescue, *Public Schools for the Middle Classes*, London, 1864, p. 18 (footnote).
55 *Bath and West Journal*, IV, 1856, p. 346.
56 Fortescue, op. cit., p. 36.
57 J. L. Brereton, 'On education as connected with agriculture', *Journal of the Royal Agricultural Society of England*, XXV, 1864, p. 59ff.
58 *Times*, 18 December 1864.
59 *Bath and West Journal*, 1857, pp. xi–xiii.
60 Ibid, T. D. Acland, 'The Education of the Farmer', pp. 252–302; also published separately under the same title, London, 1857.
61 Ibid, p. 8.
62 See below, chapter IV, p. 97.
63 J. L. Brereton, *Principles and Plan of a Farm and County School*, Exeter and London, 1858, p. 3.
64 A. H. D. Acland, op. cit., p. 140.
65 *S.I.C.*, IV, p. 606.
66 Ibid, p. 605.
67 *Journal of the Royal Agricultural Society*, XXV, London, 1864, abstract of a report of meeting of Weekly Council, 23 April 1863, pp. 539–549.
68 Ibid, p. 539.
69 Ibid, p. 544.
70 See below, chapter IV, p. 97.
71 Public Record Office, *Granville Papers*, letter from Frederick Temple, 15 August 1864.
72 Caird, op. cit., pp. 50–1.
73 Ibid, loc. cit.
74 Ibid, p. 45.
75 Ibid, p. 145.
76 J. H. Clapham, *An Economic History of Modern Britain*, Cambridge, 1938, p. 114ff.
77 Thompson, *English Landed Society*, p. 253.
78 A. Lang, *Life, Letters and Diaries of Sir Stafford Northcote, first Earl of Iddesleigh*, London, 1899, p. 75.
79 R. W. Sellman, *Devonshire Village Schools in the Nineteenth Century*, Devon, 1967.
80 The West Country members of the S.I.C. were: Henry Labouchère, (Baron Taunton), Frederick Temple, Sir Stafford Northcote, T. D. Acland.
81 *S.I.C.*, I, pp. 637–8.
82 Ibid, p. 638.
83 *S.I.C.*, IV, 31 May 1865. Robinson's opinions expressed here were part of the written evidence he submitted as Appendix B, *County Boards*, p. 623.
84 *S.I.C.*, loc. cit., also, p. 620.
85 *S.I.C.*, V, 6 March, 1866, p. 535.

86 Ibid, p. 544.
87 *S.I.C.*, II, Circular Letter, 28 May 1866.
88 Ibid, pp. 3–7.
89 Ibid, p. 25.
90 Boase, *English Biography*.
91 *S.I.C.*, II, p. 35.
92 Ibid, p. 57–8.
93 *S.I.C.*, I, pp. 637–44.
94 Report of the Endowed Schools Commissioners to the Lords of the Committee of Her Majesty's Privy Council on Education, London, 1872, p. 37.
95 Select Committee on the Endowed Schools Act, 7 April 1873.
96 J. S. Mill, *Representative Government*, 1910, p. 349.
97 J. P. Dunbabin, 'British local government reform: the nineteenth century and after', *English Historical Review*, XCII, No. 365, October 1977, p. 777.
98 Ibid, p. 779.
99 J. L. Hammond, in H. Laski, W. Ivor Jennings, and W. Robson (eds.), *A Century of Municipal Progress, 1835–1935*, London, 1935, p. 39.
100 Report from the Select Committee on County Financial Arrangements, 13 July 1868, p. ii.
101 Boase, *English Biography*. James Wyld was geographer to the Queen; he was defeated at the next election, December 1868.
102 *Hansard*, 3rd Series, 31 Victoria, 1867–8, CXCI, p. 1542.
103 Ibid, p. 1553.
104 Select Committee on County Financial Arrangements, 1868, p. iii.

CHAPTER III

County authorities

The county was often co-extensive administratively with the local organisation of the Established Church. Thus, the diocese of Bath and Wells covered the county of Somerset; the diocese of Peterborough was roughly coterminous with the county of Northants; Exeter with Devon; and Worcester with its county. Any serious consideration of practical proposals for county and diocesan activity in the field of middle-class education should begin with the initiatives taken by the National Society, the educational shock-troops of the Church, in the 1830s. T. D. Acland was involved in this initiative also, with his former Oxford friend, Gladstone, and the eminent Vicar of Leeds, later a Schools Inquiry Commissioner, W. F. Hook. The 1839 report of the Society announced the new part of its programme: the members wished to extend its work 'so as to comprehend the middle schools, and will endeavour to elevate the character of the instruction given to the children of all classes', hoping thereby to do something for those 'who are immediately above the labouring classes'. This new direction in the Society's policy was formally established at a meeting on 21 May 1839. Hook proposed,

that this meeting contemplates with satisfaction the establishment of Diocesan and Local Boards of Education in connection with the National Society, having for their object the extension of the benefits of education . . . as well as the establishment and encouragement of schools for the education of the middle classes, upon principles conformable to those which are embodied in the Society's Charter.[2]

This proposal, thoroughly endorsed by the meeting, marked the true beginning of concerted local efforts, by agencies associated with the Established Church, in connection with middle-class education. Dissenters, who did not possess the coherence to co-operate for a similar purpose, became alarmed by the Society's initiative and the subsequent evidence of its implementation. In 1841 the *Nonconformist* noted in a leading article that 'a new and ingenious mode of church extension' had been hit upon by the Bishop of London – diocesan schools for the middle classes. 'It is, we believe, the intention of the Bishop to connect one of these institutions with every district church in and around the Metropolis.'[3]

The new, or in some cases, re-vamped, diocesan boards of education under the National Society began to sponsor and encourage local efforts in middle-class schooling after 1830. The desire to get larger numbers of middle-class Anglican recruits to the trade of elementary school-teaching was an important factor in creating and sustaining the interest of the Society and its local branches in middle-class education. At Worcester, for instance, the new diocesan training college for elementary-school teachers was founded by the Diocesan Board in 1839. It also established a middle-class school within the college, with a headmaster and one assistant. In the 1840s, as well as sustaining both these institutions, the Worcester Board helped to fill the gaps in the pattern of middle-class schooling in the county. For example, in July 1844, taking account of the closure of Kidderminster Grammar School, and the controversy surrounding its management,[4] the Board granted £15 a year for two years to the Revd T. L. Claughton 'for a Middle School at Kidderminster'.[5] At various times, but usually together, Lord Lyttelton, a leading member of the S.I.C. in the 1860s, Sir John Pakington, Chairman of the 1865 Select Committee on Education, and C. B. Adderley, Vice-President of the Committee of Council in the late 1850s, were active members of the Worcester Board.

The work of the Board on behalf of middle-class schools lasted formally into the 1850s, and covered a period of considerable upheaval among local endowed grammar schools. It supplied money and advice in numerous cases; and members of the Board took their places as trustees of schools when the constitutions of institutions were revised. The Bishop of Worcester became Visitor of Kidderminster Grammar School in 1850 and was responsible for the appointment of the headmaster.[6] The Board was closely associated with the revival of Stourbridge Grammar School: 'After having remained in a depressed state, this school has lately been started afresh with handsome new buildings, and a new set of rules, framed by the governors with the consent of the Bishop of Worcester as Visitor', the S.I.C. assistant commissioner reported in 1866.[7]

Hartlebury Grammar School obtained a new scheme of government
in November 1849, and among its new governors were the Dean of
Worcester and Pakington.[8] Lord Lyttelton and the Bishop of Worcester were among the new trustees of Bromsgrove School.[9] The
Diocesan Board served as a means of reinforcing individual local
enterprise where it existed, and initiating it where it was absent. The
administrative structure of the Diocese was the only framework for
the co-ordination of enterprise and policy-making in middle-class
schooling in the county up to 1864. The leading members of the
Board had close connections with central government in its function
of making educational inquiries and providing administrative and
financial support for schooling.

As soon as it was constituted in 1838, the Bath and Wells Diocesan
Board published its own version of the general aims of the National
Society. As its third aim the Board proposed 'to build and fit up
Middle Schools.'[10] In this diocese the chief means of stimulating
middle-class schools seems to have been the awarding of prizes in the
form of books to the best pupils at middle schools in union with the
Board. This policy was the result of a motion passed in 1843. The
prizes were to be earned after examination of the schools by the
diocesan inspectors of education. The Board also supplied apparatus
for the teaching of science, as in the case of Norton Hall Middle
School in January 1846. The network of schools included institutions at Dunster, Portishead, Frome and Chewton. But the two
leading schools in association with the Board were the brothers
Brownings' famous boarding school at Weston, near Bath, founded
in 1844; and Failand Lodge, with sixty boarders and a farm, which
was commented upon very favourably in an early report by H.M.I.[11]

The Bishop brought the Brownings with him as witnesses to the
S.I.C. in June 1865. Weston and Failand Lodge were seen as serving
the needs of the tenant-farmer class, and although they were conducted on Anglican principles and were under the supervision of the
Bishop, they were open to the sons of Dissenters who used the
schools 'in large numbers.'[12] The diocese also promoted a school 'for
the lower middle class' at Wells. This had been founded by a local
clergyman, and in addition to local farmers' sons there were a few
boarders.[13] In his evidence to the S.I.C. the Bishop said he was in
favour of systematising the arrangements for middle-class education
in the diocese by encouraging groups of tenant-farmers, within
administrative areas ten miles square, to rent a small dwelling,

convert it for the purpose of boys' education, and jointly employ a certificated master at a salary of £125 per annum. 'If asked, the clergy would render their assistance most willingly in examinations.'[14]

It is clear, even thus far, that diocesan boards active in promoting middle-class education comprised a varied species: there was, as might have been expected, little uniformity, and this was partly a consequence of the breadth of the National Society's statement of policy. But certain common features of their work emerge. There was, firstly, a general concern for what they might have called the lower middle-class pupils; and the epitome of this type was the tenant-farmer's son, or, in a country town, the son of a small tradesman. Secondly, the boards were willing to supply financial assistance to middle-class schools in much the same way as they were already lending aid to local efforts in elementary education; though the giving of money was always qualified by the stipulation that the school's religious teaching ought to conform with the principles of the Church of England. Thirdly, – and here the boards were re-invoking a procedure whose passing had been regretted by Thomas Arnold – they used visitation and examination to monitor the efficiency of the education provided by schools in union with them, their approval often taking the form of prizes. Finally, at this stage – in the 1840s and 1850s – they tended to avoid becoming entangled in the complex problems posed by the unreformed endowed schools, though there were notable exceptions to this feature of their work.

The positive rôle of supervision and encouragement which the diocesan boards could play in the organisation of middle-class education is demonstrated by an episode in the development of the Winchester Diocesan Board in the 1840s. The leading permanent members of the Board, as it was constituted in 1839, were the Lords Lieutenant and High Sheriffs of the counties of Hampshire and Surrey; the Dean and Chapter of Winchester; the Warden Fellows and Master of Winchester College; the Chairmen of Quarter Sessions for the two counties; the Mayor and Recorder of Winchester; 'All Noblemen and Privy Councillors'; and the M.P.s for Hampshire, Surrey and the Isle of Wight.[15] The second stated aim of the Board was 'the promotion of schools for the commercial and agricultural classes.'

The Winchester Board involved itself thoroughly in promoting middle-class schools, whether private or endowed. The Report for

1846 noted that at Andover Grammar School the trustees had
received the co-operation of the Board in appointing a Master. There
were three other schools at that time 'whose managers united them
to the Board': the Classical, Commercial and Mathematical
Academy at Fareham, and five private grammar schools at Anstey,
Maldon, Southampton, Portsea and Dorking. The rules governing
the Southampton school had been modified by the Bishop in 1840. In
addition there was the Richmond Classical and Commercial School
which had been established by local clergy under the aegis of the
Board. The Southampton Diocesan Church School, having been
placed in the charge of a former English Master at Marlborough, had
'passed the trials of infancy', and was well established in 1846 with
thirty-eight day-pupils and eight boarders. It had been examined by
Mobberley of Winchester College.[16] In its labours for middle-class
schooling the Board showed a clear concern for the teaching of useful
subjects. In the case of Southampton Grammar School, in 1840, the
Bishop endorsed the following resolution of the trustees: 'that the
principle of the grammar school shall remain unchanged but that, as
from the altered state of society, instruction in Latin and Greek is not
desired by the inhabitants of Southampton, it is advisable to add to
the instruction in those languages instruction in other branches of
education'.[17] In the Richmond School, which was advertised in 1846
as being 'in connection with the Winchester Diocesan Board of
Education', the curriculum included, in addition to religious knowledge, 'English taught grammatically', Latin without Greek, writing,
linear drawing, arithmetic and the elements of natural history and
philosophy, French, taught by a graduate of the University of Paris,
and vocal music. Such advertisements were common at this time; but
they often promised much more than was delivered. At least, in this
case, the authenticity of the claims was guaranteed by a local and
Church institution of considerable standing. It was to be expected
that religious teaching was emphasised in the schools under the
Board. At Dorking 'Biblical knowledge and Catechism' came at the
head of the list of subjects; and at Richmond, 'as in other schools
established by the Board, the local clergy have access to the pupils as
often as is convenient and watch over their spiritual welfare'.[18] Like
Bath and Wells, the Winchester Board encouraged higher standards
by presenting prizes, usually of improving books. It was also aware
of the need to guarantee a school's standards in the eyes of middle-
class parents. At Dorking, for instance, where the fees in 1846 were

thirty guineas for boarders and eight guineas for day-boys, the parents were assured that 'the school will be periodically inspected under the direction of the Diocesan Board'.[19]

The Seventh Report, for 1847, commented upon the steadily increasing number of pupils being attracted to schools in association with the Board, but warned against complacency:

The schools . . . with the exception of Andover . . . are entirely new creations, and owe their existence to the assistance of the Board. Although, therefore, a painful sense of what remains to be done . . . cannot but exist, something has been effected, which if permitted to extend, bids fair to offer to commercial and agricultural classes in the Diocese – a class upon which the prosperity of the country under God so much depends – the means of procuring for their children a sound and useful education, according to the principles of the Church of England.[20]

An even more elaborate form of county activity, according to the National Society's model, emerged in Northants in the early 1850s. At a meeting in Northampton on 29 August 1854, the county branch of the Society transformed itself into the Northants Educational Society by adopting the recommendations of a report embodying new rules and aims. The report had been prompted by Lord Alwyne Compton, later Bishop of Ely. The aim of the Committee had been to 'consider the best means of improving and extending education in the diocese (of Peterborough) either by the establishment of training, reformatory, or middle schools, or other institutions, as well as the appointment of diocesan inspectors.[21] Here, clearly, was a body which was setting out to co-ordinate all kinds of educational work in the county, giving it coherent form. There can be little doubt, though there is no explicit evidence for the assertion, but that the motivating factor in this refashioning of a county body was the activity of agents elsewhere, particularly in the promotion of industrial schooling. There were also direct links between the leading personnel of the Northants Committee and T. D. Acland, who was at this time reviving the publishing activities of the Bath and West Society, with its special interest in middle-class schooling in the countryside.[22]

The new Northants Committee had discussed in some detail the question of middle-class schools. They considered that the heavy charges to which the middle classes were liable for the education of their children – presumably in inferior private schools – made the establishment of middle schools absolutely necessary. The extension of education among the middle classes would produce a beneficial effect, they felt, throughout the whole community:

To the supply of such schools the Society hereafter may perhaps be able to
contribute. At the same time it should not be overlooked that the endowed
schools and hospitals which exist in many large towns would, if properly
managed, serve, in great measure, to supply this want. Your Committee
therefore hope that the trustees of the charities throughout the county will
take the necessary steps for extending their advantage as far as possible, as
has recently been done so successfully in Birmingham. And they further
think that Your Society might, in many cases, lend a helping hand in this
good work.

This new desire to use the endowed schools was probably stimulated by the passing of the Charitable Trusts Act in the previous
year.[23]

Apart from its connection with the middle-class rural work being
publicised in the *Journal* of the Bath and West Society at this time,
there were two other reasons for the Northants Society taking
comprehensive action. Firstly, in relation to Reformatory and
Industrial Schools, they had now the means of responding locally to
the initiatives of Mary Carpenter, Stafford Northcote and the Revd
Sydney Turner.[24] Secondly, the passing of the Charitable Trusts Act
had released a new potential in endowed charities for secondary
education, making possible the transformation of bad institutions
into valuable educational assets.[25] There was, in fact, an awareness
in Northants of new movements and vital opportunities in a number
of educational fields, especially that of middle-class schooling. The
members of the Northants Society were conscious of the possibility
of co-ordinating, if not linking in a complete system, a wide range of
agencies for various kind of education within a considerable geographical area, under one unofficial 'local authority'.

As a result of the 1854 Report three committees were set up by the
newly constituted Society: the first for the education of the poor, the
second for industrial schools, and the third 'to promote Education
among the Middle classes'. The first action of the Middle Schools
Committee, at its meeting in December 1864, was to ask advice of
the headmasters of two of the Woodard schools in Sussex about the
expense of school management.[26]

The task facing the Committee was considerable. In the county
there were twelve schools in 1854 which could still be called 'grammar' schools, with a handful of others, like Little Harrowden, Pytch-
ley and Burton Latimer, which had given up any attempt to provide

instruction in Latin and Greek and were being conducted as elementary schools. The Court of Chancery had already been active in modifying the charters of two schools, at Kettering and Blakesley. The members of the Committee, throughout its existence to 1874, were preponderantly Anglican clergy, some of whom were trustees of local schools, with some prominent laymen, like H. P. Markham, the Clerk to the Peace.

The Committee was confronted, not only by the general disrepair of local endowed schools, but also by a particularly bitter current crisis on their own doorstep in Northampton. Earlier in the year, the Headmaster of the Grammar School had petitioned the Court of Chancery about a diminution in his salary, and a similar appeal had been made by a local solicitor about misapplication of school funds.[27] During this controversy Markham was a member of both the Middle Schools Committee and the Town Charities Committee, and was therefore the chief intermediary on behalf of the Society when it tried to help the Grammar School. The Middle Schools Committee suggested hiring a house to accommodate 200 scholars and recommended that the reformed school should by subject to a conscience clause and include the teaching of mathematics. Finally a meeting was arranged between the Middle Schools Committee and the grammar school trustees in February 1856. A scheme was fashioned which would have given the Society peculiar privileges: in return for a donation of thirty guineas it would have had the right to appoint a life-governor to the board of the new school. But this proposal, and another by the Committee which would have involved the creation of a new proprietary school in Northampton, came to nothing, and the business dragged on until 1864 when the Charity Commission accepted another plan. When T. H. Green visited the town on behalf of the S.I.C. in 1865, the grammar school was still in abeyance.

The Committee had more success in connection with the decayed grammar school at Guilsborough. A new scheme for Guilsborough was before Chancery from 1855 to 1857, and in the latter year, to help the governors out of a financial difficulty, the Committee gave the school £30. Compton, on behalf of the Society, attended several meetings of the governors at which plans for a new school building were discussed. On Guilsborough's behalf, and acknowledging its rural location, the Society wrote for advice to the Principals of the agricultural colleges at Cirencester and Kimbolton with a view to recommending the inclusion of agricultural training in any new scheme. The Revd Robert Isham stated at the February meeting of the Middle Schools Committee in 1856 that 'he would be glad of any assistance in framing . . . a scheme that the Committee could give him'; and in June he reported to the Committee that a new scheme had been drawn up 'and was likely to be adopted.' Problems persisted, however, and in July 1857, Compton reported that the Society had been instrumental in helping the trustees to raise £1,200 in support of the ailing charity. The new School seems to have started flourishing early, since in 1856 it supplied a large proportion of the candidates for the Cambridge Junior and Senior Local Examinations at Northampton which were organised by the Society.[28]

In June 1856, the Committee received a petition from the newly appointed governors of Kettering Grammar School, for which a scheme had been approved in Chancery in 1854. The Governors lacked £300 of the sum required for providing a proper schoolhouse. The Committee sent £25. In the same month the Committee received a request from the Fellows of Magdalen College, Oxford, for some suggestions as to the reorganisation of Magdalen College School, Brackley. The Committee replied proposing that some provision be made for agricultural and scientific instruction, in addition to classics, mathematics and modern languages. Also, several Committee-members promised financial support: the Earl of Ellesmere £50, Earl Spencer £25. The Society itself offered £25 annually and desired to appoint two of its members as inspectors of the School. The Fellows, however, thought the sums promised too small to give the Committee the right of inspection and interference, and negotiations were abandoned.[29]

The name of another School appears in the minutes of the Middle Schools Committee. Clipston School, near Market Harborough, founded in 1667, was conducted in the midst of a hospital for the aged; but it had long been elementary in character. In his 1859 Report the Secretary of the Society stated that the School, 'owing to the resignation of the master and the reference of its affairs to the Charity Commission, is at present in abeyance, but there is every hope that by some modification in the past mode of conducting it, it may be restored to its efficiency as a Grammar School without detriment to the claims which the poor in Clipston and its neighbourhood have upon its resources'.[30]

The Middle Schools Committee was attempting to carry out in a systematic and economical way the aims which had been set before the members in 1854. There was a responsible body keeping watch over the fortunes of the endowed grammar schools of the county. More positively, the Committee served as a source of encouragement to trustees and as an authoritiative ally in dealings with agencies of central government whose interest in education *per se* was not substantial. The Charity Commissioners and the officers of the Court of Chancery were more concerned to provide for efficient financial administration of schools than to adjust or revise their educational aims or resources. The Northants Committee, on the other hand, was consciously, in some cases, trying to modify the curricula of schools in a general way so as to meet new social requirements in a largely rural community. The greatest single achievement of the Northants Society lay in a rather different, though closely related, field; and this aspect of their work, in connection with the Local Examinations of the ancient Universities, will be dealt with later.[31] It can be argued that the clergy and laity who were leading members of the committees in Worcestershire, Winchester, Somerset and Northants were far less ignorant about contemporary local educational needs and problems than any other specific group of local citizens; there were no other groups in the local community which could have prompted useful and cohesive change.

The work of the diocesan boards formed a framework within which the Newcastle Commissioners were able to propose the establishment of what they, in 1861, called 'County and County Borough Boards of Education'.[32] Their County Board was to be appointed by the Court of Quarter Sessions from their own number and from the Chairmen and Vice-chairmen of the Boards of Guardians: six members might be chosen in this manner and they would be able to co-opt up to six additional members. The number of ministers of religion on any board would not exceed one-third of the total.[33] In corporate towns of over 40,000 inhabitants the Town Council would appoint the board, consisting of not more than six members, the number of clergy being limited to two. The boards would sit for three years, but at the end of each year one-third of the members would retire to be replaced or re-elected. An Inspector would be attached to each board by the Committee of Council; the boards should appoint examiners who would be certificated masters of at least seven years standing. The 'Newcastle' board was designed for the control of elementary education.

Earlier, in dealing with the possible forms of administration for
endowments, the Newcastle Commissioners had shown their dissatisfaction with the conduct of most local trustees. They said that
'local government, when pure and efficient, is no doubt much to be
preferred to the action of a central authority'; but the conduct of
local trusteeships did not inspire their confidence. 'The vision of
local administrators is limited to their own schools; it does not
extend to any comprehensive scheme of improvement for endowed
schools throughout the country . . . or to anything like a graduated
connection of school with school for the purpose of drafting
promising pupils from a lower place of education into a higher.'[34]
Only after the Privy Council had generally set an efficient system
working would it be found 'possible and desirable to transfer to
some local authority' a portion of administrative responsibility.[35]
These stipulations are a clear foreshadowing of the ideas expressed
six years later in the Report of the S.I.C.

The County Board idea was taken up by Pakington's Select
Committee on Education in 1865, which received evidence during
the first few months of the existence of the S.I.C. Indeed, the
Committee heard evidence from Frederick Temple, then a leading
member of the S.I.C. As Chairman of the Committee, Pakington,
evidently a supporter of the diocesan boards in principle and
practice, asked H. A. Bruce whether he had considered the possibility of establishing 'some joint action' between diocesan boards
and a central authority. The Vice-president replied that he had; but
he could see that any such arrangement, however carefully devised,
would be open to grave objection. Bruce thought, also, that the
Newcastle proposal of county boards was too complicated, and that
'it was not acceptable to Parliament or to the country' in the present
state of feeling. The chief problem, as he saw it, was religious
feeling.[36]

Another witness before the 1865 Committee also had close
associations with the S.I.C. Canon H. G. Robinson, later to become
an Endowed Schools Commissioner under the 1869 Act, gave
evidence two days after being similarly questioned by the S.I.C.[37]
Replying to Pakington, Robinson said that he had been favourably
impressed by Newcastle's county boards and wished to see the
proposal through to execution. He foresaw general public
objections to it; nevertheless he thought there would be fewer
objections to county than to municipal boards. He approved of the

plan since it marked a step towards the achievement of his desire 'to see a complete and well developed national system[38].'

It seems, therefore, that a sceptical tone characterised the comments of witnesses upon the possibility of creating local or county boards. Yet it is clear that discussions of the proposition had to continue, since the administrative alternative – the extension of the central government's powers of interference in education – was considered a worse evil. Peter Erle, the Chief Charity Commissioner and later a Taunton Commissioner, giving evidence to Newcastle, was strongly of the opinion that, in relation to charities, 'there would be great opposition to the transfer of local funds to any general fund', and that, rather than wishing for an extension of the powers of his own Charity Commission, he felt that 'the consent should be local, at least in the first instance.'[39]

The debate about the necessity for instituting some form of local administration for education, and for middle-class schooling in particular, intensified between 1859 and 1867. The S.I.C. sector of the debate has been considered already.[40] In spite of the ways in which sympathetic witnesses qualified their support for the creation of local or county boards, the S.I.C. was prepared, like its predecessor, Newcastle, to cleave to an idea which was controversial. Their confidence, such as it was, must have rested almost exclusively on the local experience of Church-based organisations in middle-class education over the previous twenty-five years, and on the security, for the time being, of the traditional structure of county government, upon which radical politicians had not yet begun to mount a serious attack.

All the organisations so far considered were operating for the most part in rural areas. One of the most interesting Anglican urban experiments in middle-class education occurred in the diocese of Chester, at Manchester in the 1840s. The Revd Frederick Watkins, H.M.I., in his report on schools in the Northern district for 1845, recorded that one Manchester clergyman had told him that there were in his district 'hundreds of men living with a community of wives'. And Watkins said that he himself had seen in another part of industrial Lancashire 'pamphlets which are largely circulated among the middling and operative classes . . . denying the sanctity of marriage' and encouraging abortion of unwanted children. In these districts, he had been told, there were tens of thousands of Englishmen who never entered a place of worship. 'It is credible that

a great many of this number never utter a word, or feel the desire, of
private prayer. Many of them spend a great part of Sunday in bed
. . . ,[41]

Watkins' anxiety about what he considered to be this canker in
industrial communities was largely related to the upper sections of
the labouring classes, and the lower reaches of the middle class. In
fact, he was happy that the most successful efforts of the Manchester
Church Education Society had been 'in a field which has as yet been
little cultivated, and yet there is ample space and sufficient depth of
soil for the most earnest and unflinching labourers': that of middle-
class education. He reported that the Society had completed one of
four proposed schools for the middle classes in Stretford New
Road.[42]

Thus Manchester, next to the Metropolis the most populous and richest of
the towns of England, may be the first, if not to design, at least to carry into
execution, a well-devised plan for the right education of that important class
which, as it has been from various circumstances little acted upon by the
direct teaching of the Church, has become impatient of her discipline and
most alienated from her communion.[43]

Watkins' enthusiasm for the Manchester experiment was loudly
echoed by the Revd Alexander Thurtell in his report for 1847.[44] The
Manchester Society had been established partly as a consequence of
the general effort of the Chester diocese, after the National Society's
new initiatives in 1838–9, in the Deanery of Manchester, and partly
as an Anglican attempt to fill the local vacuum of 'comprehensive'
effort created by the divisions over Sir James Graham's Bill in
1843.[46] The general aim of the Society was to extend elementary
education 'by stimulating not superseding local exertions.'[46]

They discovered, however, that there was one section of the community, the middle class, 'for which scarcely any public education is
provided in this parish.' Therefore, in 1845, they appointed a special
sub-committee 'to inquire into the need for Commercial Middle
Schools.' They concluded that four or more such schools were
needed in the parish of Manchester. They rejected the notion of one
large school, since four schools would better serve the needs of the
geographically dispersed lower middle-class population, and would
also encourage a healthy spirit of emulation.

Their school in Stretford New Road opened on 26 January
1846.[47] The Working Committee was dominated by the clergy; but
there was also a group of 'gentlemen' and three solicitors. It is

interesting to note, also, that a large proportion of the subscribers to the Society's funds were business firms, like 'Merec and Co., Cross St', who gave £21. It is supposed that the interest of these commercial firms had been enlivened by the prospect of a new school which would train its pupils to become more efficient junior clerks in local offices. In addition to the business subscriptions there were donations from local gentry and, indeed, from county landowners living at a distance from Manchester. Lord Francis Egerton of Worsley gave £50; Sir Oswald Moseley of Rolleston Park, £21; the Earl of Wilton, Heaton House, £105.[48] Buried in a long list of such names were two which were associated with middle-class education in entirely different, rurual contexts: Earl Ducie of Tortworth Court, Gloucestershire, who owned land in the centre of Manchester, subscribed. His son was later to play a leading part in organising 'county' activity about middle-class schools in Gloucestershire, and he was currently involved in the founding of Cirencester College.[49] Lord Ebrington, whose father also had a stake in the City, and who was later to introduce the prototype of the Local Examinations in the South-west, contributed £45. Lord Derby gave £100.

The general management of the new Schools was to be in the hands of a committee under the Dean of Manchester, Dr Herbert. The first Headmaster was the Revd J. G. Slight, formerly of the Grammar School, Barrow-upon-Soar, Leicestershire; the second master was A. T. Bramah, lately second master at the Royal Grammar School, Guildford; the third master, Mr Davis, had been headmaster of one of the Society's model schools; and there were a German and a French master. Other teachers were employed for vocal music and drawing.[50] The course of studies included Latin, English grammar and composition, history, geography, linear drawing, writing, vocal music, mathematics pure and practical, arithmetic and book-keeping, the principles of mensuration, the use of globes, mapping, and 'useful information and the elements of Natural Philosophy and General Science to the Senior Pupils.'[51] The terms were £1 15s 0d in the Upper and Lower Schools, with Greek, French, German and Drawing as extras at 10s 6d each, though there was the possibility of remitting fees in the case of orphans. In the 1846 Report the new School was acknowledged a success.

The Society then proceeded to consider the possibility of establishing schools of a second middle-class type: artisan schools for 'the smaller shop-keepers, mechanics, and other persons who find it convenient to pay for the education of their children in weekly sums'.[52] It was decided to rent premises for this 'artisans' school' in some suitable part of the town 'as an experiment of what might be expected if such second-class ... schools were established generally'. It seemed to the members of the Society that the reproach so long applied to Manchester, of doing little in the cause of education, could no longer be justified: it had already provided educational machinery 'which for comprehensiveness of purpose and capability of extension, is scarcely surpassed in any part of the Kingdom'.[53] The Society was far from implying that the Commercial and Artisan Schools were part of a 'scholarship ladder' by which lower middle-class boys could begin to ascend, via the ancient local Grammar School, to the Universities. In this sense it would be wrong to view this Manchester 'system' as an anticipation of the S.I.C.'s tripartite grading of middle-class schools as end-on institutions. The Society was contributing to the creation in Manchester of a three-tier school system in which each tier would be self-contained.

The further history of the Manchester Schools is somewhat obscure, and has been rather misleadingly interpreted. A. A. Mumford, the most famous historian of Manchester education, attributed considerable importance to the Schools as middle-class institutions up to the 1870s, saying that they 'continued to maintain a high, if not the premier, position before the reform of the Grammar School.'[54] Certainly the roll of masters during that period contains some interesting names. The third in line of succession, the Revd C. E. Moberley, appointed in 1855, had previously been head of Lancing, embodying, therefore, an intriguing connection between Woodard's Anglo-Catholicism in Sussex and Bishop Prince Lee's Arnoldian churchmanship in Manchester. Moberley moved almost immediately to Rugby School where he later served under Temple. Mumford referred to the visit of James Bryce to the Schools in 1865 on behalf of the S.I.C. Bryce not only omitted the Schools from his list of middle-class institutions in Lancashire,[55] but misunderstood their character. In his extensive discussion of the state of commercial education in the city Bryce referred to them very briefly in two footnotes: he characterised them as 'quasi-private', that is, as schools which, 'though not the absolute property of the teacher, are managed by him for his sole benefit'. He later reluctantly admitted that they were doing good in their neighbourhood '(although some of the teaching is not what it should be)' and he thought that the 'proprietors' ought not 'to fear the establishment of a new school on grander scale.'[56]

The county and diocesan committees and other off-shoots of the National Society's activity were near relatives of, or certainly members of the same species as, the groups founded for creating the array of County Schools which proliferated across the countryside in the late 1850s and the 1860s. These schools developed, by a process closely akin to cell-division, from the parent organisation in Devon.[57] They were uniformly Anglican in character, but were usually open to the sons of Dissenters, unlike the proselytising institutions of Nathaniel Woodard. It is possible, in this period, to distinguish two separate groups of County Schools: those which were associated with the parent school at West Buckland, and those which seemed or claimed to have developed independently, while adopting the same nomenclature.

The English genesis of the County School has usually been traced to the work of Fortescue and Brereton in Devon, and in particular to Fortescue's ideas expressed in his *Public Schools for the Middle Classes*.[58] In fact, while the idea was articulated for the first time by Fortescue and Brereton, the notion of the county as a unit for the organisation of schooling had its roots in the ancient administrative structure of the English counties; also, colonial Ireland, where Earl Fortescue the father had been Lord Lieutenant in the late 1830s, had been throwing up proposals for the county organisation of middle-class schooling since 1788.[59] Lamport's essay has already been noted as a comprehensive review of the ideology of county agricultural education.[60]

The foundation stone of the Surrey County School at Cranley (or Cranleigh) was laid by the Archbishop of Canterbury in November 1863. He remarked that the School was part of a large-scale attempt to fill the gap in the provision of education between the great Public Schools and the National Schools.[61] The Surrey School attracted the attention of the S.I.C. at an early stage in its investigations, for the new institution had a powerful advocate in the person of a leading witness to the Commission, E. W. Benson, then headmaster of Wellington and trustee of Cranleigh School. He was giving evidence three months before the opening of the School. Like West Buckland, it was intended for the sons of farmers and had been founded by public subscription among 'the gentry of the county'. The fees were £30 per annum.[62] But unlike Devon School, Cranleigh began by establishing its religious exclusiveness: Benson said that the religious principles were to be 'Church of England entirely': all boys would have to attend Church services.[63] He also admitted that the governors had canvassed information about school management from Hurstpierpoint, as well as from West Buckland. Replying to Edward Baines, before the S.I.C., Benson said that he thought the county was 'a very good and unobjectionable kind of division' for the organisation of middle-class schooling.[64]

The progress of the County School in Suffolk was reported to the S.I.C. by Sir Edward Kerrison, one of Acland's, Fortescue's and Brereton's colleagues on the Committee of the Royal Agricultural Society.[65] The School at Framlingham had been opened in April 1865, with a subscription of £22,000, provided by the gentry of Suffolk and also by Suffolk businessmen who had made their fortunes in the London trade. The School began with 270 scholars, but like West Buckland, and unlike Cranleigh, it had a conscience clause and the master did not need to be a beneficed clergyman.[66] Lord Lyttelton asked Kerrison whether he had been in touch with any other schools of a similar type, and he replied that he had personally visited 'several of them', including West Buckland and, once again, Hurstpierpoint; though he thought 'our school is perhaps more formed after West Buckland than any other school.'[67]

Later, in March 1866, the Commissioners called Framlingham's Master, the Revd A. Daymond, to give his account of the School's progress.[68] He had taught briefly at Eton under Hawtrey, but mainly at St Mark's College, Chelsea, 'where we had a very large school of over 600 boys, consisting principally of the upper middle, middle class and lower class.'[69] He had been *ex officio* headmaster of the college schools at Chelsea. Daymond, like Kerrison, seems to have favoured a thorough general education, rather than a special preparation for later vocational needs. He thought that in middle-class schooling there was generally 'a want of thoroughness, a dabbling in a great many subjects, and a good knowledge in very few'. He favoured the Framlingham type of curriculum, with its thorough grounding in Latin, English, French and German.[70]

West Buckland also had imitators close at hand. In February 1863, a joint stock company was registered as the 'East Devon County School, Ltd.' to supervise the affairs of a middle-class proprietary school at Sampford Peverall in Devon which had been open since May 1860. The stated object of the School was 'the instruction of the sons of the middle classes, especially of the agricultural classes'.[71] The boarding fees for older boys, at nineteen guineas, compared favourably with the twenty five guineas at West Buckland. The education provided was what would have been called 'English' in character, with Latin as an 'extra' at two guineas. Judging by the limited tables in the S.I.C. Report, over half the pupils were the sons of farmers from Devon and Cornwall. There were nine trustees who were also owners of company stock; but no attempt seems to have been made to enlist the support of the county 'grandees'. The School had been established on the initiative of the Revd C. S. Bere, rector of Uplowman, near Tiverton, and he and C. A. W. Troyte, a gentleman-farmer and member of the Bath and West Society, had endowed scholarships of £5 and £10 respectively.[72]

Another School in the West Country, established on similar lines, and registered under the Companies Act, 1862, was the Dorset County School, near Dorchester. The stated objects were to provide a general education for the sons of 'yeomen, tradesmen, merchants and professional men'.[73] The School was begun by the Revd Thomas Sanctuary, Archdeacon of Dorset. In a printed letter of May 1863, which accompanied the first Prospectus of the School, he said that he had been motivated by 'the repeated communications' of 'influential members of the middle classes'. He was aware that yeomen especially in the county were not satisfied with the existing provision of education for their sons. He said that he could produce testimonies to this effect 'from men of almost every shade of opinion in other matters'. A further encouragement to activity had been the recent great advancement in the instruction of 'the peasantry'. Though he had met with no jealousy towards the National schools among the middle classes, yet,

While ... it is a matter of thankfulness to see the families of the day-labourers making efforts to take advantage of the good instruction which is now almost everywhere generously provided for them; and while almost everyone would regret that any single child of that class who may be gifted with special talents should, from lack of education, miss the opportunity of exercising them, and of rising in the social scale; at the same time it cannot be right that one *Class* should be gradually taking a place in intelligence beyond another which is above it in other respects. And yet it is acknowledged that there is a tendency in this direction, because in very many circumstances the education of the peasantry is thoroughly substantial and good, while the children of their employers are far less well instructed.

He was therefore enlisting the sympathy of 'the county', with a view to steering clear of all political and religious differences. He had not envisaged creating a charitable institution, since it 'would not be acceptable to those for whom it is intended. . . .' He wished that the School should come to resemble those at Marlborough and Cheltenham.

> In other counties, such as Devon and Suffolk, schools of the kind now proposed have started with a good prospect of success, and there can be no reason why the county of Dorset need hold back. To those who object to class education, I should reply that a school that should include the sons of the average yeoman, the average man engaged in general business, the average county professional man, would have at least as broad a foundation as the schools to which I have referred.

And far from discouraging other enterprises, the County School would, he thought, stimulate by competition the growth of good private middle-class schools and eradicate useless ones.[74]

The Prospectus of the School proposed a Council of nineteen members, nine of whom were to be chosen 'in virtue of their offices': the Lord Lieutenant, the Sheriff, the three M.P.s, the Chairman and Vice-chairman of Quarter Sessions, and the Archdeacon of Dorset. This plan was followed after the opening of the School, with the qualification that, in addition to the officials, fifteen members were to be elected by the shareholders. The School was opened at Michaelmas 1863, and by 1867 had seventy five boarders, more than half of whom seem to have been the sons of Dorset farmers.[75] Religious knowledge was an optional subject, though only nine boys did not take it. The headmaster had to be an ordained clergyman. There were six masters and a drill sergeant in 1867.

A school which attracted the attention of the S.I.C. from a number of directions, and which shared many of the features of the County School and the National Society schools, was the Yeoman School at York. It was described in Fitch's Report to the S.I.C. as Archbishop Holgate's School.[76] The explanation for this confusion of names was provided in H. S. Thompson's evidence to the Commissioners in December 1865. Thompson had been one of Acland's associates in the conduct of the Royal Agricultural Society's *Journal* in the 1850s.[77] His chief educational concern was for the lower division of the middle class, the farmers, who could not afford to pay a high rate to secure a good schooling for their sons: 'tenant-farmers have from time to time asked me if I could recommend them any school where their children might receive a good education.'[78] Thompson's desire to create boarding schools for farmers' sons had first been embodied in his establishing, with a committee of local gentlemen, including the Earl of Carlisle, the Yeoman Proprietary School in York in 1849. A site and buildings were acquired and the fees fixed at £22. The headmaster was the Principal of the Diocesan Training College at York. Despite help from the College, the new School got into difficulties.[79] Consequently in 1857 a new scheme for the management of the School was prepared in Chancery. Archbishop Holgate's Free School, also in York, had fallen into decay. The Chancery scheme arranged that the trustees of the Free School should pay the debts of the Yeoman School; that certain of the trustees and subscribers of the Yeoman School should be appointed as trustees of the Charity;[80] and that the fees should not exceed £30 a year. A conscience clause was incorporated in the scheme. His experience of this York scheme had led Thompson to believe that 'it would be desirable to amalgamate these various endowments for educational purposes which are now scattered throughout the country.'[81] But he admitted that the original Yeoman School had failed because of its clear connection with a Church Training College.

Canon H. G. Robinson, an Endowed Schools Commissioner after 1869, went to York as Principal of the Training College, and therefore as headmaster of the Yeoman School, in 1854.[82] He resigned in 1863. He made it clear, in his evidence to the S.I.C.,[83] that there were in fact three foundations in York: the Yeoman Proprietary School with its boarding pupils; the Holgate Charity School; and a model school attached to the Training College as a day-school for middle-class boys from the City. He mentioned that it had been intended by the subscribers that there should be a farm established in connection with the Yeoman School; but this scheme had never come to fruition. He had told the Social Science Association meeting at York in 1864 that such a complex of schools might be established in every town throughout England by voluntary local efforts.[84] Robinson had also been responsible for recommending the first headmaster of West Buckland to J. L. Brereton: '. . . the master was sent there by me and I have had constant communication with him.'[85]

In February 1870, the *Northampton Mercury* carried an item headed, 'The Bedford Middle Class School':

A public school has been founded in Bedfordshire to suit the agricultural and other middle-class inhabitants of the county. The education of this class has had a large share of discussion in the last few years; and the land-owners, tenant-farmers and professional and trading classes of Bedfordshire have taken a practical step to meet the demand now generally felt.[86]

Just over a year earlier the *Times* had reported the founding of a large school for 300 boarders at Kempston, near Bedford. The funds had been raised through shares purchased by landed proprietors and leading farmers of the county. The Duke of Bedford, who had earlier endowed exhibitions at West Buckland, had supported the movement by taking shares worth £10,000; Lord Cowper, the Lord Lieutenant, subscribed £1,000, and Samuel Whitbread, M.P., £2,000.[87] The School was to be governed by a board of 'Noblemen, Gentlemen, and farmers of the county', with Cowper as Chairman. The fees were 'moderate' at £33 10s 0d per annum. 'It is right to say that the religious principles upon which the school is conducted are free altogether from sectarian bias.'[88] Since the Harpur Trust was one of the wealthiest educational endowments in the country, the need for such a school as Kempston may be questioned. However, the great Bedford Trust was as yet unreformed, and Kempston can be seen as a rustication of middle-class schooling outside the narrow controversies then raging in the town of Bedford over its trusts.[89]

While Fortescue and Brereton relished receiving news of the expansion of the movement they had initiated, this Bedford County School was not completely to their liking. In a letter to his colleague in 1867, when Kempston was first proposed, Fortescue likened the non-sectarian religious character of the projected school to that of the schools of 'Hang Theology' Rogers in London.[90] Yet it seems clear that by the time the Report of the S.I.C. was published, a varied and widely dispersed pattern of county schools for the middle classes had been established. The original model was West Buckland. They had been conceived as boarding schools for the sons of farmers and other members of the rural middle classes, with fees set at a moderate level, and curricula which, though general rather than vocational, were devised with the aim of preparing boys for local middle-class occupations, as distinct from entry to the Universities and the higher professions. In most cases they were proprietary in principle and were governed by boards of varying sizes whose composition was nevertheless uniform in the sense that their members were usually local or locally connected noblemen and gentry. They were not elementary in character; and their religious teaching was of a broad Anglican kind, tempered by a conscience clause in most cases, unlike the aggressively exclusive Woodard schools. In fact, the contrast between the Woodard model and its Brereton counterpart has been highlighted by Brian Heeney in his brief comparison of the St Nicholas foundation at Denstone in Staffordshire and the more moderate Trent College established not far away in Nottinghamshire in 1868, the latter supported by the Duke of Devonshire who had connections with West Buckland. Lord Harrowby, alluding to the religious principles operating at Trent College, said, 'I hope we are doing good work here and are enduing the middle class with a sound religious education without any animosity towards our Nonconformist brethren and without enforcing our opinions upon those who object to the principles of the Church of England.'[91]

Brian Heeney has shown that Woodard and Brereton had much in common – their middle-class target, their aversion to state interference, and their espousal of the boarding principle. But they differed markedly on other matters, particularly in Brereton's willingness and Woodard's adamant refusal to compromise with Dissent.[92] Of the two, Brereton would seem to have been the more typical leading Churchman of his time: he was essentially part of the mainstream which flowed through Tait and could be traced back to Thomas Arnold. Heeney, with his scholarly devotion to the cause of Woodard, is substantially correct when he says that 'on the whole, the practical results of the County School plan were small when compared with the success of St. Nicholas College.[93] But it is equally true to say that the functions of the county school did not die, but became transmuted in the form of the country grammar school which gradually emerged to serve the rural community between 1869 and 1902.

Even Fortescue at his most pessimistic in 1868 told Brereton that he had glanced briefly at the S.I.C. Report and seen in it 'more mention a great deal made of Woodward (sic) (thanks to Lyttelton and Acland) than of us a good deal'. But his preliminary judgement was wrong, since in Volume I at least as much space was devoted to the County Schools as to the Woodard foundations. And Fortescue said later that 'the truth must come out in the reports of the District commissioners', and in this anticipation he was more correct.[94] The remarks of assistant commissioner Stanton, and of Giffard and Hammond on other schools at Framlingham and Cranleigh, were moderately favourable.[95] On the other hand, assistant commissioner Giffard's remarks on Woodard's schools in Sussex emphasised the bogey of the religious problem:

> The close adherence of the (Woodard) schools to the discipline of the Church of England obviates many of the difficulties which are complained of in mixed schools; but this rigid adherence has given rise to apprenhensions in the minds of many churchmen as well as dissenters, who, though they may acknowledge the truth of the doctrines of the Church, are indifferent or averse to its ritual. This is the case especially in the county of Sussex, which has a strong evangelical *penchant*; and there ... the schools have not yet shaken off the unpopularity which certain accusations, made some years back, created.[96]

Despite Fortescue's apprehensions, and whatever Acland's and Lyttelton's personal sympathies – both had in fact been subscribers to Woodard's more recent campaigns – the S.I.C. Report seems to have embodied an impartial evaluation of the two sets of schools, not favouring one above the other. Fortescue and Brereton, Woodard, and the exponents of National Society policy had all conceived their plans for the organisation of middle-class schooling in the era before reasonably efficient central agencies for the reform of education had been created. The advent of the Charity Commission in the early 1850s had meant that it would be unlikely that England would soon be covered by a network of proprietary schools, whether based on the diocesan, county, or Woodard model. Fortescue's and Woodard's plans were based on the assumption that no good could come of a mass of ancient educational institutions; that the endowed grammar schools were incapable of being reformed *en masse*. The S.I.C. accepted the possibility of reform, and also the idea that a temporary department of the central government was the appropriate body for undertaking reform. For different reasons Fortescue and Woodard found the prospect of government interference in the development of middle-class schooling distasteful.

The chief importance of the County School movement and the work of local diocesan committees was that they suggested to the Commissioners the possibility of creating official local agencies, or boards, based upon the county, or a group of counties, for managing a system of middle-class education, the greater part of which would rely on existing endowments. The S.I.C. accepted the probable necessity for supplementing the endowed schools with existing private or proprietary, or rate-aided secondary schools in urban areas, with appropriate guarantees of educational standards.[97] They also accepted the need for creating a graduated system, with centrally located second-grade schools, like West Buckland, serving a wide geographical area within a county.[98] Further evidence in support of the county board proposal was provided by the comments of the Newcastle Commissioners in 1861 and the evidence to Pakington's Committee in 1865. In their different ways the National Society's local committees and the County School movement encouraged the S.I.C. to adopt the proposal of provincial boards which was a crucially important component of their overall scheme for creating a graduated system of middle-class schools.

A link between the kinds of schools and local agencies discussed above and a further provincial development in middle-class education between 1845 and 1864 is suggested by the S.I.C.'s consideration of two other schools which fell into the 'county' category. Volume XIV included a report upon Callington Proprietary School in Cornwall, founded in 1864 by the Revd F. V. Thornton, whose object was to educate 'all classes in the immediate neighbourhood, and the upper and lower middle classes at a distance'. Callington partook of the character of a County School since the governors were to be 'gentlemen of position in the county and neighbourhood'.[99] Volume I of the S.I.C. Report contains a brief reference to the foundation of a County school in Herefordshire; Dean Dawes' proxy written evidence to the Commissioners also mentioned this school 'designed to meet the needs of the lower middle classes', and there was a short report upon the School by assistant commissioner Bompas.[100]

This conjunction between Dawes and Thornton, the result of their common concern for the education of the sons of farmers, was not fortuitous. They shared interests which lay outside the environs of the County School movement. In a later chapter Thornton's work is touched upon in relation to his pamphlet, *The Education of the Middle Classes in England*, written in December 1861, when he was rector of Brown Candover in Hampshire.[101] In this and in his later evidence to the S.I.C. he revealed his debt to Richard Dawes, formerly, though briefly, his neighbour in Hampshire.

Dawes was born in Wensleydale in 1792, the son of a freeholder. The foundations of his mathematical prowess were laid at John Gough's famous school in Kendal. He went up to Downing College, Cambridge, becoming fellow and Bursar in 1818. His earliest biographer wrote that the College's depleted funds had benefited from Dawes' 'active and vigilant stewardship'. Much of the College estate property lay in Cambridgeshire and from his management of it he may have gained his sympathy for the tenant-farmer and some vicarious experience as a landlord:

> With the tenantry Mr. Dawes conducted relations of a most friendly character, making them free of the hospitality of the College. . . . The estate soon found itself in the hands of a man who played the part of a landlord for the College precisely as he would have done for himself, and who scrupulously and rigidly maintained all rights of ownership, while showing all fairness, justice and even leniency, when needed, towards the tenants.[102]

An interesting foretaste of Dawes' staunchly tolerant religious opinions came in 1836, when it was thought that he was sure to succeed to the Mastership of Downing. But he had voted earlier, along with Professor Sedgwick, for the admission of Dissenters to the University, and in the eyes of some of the electors, the Master of Clare particularly, this action disqualified him. In the following year he was presented to the living of King's Somborne in Hampshire by Sir John Mill, one of his former pupils at Downing.[103]

The features of Dawes' school at King's Somborne, and the public praise raised upon it by H.M.I.s Moseley and Allen, are well known.[104] It was in order to publicise his experiment even more widely, 'giving some assistance to those who have the same object in view as myself', that he prepared his *Hints on an Improved and Self-Supporting System of National Education* in 1847. His chief aim, as rector of a scattered rural parish, was to provide a self-sufficient and economical form of education which would meet the needs of children of the labouring classes and also of the tenant-farmers in the neighbourhood. The scheme therefore ran contrary to the currently accepted convention that even the smaller tenant-farmers would not countenance such a blending of social classes in schools attended by their children. Dawes thought that a realistic inducement for its acceptance by farmers might be offered by the provision of a curriculum which would be seen to prepare children for their practical occupations in life. If the quality of the secular education thus provided was found to be good, then, he argued, one would be able to 'promote the blessing of a sound scriptural education' to a higher degree than was possible in an ordinary National school. A further inducement, to the practically minded farmer, might be that the fees would be lower than those exacted by local private schoolmasters.[105] And since the farmer would be able to maintain his children at school longer than the labourer, an important social and intellectual aim would have been achieved: the labourer's son would no longer be, in point of education, the superior of his employer's child.[106] 'Why discontent these adjoining and important links in the social chain – the very mainstay and support of the whole fabric – when they might be united by a much stronger tie than any which binds them together at present; that of an education in common?'[107]

The school-fees were fixed on an ascending scale: 2d per week for the first child of a labourer; 6s 0d per quarter for parish children above those of the labouring class. The curriculum at King's Somborne has been treated comprehensively by David Layton;[108] and it is worth mentioning that the secular books used were the publications of the Irish National Board of Education. The chief significance of the School, for the present purpose, lies in its effect, as Dawes suggested, upon a number of neighbouring schools, and even upon schools in distant parts of the Kingdom. Dawes became a leading member of the unofficial rural 'establishment' of education, particularly through his association with Acland and the Bath and West Society, for whose *Journal* he contributed a number of articles on topics relating to rural education.[109]

He lectured widely, on adult 'secondary' education as well as his elementary schemes. He not only introduced, but himself taught, scientific subjects in the School, and he attracted there lecturers of considerable reputation; for example, Professors Frankland and Tyndall, later to fill the places of Davy and Faraday at the Royal Institution, were, in the late 1840s, lecturing at the nearby Queenswood Agricultural College, and both went to give courses of lectures to the junior and adult pupils at King's Somborne.[110]

On Russell's recommendation, Dawes became Dean of Hereford in 1850. Besides the restoration of the Cathedral building, he continued his educational work in his new place. In particular he personally supervised the reform of the Bluecoat and Scudamore charity schools in the City of Hereford. The improved condition of the schools soon attracted to them 'the children of the tradespeople' who were admitted after 1856 on payment of moderate fees, alongside the free children. In 1863 the usefulness of the schools was extended by the introduction of a plan of payments graduated according to the means of the parents; while seventy free scholarships were still reserved for children of the poorest class.[111] Dawes chose the certificated masters and pupil-teachers. In addition he managed the Cathedral School and took a close interest in the Proprietary School (the County School mentioned above).[112] Thus Mr. Bompas, on behalf of the S.I.C., could say of Hereford that it already possessed a graduated system of middle-class education in 1866: there was the Cathedral School for classical instruction; the Proprietary School for higher commercial education; and there were also 'very good free elementary schools, to the upper classes of which the sons of the lower middle classes are sent'.[113] It is interesting to speculate upon the extent of Dawes' interference in the appointments to the Proprietary School, for the Headmaster in 1859, J. J. Lomax, had formerly been supervising master for the National Society in the Hereford diocese, while the 'Professor of Chemistry and Machinery', Robinson, had come from the Diocesan Training College at Chester.[114] All the Hereford schools, save the Cathedral School, operated conscience clauses. He also founded the Ledbury National schools which had similar social and religious characteristics.[115]

Dawes died, after long and painful illness, in March 1867. His biographer provided a fittingly broad evaluation of his influence on educational development:

> Nor was the Dean's zeal in promoting education confined to schools founded or organised by himself – his friends, whether near or remote, were always sure of his sympathy, advice, and active aid, in the management of their schools, and in the careful selection of teachers. In fact he had become a kind of minister of public instruction, not merely for the diocese of Hereford, but wherever in England or Scotland he had friends engaged in this noble work. . . . And during the later years of his life he was constantly receiving letters from persons whom he had raised from humble stations into competence and respectability.'[116]

Prominent among Dawes' education 'friends' was the Hon. and Revd J. Best, rector of Abbot's Ann, Hampshire, a neighbour of Dawes in the 1840s and with him a supporter of the Hants and Wilts Education Society. When he gave his evidence to the S.I.C. in 1865 Best had held his Hampshire living for thirty-four years. It is clear from his account of the School at Abbot's Ann that it resembled very closely the institution at King's Somborne: the sons of farmers and labourers were educated together; there was a system of graduated fees; the rudiments of agricultural chemistry were taught; a master from the Andover School of Art came over to teach the pupils and a conscience clause was in operation.[117]

Thornton gave his evidence to the S.I.C. in March 1866. At that time he had been rector of Callington for two years, having held his living in Hampshire for the previous fourteen years. Lord Taunton described Thornton's school at Callington as one in which 'there is a mixture of the children of different classes of society'. The nucleus of the school had apparently been brought from Hampshire.[118] It had soon attracted the sons not only of the lower middle but of the higher classes. A boarding house had been added to the school, and in this case, too, the fees were graduated according to the parents' income. An assistant master from Marlborough had been appointed head-master. As evidence of the successful mixing of social classes at Callington Thornton recorded that 'the captain of the school at the present moment is a labourer's child'.[119] He had instituted a con-science clause. Greek was taught: one of the local pupils had got on to the foundation at Eton. But he admitted that good teachers of chemistry were hard to find, and that consequently there was no systematic science teaching.[120] Thornton's own sons had attended the school, and one of his daughters had remained a pupil there till she was eighteen.

Dawes was mentioned neither in Thornton's evidence nor in his pamphlet. Yet, if only circumstantially, because of the basic common features of their schools, and the geographical coincidence, it seems likely that King's Somborne and Abbot's Ann were models well known to Thornton. A school of a different, though closely related, type came to the notice of the S.I.C., and in this case, too, there is no evidence of direct connection with the work of Dawes. The ancient Aldersey School, at Bunbury in Cheshire, differed from King's Somborne in that it had begun its career as an endowed grammar school. The trustees were the Haberdashers' Company of London. The S.I.C. summoned the Revd W. B. Garnett Botfield as witness in 1866. He described the School as being 'at present carried on more like a National school . . . a school for all classes'.[121] R. S. Wright, the S.I.C. assistant commissioner, had described Bunbury as 'a National school rising into a middle school'.[122] It contained the sons of labourers, of tradesmen, of farmers and professional men, of clergymen and merchants. The higher classes among the pupils represented one-third of the whole. As at King's Somborne the fees were fixed according to parents' means, the highest at 15s a quarter, the lowest 2d a week.

Bunbury had been brought to the notice of the S.I.C. early in its proceedings by the former H.M.I., the Revd J. P. Norris. Commenting on the work of Botfield and his single-minded transformation of the school from one for twelve boys conducted in a barn to an institution of 100 pupils serving a rural parish of 5,000 people, Norris said that 'what has been done at Bunbury might be done in 400 or 500 of such schools all over the country to the greatest possible advantage'.[123] Latin was taught, if required, with chemistry, land-surveying, and 'the English education', all by a 'highly trained certificated master' from Battersea.

In the matter of the school's endowment and its nominal trustees, the Haberdashers, Botfield seems to have shown a judicious ignorance. Replying to Lyttelton before the S.I.C. he admitted that he had neither consulted the trustees nor made any application to Chancery before making radical changes in the character of the school.[124] Surprisingly the Commissioners pursued further neither this point nor the rather doubtful conjunction of a £50 endowment and receipt of the Government grant to elementary schools. It is impossible to be sure whether these matters are connected with the complete absence of any information about the Bunbury charity in the Charity Commission files at the Public Record Office. Botfield was a school patron of considerable energy, willing to use, illegally it seems, whatever resources were to hand in order to create a school which served what he considered to have been the best educational interests of the local rural community. He ended his evidence saying, 'I would suggest that in all National schools and others receiving the government grant there should be a scale of payments for the better classes, so that if the schools were efficient and satisfied the requirements of such classes in the district, they might avail themselves of it at a fair charge'.[125]

The significance of Norris's reference to Bunbury lies in a wider context than the comment of one H.M.I. upon an isolated example of educational enterprise on behalf of the lower middle classes. Comments such as his occur in the official reports of his Inspector colleagues in the period from the mid-1840s till the 1860s. Their references were to a system of schools which would establish some connection between elementary education up to eleven or twelve, and a higher department of upper standards providing a fundamental secondary education for children in country towns and rural areas. The Revd H. Sandford, H.M.I., sent an unsolicited letter to the S.I.C. in September 1866, in which he claimed that, to a certain extent, the elementary schools of his acquaintance were attended by the children of the middle classes: 'farmers, tradesmen, well-to-do mechanics . . . furnish a considerable proportion of the scholars in our National schools'.[126] The main defect of the system, as he saw it, was that 'in cases where there are two or more institutions under public management they do not work harmoniously together, there is no proper division of labour, no graduated system of instruction, by means of which one class of schools might take up and carry forward the work begun by others.'[127]

He reiterated his plan for creating higher departments and a graduated system in his report to the Committee of Council in 1868,[128] and showed that his idea was not new by referring to earlier statements of similar views by other H.M.I.s. He quoted Mr Kennedy's report for 1855:

> Our voluntary system, by connecting the whole course of elementary instruction with an ecclesiastical district, prevents our having three or four series of graduated schools, and chains the schools down to a uniform dead level. There is not sufficient scope, there is not a sufficiently high style of school, for boys ranging from ten to fourteen years of age. We want at least three grades of schools, an infant, a first school, a second school, and a third school.[129]

Sandford also referred to Norris's report of 1857 in which he mentioned a letter from the Secretary of the Education Department to the Vice-President; Lingen had said,

> The Lord President thinks that a system of secondary schools might with great advantage be added to the present system of primary schools, in all those localities where schools of the latter kind are sufficiently large or sufficiently numerous to afford a supply of children who have mastered the common elements of instruction, and are prepared to proceed with more specific studies.[130]

These kinds of opinions, held by educationalists employed by the central government, were taken up by the Newcastle Commissioners.[131] When the S.I.C. interviewed Sir John Pakington in 1865, he stated firmly that, if a proper system of elementary education were to exist, then the lower middle class – 'the farmers to a great extent certainly' – would be willing to send their children to the National schools for their elementary education.[132] He referred to a school with which he was connected at Cutnall Green in Worcestershire where there was a mingling of social classes and a graduated system of payments. He had received evidence from the counties of Lincoln,

York and Oxford about the operation of similar schools, and he mentioned also the case of St Peter's School Droitwich, 'which Lord Lyttelton is well acquainted with', run according to the same principles.[133] Lyttelton himself, in his written evidence to the Newcastle Commission in 1859, had said of his own elementary school at Hagley: 'A large proportion of the children . . . 'belong to the lower part of the middle classes . . . as well as to the labourers'. Though he went on to admit that, given the present state of elementary education, he could not imagine there ever being numerous imitators of 'the remarkable case of King's Somborne School'.[134] Of Pakington's long-standing commitment to the idea of this extended form of elementary education there can be little doubt; for in his address to the Education Department of the first conference of the Social Science Association at Birmingham in 1858 he said, 'I believe there is no greater error than that of supposing that it is impossible to get the middle classes to associate with the working classes for the purpose of education'.[135]

The 'liberalism' of the views put forward by Pakington, Acland, Sandford and others is open to misinterpretation. The opinions ranged against them – that the middle classes did not want their children to mix with their social inferiors – were conservative, and could be substantiated by statistical evidence and by the existence of a thriving market providing ineffectual private schools for the lower middle class. But their liberal schemes, for the extension of the scope of the elementary school in an upward social direction, in conjunction with the supervision of that schooling by 'county authorities', were part of a broader plan for controlling social movement and preserving the balance of traditional elements in the structure of rural society. This policy of social containment became part of the underlying philosophy on which the apparently radical proposals of the S.I.C. were based. The local boards which had existed and the provincial boards which the Taunton Commissioners wished to see established were, or would have been, dominated by the traditional leaders of county society.

Brian Heeney has stated that the National Society's concern for middle-class education resulted in 'comparatively little action between 1839 and 1860'.[136] The first part of this chapter went some way towards providing evidence for a considerable modification of that judgement. One of the mysteries enveloping the work of the S.I.C. has been the question of why that mixed bag of

Commissioners collectively and doggedly clung to the proposal for county and provincial boards which they had begun to discuss in 1865. A considerable part of the answer to that question is provided by the evidence of widespread and varied activity, at a local level, described here. The National Society's efforts of 1839 were not sustained at the centre; but they were continued strenuously by local agencies like the Northants Society. The original impulse of the National Society was represented on the S.I.C. by Acland, one of the 1839 group: the local initiative by Lyttelton and all those who regularly attended local meetings of the National Society. The County School movement had its roots in a related field: a liberal alliance of Anglicans sharing an interest, founded upon economic self-interest, in the well-being of the tenant-farmer class and its sons. The schemes for lower middle-class elementary education, which seem to have owed so much to Richard Dawes, were similarly based upon Anglican effort in rural communities. It can be argued that, under the combined and connected pressures of the experience of these movements, all of which had originated in the quarter-century before 1864, the S.I.C. could hardly fail to grasp an idea for the local management of middle-class education which originated in the kinds of rural county communities from which most of the leading members of the Commission came. Certainly, the urban industrial communities of mid-nineteenth-century England could offer no coherent or systematic alternative for educational reform. When the S.I.C. made proposals about lower middle-class education, their examples were almost invariably the tenant-farmer and the rural tradesman.

Notes

1 National Society, Annual Report for 1839, p. 9.
2 Ibid, Appendix XVI.
3 *Nonconformist*, 10 November 1841, p. 574.
4 *S.I.C.*, XV, James Bryce's Report on Kidderminster Free School, pp. 541–6.
5 Worcester Diocesan Library, Minute Book of the Diocesan Board of Education, I, 31 July 1844.
6 S.I.C., XV, p. 590.
7 Ibid, p. 602.
8 Ibid, p. 581.
9 Ibid, p. 549.
10 Wells Chapter Library, Minute Book of the Bath and Wells Board of Education, 1857–74; a copy of the printed Aims is pasted inside the cover.

11 For an account of Failand Lodge's early history, see Committee of Council Minutes, 1844–5, pp. 114–15.

12 S.I.C., IV, p. 694.

13 Ibid, p. 692.

14 Ibid, loc. cit.

15 Hants County Record Office, Winchester, pamphlets reserve Box C, Sixth Report of the Winchester Diocesan Board of Education, May 1846, p. 2.

16 Winchester Board, Sixth Report, loc. cit.

17 S.I.C., XI, p. 353.

18 Winchester Board, Sixth Report, p. 5.

19 Ibid, pp. 9–10.

20 Winchester Board, Seventh Report, 1847, pp. 5–6.

21 Northants County Record Office, Box 306, Minutes of the Middle Schools Committee of the Northants Education Society, 1854–73, printed Report of a Special Committee, 1854, pp. 10–11.

22 Revd H. J. Barton was a contributor to Acland's revived Bath and West *Journal*.

23 Northants, Report of a Special Committee, II.

24 These were the leading figures in the promotion of the Industrial Schools Act, 1854.

25 See below, Chapter V.

26 Northants Middle Schools Committee Minutes, 30 December 1854.

27 PRO ED 27/3672, Northampton Grammar School File, Charity Commission Inquiry, 1854–6.

28 The foregoing information is taken from the sequence of reports in the Minutes of the Northants Education Society. See also, T. C. Lees, *A Short History of Northampton Grammar School*, Northampton, 1947, p. 53.

29 *Victoria County History of Northants*, IV, p. 293.

30 Northants Education Society, Annual Report, 1859.

31 See below, Chapter VI.

32 *Report of the Commissioners appointed to Inquire into the State of popular education in England* (the Newcastle Commission), 1861, I, p. 545.

33 See below, Chapter VII, p. 156, for George Griffith's notion of a representative local body.

34 Popular Education Commission, I, pp. 480–1.

35 Ibid, p. 481.

36 Select Committee on Elementary Education, 1865, p. 52.

37 S.I.C., IV, pp. 602–3.

38 Select Committee, 1865, p. 48.

39 Popular Education Commission, 1861, VI, pp. 452–3.

40 See above, Chapter II, pp. 49–50.

41 Minutes of Committee of Council, 1845–6, pp. 60–1.

42 Ibid, p. 173.

43 Minutes of Committee of Council, 1845–6, loc. cit.

44 Minutes of Committee of Council, 1847–8, p. 34.

45 Manchester Church Education Society, Report for 1845, p. 34. (Copy

in Manchester Central Reference Library.)

46   Ibid, p. 7.
47   Special Report of the Working Committee of the Manchester Church Education Society, I.
48   Manchester Society, Annual Report, 1846, pp. 31–8.
49   See above, Chapter II, pp. 37–8.
50   Manchester Society, Annual Report, 1845, Appendix A, p. 32.
51   Ibid, p. 33.
52   Manchester Society, Annual Report, 1847, p. 23.
53   Ibid, p. 26.
54   A. A. Mumford, *The Manchester Grammar School, 1515–1915, a Regional Study of the Advancement of Learning in Manchester since the Reformation*, London, 1919, p. 297.
55   Ibid, pp. 296–8; see also, *S.I.C.*, XVII, pp. v–vii.
56   *S.I.C.*, IX, p. 714; p. 727.
57   See above, Chapter II, pp. 43–4.
58   For other comments on Fortescue's *magnum opus*, see John Roach, op. cit., pp. 50–5; B. Heeney, op. cit., pp. 160–1. Also, Spens Report, 1938, pp. 26–7.
59   See below, Chapter IV, p. 97.
60   See above, Chapter II, pp. 30–31.
61   Fortescue, op. cit., 170.
62   *S.I.C.*, IV, 23 May 1865, p. 478.
63   Ibid, p. 478; p. 481.
64   Ibid, p. 483.
65   Ibid, pp. 645–62. For links between these persons, see above, Chapter II.
66   Ibid, p. 645; p. 648.
67   Ibid, p. 653.
68   *S.I.C.*, V, pp. 588–605.
69   Ibid, p. 589.
70   Ibid, p. 604.
71   *S.I.C.*, XIV, p. 516.
72   Homerton College, Cambridge, Fortescue–Brereton Papers, letter from Fortescue, 21 August 1866, arranging meeting with Troyte at Sampford Peverall.
73   *S.I.C.*, XIV, p. 471.
74   Dorset County Record Office, P97/SCI, letters concerning proposed County School; printed letter of Archdeacon Sanctuary.
75   *S.I.C.*, XIV, pp. 471–2.
76   *S.I.C.*, XVIII, p. 429.
77   See above, Chapter II, p. 39.
78   *S.I.C.*, V, p. 269.
79   *S.I.C.*, loc. cit.
80   *S.I.C.*, XVIII, p. 429.
81   *S.I.C.*, V, p. 271.
82   See below, Chapter X, p. 248 for further details of this passage of events which links the Yeoman School with Cirencester College.

83   S.I.C., IV, p. 602.
84   Transactions of the National Association for the Promotion of Social Science, conference at York, 1864, London, 1864.
85   S.I.C., IV, p. 606; see also Brereton's evidence, ibid, V, p. 129.
86   *Northampton Mercury*, 12 February 1870.
87   *Times*, 29 January 1869; also, *S.I.C.*, I, p. 311 (footnote).
88   *Northampton Mercury*, 12 February 1870.
89   S.I.C., XX, 352.
90   Fortescue–Brereton Papers, letter of 30 June 1867. For Rogers, see below, Chapter IX.
91   A. J. Tawer, *Trent College, 1868–1927*, London, 1929. Quoted in Heeney, op.cit., pp. 161–5.
92   Heeney, op. cit., p. 167.
93   Ibid, p. 165.
94   Fortescue–Brereton Papers, letter of Fortescue, 23 March 1868.
95   *S.I.C.51, (i) VII, pp. 62–3; (ii) XI, pp. 157–8; (iii) VIII, pp. 370–8.*
96   S.I.C., VII, p. 146.
97   S.I.C., I, pp. 652–9.
98   *Ibid*, pp. 580–1.
99   S.I.C., XIV, p. 520.
100 S.I.C., I, p. 311; II, 28; XV, p. 810. See also *Hereford Times*, 29 October 1859.
101 For Thornton's general views, see below, Chapter VI.
102 William Charles Henry, FRS, A Biographical Notice of the late Very Revd Richard Dawes, MA, Dean of Hereford, London, 1867, for private circulation, 9. (Copy in Hereford City Reference Library.)
103 Ibid, p. 10.
104 See (i) W. A. C. Stewart and W. P. McCann, *The Educational Innovators, 1750–1850*, London, 1967; and (ii) David Layton, *Science for the People*, London, 1973, Chapters II and IV.
105 Richard Dawes, *Hints on an Improved and Self-supporting System of National Education, suggested from the working of a village school in Hampshire*, 1847, pp. 1–4.
106 Ibid, p. 5.
107 Ibid, p. 7.
108 Layton, loc. cit.
109 See above, Chapter II, p. 39.
110 Henry, op. cit., p. 14. This passage was contributed by the Hon. and Revd J. Best.
111 Ibid, pp. 16–17.
112 See above, this Chapter, p. 81.
113 S.I.C., XV, p. 215–16.
114 Advertisement in *Slater's Royal National and Commercial Directory and Topography of the Counties of Gloucester, Hereford . . .*, Manchester and London, 1859, p. 66.
115 Henry, op. cit., p. 19.
116 Ibid, p. 24.
117 S.I.C., IV, pp. 668–701.

118 *S.I.C.*, V, p. 685.
119 Ibid, p. 692.
120 Ibid, p. 695.
121 Ibid, p. 579.
122 *S.I.C.*, XVII, p. 21.
123 *S.I.C.*, IV, p. 59.
124 *S.I.C.*, V, p. 584.
125 Ibid, p. 587.
126 *S.I.C.*, II, Miscellaneous Letters, p. 106.
127 Ibid, p. 109.
128 Minutes of Committee of Council, 1868–9, p. 201.
129 Minutes of Committee of Council, 1855–6, p. 359.
130 Quoted in Minutes of Committee of Council, 1868–9, p. 202.
131 See above, this Chapter, p. 68.
132 *S.I.C.*, V, p. 674.
133 Ibid, pp. 667–8.
134 Popular Education Commission, 1861, V, p. 277, 288.
135 *Transactions of the National Association for the Promotion of Social Science, at Birmingham, 1857*, London, 1858, p. 41.
136 Heeney, op. cit., p. 169.

CHAPTER IV

'Fiat experimentum in corpore vili'
Irish models for middle-class education in England

. . . Ireland would ever seem to be the place of experiments, both of politics and of education, and a cloud of never-ending failures has encompassed her in both . . .

W. J. Bennett, *Crime and Education: the Duty of the State Therein*, London, 1846.

Despite the conscientious work of recent Irish scholars, particularly Donald Akenson,[1] the significance of Ireland in the nineteenth century as a laboratory for conducting educational experiments has been largely overlooked by British historians. But the forms of schooling and educational administration which were implanted there between 1800 and 1880 by English politicians were studied closely by contemporary educationists in England, since they were seen as experimental devices for solving problems similar to those being encountered on the larger island: the education of the lower orders and the curriculum appropriate to working-class schooling; the problem of the relationship between an Anglican Establishment and Dissent; the types of schools best suited to the needs of the middle classes; and University provision.

Peel, as Chief Secretary for Ireland, had acknowledged the work of voluntary educational agencies in Ireland by making a Government grant of £6,980 in the 1814–15 Session towards the cost of popular schooling. Irish educational administration developed in advance of the system in England and was completed at elementary level by the liberal compromise of the National Board of Education in 1831, which was based upon the generous assumption that 'no system can be expedient which may be calculated to influence or disturb the peculiar religious tenet of any sect or denomination of Christians'.[2] Peel had also presided over the early attempts to put Irish middle-class education in order, a process which continued until the Irish

Intermediate Education Act of 1878. Nevertheless, little has been written about the extent to which Ireland provided substantial models for reform of middle-class education in England and Wales.

When Granville, Lord President of the Council, was trying to fashion terms of reference for the Schools Inquiry Commission in the summer and autumn of 1864, he sought advice from, among others, Henry Austin Bruce, then Vice-President of the Committee of Council on Education. At one point in the correspondence Bruce suggested that the best form of words might by 'to inquire into the State of Middle-class Education in England and Wales, and into the application of endowments designed to promote it'. He continued, 'Some such inquiry was made, into similar schools in Ireland by a Commission presided over by Lord Kildare (in 1858) . . . perhaps a reference to the terms of that Commission would supply a useful limit'.[3] Advice was offered, too, by Ralph Lingen, Kay-Shuttleworth's successor as Secretary of the Committee of Council, who referred Granville to two recent essays on middle-class education in the *Cornhill* written by Harriet Martineau.[4] These were not Martineau's first writings on the subject: for the *Daily News* in 1858 she had compiled a series of twelve articles which were subsequently published under the title 'Endowed Schools of Ireland.'[5] In her Preface she directed the attention of 'the friends of education in general' to the 'misapplication of Irish endowments' and to 'the educational interests of the great middle classes'.

She pointed to the gulf which then existed in Ireland between the efficient National elementary schools and the recently founded Queen's Colleges of higher education. This kind of analysis had already been applied to the decadent state of middle-class schooling, compared to elementary provision, in England. The need to reinforce the relative social standing of the English middle class was a central feature of the debate about educational provision in the 1850s and 1860s, and had been anxiously uttered by Thomas Arnold in 1832. Martineau said that an outstanding reason for the appointment of the Kildare Commission had been an awareness that, in their preparation for business life, the children of 'peasantry, artisans, and labourers' had a distinct advantage over those of the 'shop-keeping, manufacturing and professional orders'. As in England, if Irish endowments were put to more efficient use, they might form the core of a strong system of middle-class schooling, and would thus reinforce the existing social fabric. Looking to the Irish endowed schools, she anticipated the thinking of the Taunton Commissioners:

> At present the wisest way appears to be, to see what can be done with the
> old, in order to ascertain what more is wanted. To restore the institutions
> which have lapsed, to recover those which have disappeared, to extend such
> as have been redeemed, to verify those which are traditional, and build up
> those which are insecure, adapting all to the needs of the time, as those needs
> would be regarded by the founders if they were living now – these are the
> means of providing for a good deal, though not nearly all of that intermedi-
> ate education which the middle classes of Ireland are in distressing need of.[6]

While acknowledging the value of classical instruction, she said that
Irish employers wanted 'young men who can not only tell how many
years they have been learning French, but read and reply to a French
letter, or conduct purchases or sales in French. . . . The farmer is not
taught the chemistry of agriculture, the shopkeeper the laws of life
and health'. By contrast, the products of the elementary agricultural
schools at Templemoyle and Glasnevin were snapped up as valuable
fodder for nourishing the rural economy.[7] It is clear that she
intended that her remarks should be seen as having a parallel relevance to the improvement of similar institutions in England and
Wales.

The outstanding native figure initiating Irish educational progress
in the first half of the century was the extraordinary Thomas Wyse, a
member of the Catholic gentry educated at Stoneyhurst and Trinity
College, Dublin. He was aware that Irish rural society was riven by 'a
large floating mass of turbulence and violence': the more education
could be infused, he thought, 'the more tolerance and smoothness
you give to all popular movements'.[8] Peel, in the second decade of
the century, had at first tried to mitigate Irish social turbulence by
police legislation. But this had been ineffective in the face of the
underlying problems of a largely indifferent landowning class,
unwilling to invest capital in farming for their tenants, and a sullen
peasantry who resisted the scarce attempts from above to improve
their condition. Norman Gash has suggested that the simplest solution to the Irish problem would then have been to consolidate
holdings and invest more capital in large-scale farming.[9] But this did
not happen.

In 1813, however, Peel carried an Act which has been largely
ignored by recent social and educational historians, an 'act for the
Appointment of Commissioners for the Regulation of the several
Endowed Schools of Public and Private Foundation in Ireland'.[10]

This was the direct result of revelations by the Commissioners of Education for Ireland, among them Richard Lovell Edgworth, in their reports made between 1809 and 1812.[11] Even earlier, in 1788, an Irish Act (28 George III, cap 15) had appointed commissioners to investigate educational charities, and they had issued a startlingly radical report in 1791.[12] Their chief suggested remedy for the abuses they had discovered was the endowment of a 'Collegiate School' connected with the University. In addition they proposed 'a professional academy or academies' for instruction in mathematics and science, 'to initiate (young men) in the principles of chemical knowledge, with its application to arts and manufactures', to prepare soldiers, seamen and merchants for their respective businesses, 'to give a general account of the manners, customs and governments of different nations, with a short abstract of their history', and to teach French, German and Italian. They hoped for a model school, which would have been equalled only by a handful of Scottish academies, like Dundee, and a few English dissenting academies.[13] No system of schools, the commissioners thought, would thrive without close supervision; so they proposed a 'Board of Control' for inspection, for deploying surplus revenues, and even for setting up new schools. The 1791 Report provided a matrix for the work of the board of reforming Commissioners set up under Peel's 1813 Act.

The 1813 Commissioners for Irish endowed schools began promisingly. They had legal power to interfere in the management of schools and by-pass the Irish Court of Chancery, a feature which was not incorporated in legislation for England until 1853; and they could amalgamate existing schools and establish new ones by raising a rate on the county through the Grand Jury. However, while they were able to make marginal changes of detail, and indeed transform individual schools, they found the Grand Juries impossibly obstructive over finance. By the time Wyse's Select Committee on Irish Education reported in 1838, the Commission was for all practical purposes dormant.[14] Its failure was partly due to local obstructiveness and to the other business concerns which pressed upon the time of the unpaid Commissioners – led by the Primate, the Lord Chancellor, the Lord Chief Justice, and the Provost of Trinity. But two other factors probably carried great weight: all the Commissioners were Anglicans; and they had to work during a period of volcanic political and constitutional disturbance in Ireland, with rebellion and Union as its main features of cause and effect.

Nevertheless, unsuccessful as they ultimately were, the 1813 Act and its Commissioners prefigure remarkably the intentions and functions of their later English counterparts, the Endowed Schools Act, 1869, and the three reforming Commissioners appointed under it. There is no evidence that the architects of the English Charitable Trusts Acts in the 1850s had any precise knowledge of the work begun in Ireland forty years before; but the parallels between the weaknesses they were separately trying to eliminate, and the problems confronting them at different times, are clear.

Thomas Wyse was active not only on behalf of Irish education but in politics. The Revd James Bryce, President of the Belfast Academy (and uncle of another James Bryce who, early in his distinguished career was to be an assistant commissioner for the S.I.C.), said that Brougham had been an enthusiastic educationalist, but that "with Mr. Wyse it was a veritable passion."[15] The main objects of his Irish education policy owed much to Dr Doyle, Bishop of Kildare and Leighton, who had told him that, if he wished to promote education, he should look above the elementary schools and turn the Government's attention to founding 'four Provincial Academies' where non-classical subjects would be taught to 'the middle classes of society'. Doyle also required 'Agricultural Schools' on the joint-stock principle for the same class.

After providing much of the initiative which gave Ireland its first Board of Education, Wyse published his *Education Reform* in which he proposed a 'middle term' of Government intervention of the kind, one suspects, which Arnold earlier had in mind: that is, close co-operation between central authority and existing local voluntary agencies. 'Let the Government provide and extend a good system of education to all the people (it is the Government of all), and let all the people, in return, support and perpetuate such a system when provided by the Government.' This would apply to all three areas of schooling, elementary, middle-class and University.[16] In 1837 he became Chairman of Committees for the Central Society of Education, the most powerful educational pressure-group of the time, dominated by English Whigs and Radicals. The views he expressed in Central Society publications cannot have been overlooked by other members, like Harriet Martineau, William Ewart, Lord Ebrington (soon to become Lord Lieutenant of Ireland) and Lord Lansdowne (later Lord President of the Council and therefore responsible for education).

According to Wyse's niece, he was responsible for writing the report of the 1838 Select Committee on Irish Education.[17] It is hardly surprising, therefore, that the report recommended the reconstitution of the Irish National Board, with wider powers, embracing secondary and University education.[18] The section on elementary schooling owed much to B. F. Duppa's evidence about de Fellenberg's schools at Hofwyl.[19] Like the S.I.C. in the 1860s, Wyse dismissed the notion of completely gratuitous schooling because of its tendency to 'pauperise' the recipients.[20] The Government ought to aid secondary education since it was only by an efficient system of schooling that the Irish middle class might 'acquire and maintain that proper position in society to which they are entitled, and by means of which the community can be fully protected from the chaos of internal disorder'.[21] There should be County Academies, with admission by scholarship, administered by the county Grand Juries, and County Colleges providing advanced instruction. He thought there should be an agricultural school, on de Fellenberg lines, attached to each County Academy, to provide 'an educated class of farming bailiffs'.[22]

As in Wales later in the century, the 'top' of Wyse's plan was executed first. In May 1845, Sir James Graham piloted an Act through Parliament which instituted the Queen's Colleges in Ireland.[23] However, Wyse's tolerance, though shared by a number of Catholic bishops, was resented by Bishop McHale who, with O'Connell, opposed the measure, and succeeded in enlisting papal support. The Irish Catholic community had to turn their backs on Wyse; his career was ruined and he retired to the obscurity of diplomatic office in Athens.[24] But his influence prevailed: the Queen's Colleges, in a modified form, were established and have prospered; and, after Hugh Owen's examination of them, they served as the model for the federal University of Wales.[25]

After Wyse's level-headed, radical proposals in 1838, the Report of the Kildare Commission twenty years later hardly constituted a significant advance. It proposed adequate inspection of schools and proper qualifications for school-masters. Beyond this, and a heavy preoccupation with the interests of the tenant-farmer and shopkeeper class, it uttered little that was new or invigorating.[26]

The sequence of educational proposals and practices in Ireland between 1788 and 1858 comprise an important epoch in the history of middle-class education in Britain. Ireland was not so much a theatre for debate, as an area for which remedies could be suggested without inhibition, since they applied to a social system whose governors were invariably on the brink of despair. In outline, Irish middle-class schooling had problems and weaknesses in common with its neighbours in England: outmoded, often corrupt endowments which nevertheless dominated thinking about a possible future framework for reform; sectarian strife and intolerance; an archaic curriculum; an unrepresentative system of local government; inexpedient and expensive laws of charitable uses. The dissimiliarities were more deeply rooted in the different textures of the two communities.

In Ireland the need – or rather, the need felt by Anglo-Irishmen who mattered – was to create, not just reinforce, the middle-class part of the social fabric. The economic inertia of southern Ireland had no parallel in England. The notion of the Two Nations had a much more than metaphorical significance for Ireland. Proposals for reform were treated by the officers and supporters of a popular indigenous Church as alien impositions; and even the apparent deliverer, Wyse, the Catholic apostle of tolerance and compromise, was eventually driven into the wilderness. The visit of the Social Science Association to Dublin in 1861 only served to disguise the dissimilarities.

Yet the parallels, such as they were, remain remarkable, as were the anticipations of English schemes. As early as 1788 a supervising authority specifically for endowed schools was being officially suggested for Ireland; by 1813 the country had a permanent statutory commission for dealing with endowed-schools reform which, in a limited way began to co-operate with 'local authorities' in the form of Grand Juries; a Select Committee in 1838 prepared a blueprint for a complete system of national education in Ireland; and, by the late 1840s, the country had gained an elementary system and series of middle-class institutions for higher education.

If only because of these achievements and experiments Ireland became a touchstone for the solution of English educational problems and was a source of promising ideas and of despair for those who were announcing propositions in the middle-class debate. There was the continuing hope that Irish experiments might prove that a paternalist–collectivist alliance of aristocrats and intellectuals might succeed in promoting a system of education suitable for and acceptable to those in the middle ranks of society in England.

Writing of early nineteenth-century Ireland, Oliver MacDonagh has asserted that, whereas after the 1707 Act of Union Scotland remained *sui generis* in many respects, Ireland was, even by then, another England, legally and governmentally. This feature, reinforced by the 1801 Act, he says, is what makes Irish developments particularly relevant to the study of English government in the nineteenth century: they were readily transferable to the parent system; 'and where they were not so transferred, they raised challenging and penetrating questions'.[27] He points to the collectivisation of the Irish health service – in the early nineteenth century probably the most advanced in Europe – and to other collectivist features like fisheries, drainage and prison administration, as forerunners of similar, later developments in England.[28] Although McDonagh does not mention Irish education, the experiments and principles of reform which have been described in this chapter suggest that the collectivist tendencies in Irish educational administration provided both models for possible imitation and serious points for discussion and consideration in England.

Notes

1   See especially D. Akenson, *The Irish Education Question: the National System of Education in the Nineteenth Century*, London and Toronto, 1970.
2   The foregoing summary is based largely upon Akenson, op. cit., and upon G. Balfour, *Educational Systems of Great Britain and Ireland*, Oxford, 1903.
3   Public Record Office, Granville Papers, letter from H. A. Bruce, Duffryn, Aberdare, 15 August 1864.
4   Ibid, letter of R. R. W. Lingen to Granville, 7 October 1864. Lingen's judgement of the authorship of the articles is confirmed in Wellesley's *Index of Nineteenth-century Periodicals*.
5   H. Martineau, *Endowed Schools of Ireland*, reprinted from the Daily News, London, 1859.
6   Ibid, pp. 30–1.
7   Ibid, pp. 43–4.
8   T. Wyse, *Education Reform, or the Necessity of a National System of Education*, I, (there was no second volume), London, 1836, pp. 429–35.
9   N. Gash, *Mr. Secretary Peel: the Life of Sir Robert Peel to 1830*, London, 1961, p. 195.
10   The Act is ignored by Gash, op. cit. It is, however, mentioned in R. J. MacDowell, *Public Opinion and Government Policy in Ireland, 1801–46*, London, 1952. See, The Statutes of the United Kingdom of Great Britain and Ireland, V, Containing the Acts of 53 George III and 54

George III . . ., London, 1814. The Act in question is 53 George III, cap CVII, pp. 215–21.

11 Report from the Commissioners of the Board of Education in Ireland, 1809–12, reprinted 7 December 1813, Dublin.

12 Report of Her Majesty's Commissioners appointed to inquire into the Endowments, Funds, and actual Condition of all Schools endowed for the purpose of Education in Ireland, II, 1858, Document XIX (the 1791 Report), p. 341.

13 Ibid, p. 354, 355.

14 Report of the Commissioners of Education in Ireland to His Excellency the Lord Lieutenant, of the Proceedings of the Board from the 18th November 1813 to the 25th March 1814; published in the Reports of the Commissioners of National Education in Ireland from the year 1834 to 1842 inclusive, Dublin, 1844, pp. 3–6.

15 Quoted in W. M. Wyse, Notes on Education Reform in Ireland, during the first half of the nineteenth century. Compiled from the Speeches, Letters, etc., . . . by his niece, Winifrede, M. Wyse, Waterford, 1901, p. 6.

16 Central Society of Education, First Publication of 1837, Sir Thomas Wyse, 'Education in the United Kingdom. Its Progress and Prospects', p. 55.

17 W. M. Wyse, Notes, 51.

18 Report from the Select Committee on Foundation Schools in Ireland, 1838, p. 21.

19 Ibid, pp. 34–6. See also above, chapter II.

20 Ibid, p. 65.

21 Ibid, loc. cit.

22 P. J. Dowling, *A History of Irish Education: a Study of Conflicting Loyalties*, Cork, 1971, pp. 128–9.

23 Hansard, Third Series, LXXX, May–June 1845, p. 345.

24 W. M. Wyse, Notes, p. 102.

25 See D. Lewis Lloyd, *The Missing Link in Education in Wales*, Banglor, 1876. For Hugh Owen, see Report of the Committee appointed to Inquire into the condition of Intermediate and Higher Education in Wales (the Aberdare Report), 1881, II, Appendix I, p. 865.

26 Kildare Report, I, pp. 267–8.

27 O. MacDonagh, *Early Victorian Government, 1830 to 1870*, London, 1977, p. 179.

28 Ibid, pp. 184–7.

CHAPTER V

Equity Courts and Charity Commissions

What in the name of all that is wonderful, Mr Bluenose,' said the Reverend Dr Folliott, as he walked out of the inn, 'what in the name of all that is wonderful, can those fellows mean? They have come here in a chaise and four, to make a fuss about a pound per annum, which, after all, they leave as it was. I wonder who pays them for their trouble, and how much?

Thomas Love Peacock, *Crotchet Castle*, 1891 edition.

Dr Folliott's incredulous comment upon the visit to his village of the first Charity Commissioners was surely echoed, in reality, by harassed trustees of charities small and large during the 1820s and 1830s. It is remarkable that, during a period in which the Tory party largely dominated English political life, a temporary commission should have been allowed to spend £250,000 out of public funds upon a comprehensive investigation of another species of public funds.[1] The Brougham Inquiry, between 1818 and 1837, helped to create a climate of opinion about educational charities and their potential usefulness.

Yet it is hardly surprising that, in an age when men who mattered were aware of the increasing erosion by government of the principle of *laissez-faire*, Daniel Whittle Harvey, M.P., newspaper proprietor and proponent of economy and efficiency, fearing that the Commission might become permanent, petitioned successfully for a Select Committee to examine its work up to 1835.[2] Harvey himself became chairman of the Committee, and it was a powerful one, with Peel, Russell and Joseph Hume among its members. They succeeded in promoting Harvey's original aim: to terminate as soon as possible the work of the Brougham Commissioners. But, aware perhaps of the efficiency of the new Poor Law Commission, and anticipating the appointment of the Ecclesiastical Commission, Harvey and his colleagues proposed the creation of a skeletal Charity Commission of three members to supervise the sale and financial management of charity property.[3]

There were precedents for the Brougham Commission. One of the earlier inquiries, which had produced the Gilbert Returns after 1787, had helped to arouse a more general interest in the conduct of charities, and had shown that there were often anomalies in their local administration. The Gilbert Returns were not finally completed until 1803, and were reprinted in 1816, providing in that year the immediate stimulus for a new round of more accurate inquiries.[4] Only a little less pertinent to the promotion of inquiry was the sequence of events in Ireland between 1788 and 1813 which had led to the creation of a permanent Charity Commission in that part of Britain.[5] The chief aim of the instigators of the Gilbert and Brougham inquiries was of limited scope: it was to record some of the worst abuses of charity administration. In accordance with this aim the Charities Procedure Act and the Charitable Donations Act, which required the central registration of all existing charities, were passed in 1812; but neither Act was in any significant way effectual, the first perpetuating the use of Chancery as the sole and cumbersome means of reform, the second doing nothing to enforce registration effectively.[6]

In its educational work the Brougham Inquiry had been immediately preceded by the independent investigations of Nicholas Carlile whose findings were published in 1818.[7] His inquiry could hardly be called systematic; but despite its failings it provided some detailed descriptions of the subjects taught in endowed schools and their general condition, and created the only broad context for the growing debate about the inadequacies of the ancient curriculum in a changing society.

One of the effects of the Brougham inquiries was to reveal problems which affected all educational endowments in need of reform or modification. These were the interrelated problems of, firstly, *cy près*, and secondly the slowness and expense of proceedings in the Court of Chancery. Both were dealt with by Brougham himself in an *Edinburgh Review* article of 1823.[8] His attack was concentrated on Lord Eldon, the notoriously reactionary judge in the Leeds Grammar School case of 1805:

> . . . it is difficult . . . to deny that he more frequently gives proof of caution than of boldness, of subtlety than of vigour in his reasoning . . . that he confines himself too rigidly to the decision of special matters that come

before him, without aiming either at the establishment of general principles and the improvement of the Science he professes, or at the correction of those vices in the constitution and administration of his court, of which he daily sees and hears too much to make it conceivable that he should be ignorant ...[9]

An earlier article, similarly drawing attention to Chancery proceedings, had begun with a quotation from *Blackstone*:

> Our system of remedial law resembles an old Gothic castle erected in the days of chivalry, but fitted up for a modern inhabitant – the moated ramparts, the embattled towers, and the trophied halls, are magnificent and venerable, but useless, and therefore, neglected: the inferior apartments accommodated to daily use are cheerful and commodious, though their approaches may be winding and difficult.[10]

The Scottish-Whig-Utilitarian group which maintained interest in the reform of educational endowments between 1816 and 1830 was succeeded by two other Whig-Radical pressure-groups in the 1830s, though both these groups shared personnel in common with the earlier one. The *Quarterly Journal of Education* in 1831 contained an article complaining about the difficulty of revising the curricula of endowed schools.[11] This theme was developed more fully in the same journal three years later when it was admitted that 'it is more easy to point out the causes of decay, than to suggest remedies which are likely to be speedily applied.'[12] This later article, which had been occasioned by the publication of a digest of Brougham statistics in 1832, contained an expression of the hope that the State would intervene in the management of every endowed school, 'without giving itself the trouble to answer all objections that may be raised'.[13] Brougham was chairman of the *Quarterly Journal*'s management committee.

The second pressure-group was the Central Society for Education which published three volumes of essays in the late 1830s, each dealing with a broad range of topics. By far the longest in the second volume was by George Long, an inspector of Municipal Charities and formerly a member of the committee of the *Quarterly Journal*. His article, on Endowments, demonstrated his debt to the Brougham Returns and to detailed reporting of Chancery cases. He went further than the *Quarterly Journal* and demanded the appointment of a Minister of Education with a seat in the Cabinet. In addition he required a 'central authority which shall exercise superintendence over all charities'.[14]

In the early 1840s these utopian schemes, either for cutting through the knot of *cy près*, or for by-passing Chancery by means of government action, were superseded by legislative attempts to simplify equitable jurisdiction. Fuel for the government's advance upon the problem in England had been provided, not only by the Brougham investigations, but by the inquiries before the introduction of the Municipal Corporations Act in 1834 and 1835.[15] A further encouragement for the development of new legislative policies was provided by the Poor Law Commission whose 1834 Report had been signed by the Archbishop of Canterbury and the Bishop of London. The Commissioners had concluded, '. . . if the funds now destined to the purposes of education, many of which are applied in a manner unsuited to the present wants of society, were wisely and economically employed, they would be sufficient to give all the assistance which can be prudently afforded by the State'.[16]

In July 1840, Sir Eardley Wilmot's Bill, soon to become known as the Grammar Schools Act, was referred to a Select Committee which included the youthful Lord Lyttelton, Lord Lyndhurst, Brougham and the Bishop of London. Much was expected of this Act. Wilmot declared that the only purpose of his Bill had been 'to give a remedy to trustees of grammar schools for the better application of the funds' at a cost of £30 or £50, the current expense being much greater in Chancery.[17] A cursory examination of the terms of the Grammar Schools Act might suggest that it is a document of transparent simplicity and directness, and that it should have been able to reach the roots of the problems afflicting the endowed schools. It stated that a Court of Equity, when a question came before it, could henceforward make schemes for grammar schools, extending the course of study, changing the rights of admission, and amending the application of revenues. The Court might suggest substituting 'useful branches of literature and science' for Latin and Greek.[18] The Act seemed also to abolish the freehold right of the Master, and, on the other hand, provided machinery for superannuating aged or infirm masters. It seemed to permit that 'where several schools are in one place, and the revenues of any are insufficient they may be united'; the sting in this particular tail, however, lay in the proviso that all interested parties had to agree to the amalgamation.[19] Most of the recent commentators upon the Grammar Schools Act have discussed it very briefly. George Griffith, whose interest in the grammar schools in the middle decades of the century amounted to an obsession, said that 'unfortunately the provisos and exemptions of that Act rendered its good clauses almost nugatory'.[20]

The fundamental weakness of the Act, however, lay in Clause III which stated that the Court was not to dispense with Latin and Greek, or with the qualifications of masters, 'unless revenues are insufficient'. In practice this would have meant that the only schools which could have hoped to benefit by the Act had to be direly impoverished and no longer able to maintain themselves above the level of elementary schools in any case. Soon after its publication, however, inhabitants of some towns with grammar schools in need of reform or modification seem to have overlooked Clause III. In the case of Laxton's Oundle Charity, in 1843, the Attorney-General filed an information on behalf of the inhabitants of Oundle against the Grocers' Company, the school trustees. They wished the Company to apply the whole rent of Laxton's bequest to the charitable purposes stated in his will, namely, to the upkeep of a school for the inhabitants of Oundle. Giving judgement, Lord Langdale, Master of the Rolls, said that the Grammar Schools Act could have 'no application to any case whatsoever', except 'where there are certain revenues appropriated to the instruction there pointed out'.[21]

It is the opinion of David Owen that, although it was not a primary cause of the condition of the endowed schools discovered by the Brougham Commissions, 'the Eldonian strait-jacket became more irksome as the century advanced'.[22] The more extensive implications of this historic judgement will be examined later; but even before 1840 there were periods of remission from the constricting effects of Eldon's treatment. In the 1830s, particularly during Brougham's period of office as Lord Chancellor from 1830 to 1834, a variety of judgements, based on conflicting principles and precedents, were given in the courts of equity. In the case of Brentwood Grammar School in 1833 the Master of the Rolls, Sir John Leach, making judgement on the informants' petition that 'there was no demand for the instruction in the learned languages', said that, 'the school must necessarily be confined to the character of a grammar school', and thought that any radical changes would have to be embodied in an Act of Parliament.[23] Yet six months later, in the Market Bosworth case, Leach gave permission for the course of instruction to be extended 'beyond the mere literally expressed intentions of the testator'. But he admitted he was taking account of an earlier scheme of 1825.[24] On that earlier occasion Eldon had produced a judgement remarkably different from the classical precedent of the Leeds case: his remarks almost amount to an extraordinary example of Tory democracy in action. He said in 1825 that the Master should inquire how far any provision for instructing the children of the parishes of Bosworth and Cadeby would be consistent with the proper execution of the charity, as founded by the testator; and that the Master, in settling upon a scheme, should have 'due regard to the result of the inquiry'.[25] Three years later Eldon reverted to the classical principle in the Highgate school case which was before the courts for two years.[26] Giving judgement in the Rugby School case in 1839 Lord Langdale demonstrated that 'the principle laid down by Lord Eldon was departed from in some recent cases' – he quoted three – but he said that it was 'doubtful whether, in those cases, the Court had not extended its jurisdiction'. Reinforcing Brougham's earlier point, he judged the question to be 'not so much one of authority, as of jurisdiction'.[27]

In the years 1844 to 1846 Lord Lyndhurst put forward three legislative proposals in the Lords. In the second of these measures, based upon the recommendations of the 1835 Select Committee, he introduced the notion of a one per cent tax on charities as a means of financing the supervisory board,[28] a proposition which anticipated by nearly twenty years Gladstone's Budget scheme of 1863.[29] The 1845 Bill was defeated in the Commons. More promisingly, his 1846 attempt, which would have passed the Lords, was borne down by the gale of the Corn Law controversy. Lyndhurst's Bills were attempts to circumvent speedily the painful and expensive passage of a suit through Chancery. In the *Edinburgh Review*, 1846, Nassau Senior said, 'The Court can give no relief. The purpose is lawful – the trust is explicit. It must be performed whatever the consequences'.[30] The costs were often crippling to smaller charities. 'As a general rule it may be laid down, that the instant a charity not exceeding £30 a year becomes the subject of a suit, it is gone.'[31] So the 'prudent friends' of such a charity were often willing to countenance its continued mismanagment, rather than risk its utter annhilation by Chancery. Lord Chancellor Lyndhurst had corroborated Senior's description when he said, in presenting the 1846 Charitable Trusts Bill, 'My Lords, no man of intellect, or of tolerable experience, would recommend an application to the Court of Chancery in the case of small charities. The consequence is an absolute denial of justice'.[32]

Explaining the failure of each of Lyndhurst's Bills, George Griffith spoke generally of 'opposition from various interested quarters' in the Commons, and particularly of the power of the City Companies.[33] In fact, on 14 May, ten of the leading Livery Companies presented petitions against Lyndhurst's 1845 Bill 'praying that the Charitable Trusts confided to their administration may be exempted from the operation of the Bill'.[34] A week later three more Companies petitioned, along with the governors of St Olave's Grammar School, Southwark.[35] On 26 May there were petitions from, among others, the Mayor and Commonalty of the City of London, from the Brewers' Company, and from the Merchant Venturers of Bristol.[36]

The massed battalions of the Companies and the City Corporation repelled further attempts to push forward reform in the 1840s. But in September 1849, the Queen appointed a temporary Commission 'to inquire into those cases which were investigated and reported upon by the Charity Commissioners (Brougham), but not certificated to the Attorney-General, and to report what proceedings, if any, should be taken thereupon. . . .'[37] Among the 1849 Commissioners were Earl Ducie and Lord Wharncliffe. Early in their proceedings the Commissioners decided to report upon a number of selected cases which seemed to require 'immediate interference or regulation'. They published a remarkable statistic: the Brougham Commissioners had reported upon 28,840 charities; of these about 400 had been certified by the Attorney-General; and about the same number had been the subjects of proceedings in Chancery on the instance of relators or petitioners since 1838. Conflagration seems to have played an important rôle in the history of charity trusteeship: the 1849 Commissioners had a necessarily imperfect knowledge of case law between 1819 and 1838 'owing to the destruction by fire of the papers'.[38]

Many of the abuses they found were attributed to nothing more than the ignorance of trustees. A remedy might be obtained by creating 'some public and permanent authority' charged with the duty of supervising the administration of all charitable trusts. They suggested that all trusts be compelled to keep accounts, and that these should be audited 'by some local authority'.[39] They also foreshadowed Gladstone's 1863 plans for taxing charities by indicating that a penny in the pound levy on charities with incomes of £10 a year or less would produce an annual income of £5,000, out of which a central board might be maintained.[40]

The Charitable Trusts Acts of 1853, 1855 and 1860[41] have been

considered in some detail by David Owen.[42] The Board created
under the 1853 Act consisted of three paid Commissioners – two
barristers, Peter Erle and James Hill, and a clergyman, Richard
Jones, who had been Professor of Political Economy at King's
College, London, and an academic collaborator with Karl Marx, –
an unpaid Commissioner, Sir George Grey; and two paid Inspectors,
one of whom was the gifted and original Thomas Hare. But the
Charity Commission as it was constituted under these three Acts was
a muted instrument. The 1860 Act did extend its powers beyond
those of mere inquiry; but Lord Lyndhurst, moving the second
reading of the 1853 Bill, set the tone of the new institution when he
said that the new Commissioners would have power '. . . not to
inquire into the administration of the charity . . . but merely to call
for an account; because I am satisfied with this, that if any charity has
from year to year to render an account of its receipts . . . that will be
the best and greatest security against abuse'.[43]

The most extraordinary feature of his speech, however, was the
open attack he mounted upon the City Companies who were, he
said, 'by far the greatest opponents of this measure'.[44] He directed
special attention to the abuses and perversions of which the Mercers'
Company was alleged to be guilty. Lord Cottenham, speaking from
the opposite side of the Chamber, expressed surprise at this anomaly
in Lyndhurst's performance:

> The greater part of the speech of my noble and learned friend went to
> show that some of the great London Companies had been guilty of very great
> malversation; that that fact had been duly established by the inquiries of the
> Commission (of 1849–51). . . . My noble and learned friend does not ask us
> to include, because they have abused their trusts, the Mercers' Company, or
> the other companies he particularised; the Bill is not to operate upon them![45]

Cottenham's ironic challenge was to reverberate through the next
sixteen years of the Charity Commission's career until, in 1869, the
newly-created Endowed Schools Commission, with much sharper
tools, was to make deep incisions in the plumper educational charities administered by the Livery Companies and the City of London
Corporation.[46]

The most powerful and extraordinary evidence submitted to the
S.I.C. by a legal witness took the form of an extended affidavit by
Lord Westbury, who had been variously Attorney-General and Lord
Chancellor. Westbury began by seizing the initiative, asking Lord
Taunton, 'Is the principal object of your inquiry the improvement of

Tables I–VI *representing the incidence of reform of secondary schools in 6 counties, 1800–67.*

I. *Gloucestershire*: 26 schools were classified as being above elementary in 1866.

	1. Statute	2. Chancery	3. Trustees' Rules	4. County Court	5. Ch. Comms.
Before 1800	—	1 (Henbury)	—	—	—
1800–1809	—	—	—	—	—
1810–1819	—	—	—	—	—
1820–1829	—	1 (Tetbury)	—	—	—
1830–1839	—	2 (Wickwar, Chipping Sodbury)	—	—	—
1840–1849	—	1 (Bristol Grammar School)	—	—	—
1850–1859	—	3 (Cheltenham, Tewkes'y, Colston's)	—	—	—
1860–1867	—	1 (Bristol – amendment)	—	—	2 (Woodchester, Chipping Sodbury)

SOURCE: *S.I.C.*, XV, West Midland Division, pp. 19–130. C. H. Stanton's reports.

II. *Staffordshire:* 26 schools were classified as being above elementary in 1866.

	1. Statute	2. Chancery	3. Trustees' Rules	4. County Court	5. Ch. Comms.
Before 1800	—	—	—	—	—
1800–1809	—	—	—	—	—
1810–1819	—	—	—	—	—
1820–1829	—	1 (Bradley)	—	—	—
1830–1839		2 (Newcastle, Kinver)	—	—	—
1840–1849	—			—	—
1850–1859		5 (Handsworth, Dilhorne, Burton, Audley, Stafford)	2 (Uttoxeter, Stone)	—	1 (Aldridge)
1860–1867	—	—	—		5 (Abbots Bromley, Kinver – revision, Tamworth – 2, Wolverhampton)

SOURCE: S.I.C., XV, West Midland Division, pp. 365–485. T. H. Green's reports.

III. *Worcestershire*: 19 schools were classified as being above elementary in 1866.

	1. Statute	2. Chancery	3. Trustees' Rules	4. County Court	5. Ch. Comms.
Before 1800	—	—	—	—	—
1800–1809	—	—	—	—	—
1810–1819	—	—	1 (Hanley)	—	—
1820–1829	—	—	1 (Martley)	—	—
1830–1839	—	1 (Evesham)	—	—	—
1840–1849	—	4 (Dudley, Hartlebury, Worcester Gr. Sch. Old Swinford)	—	—	—
1850–1859	—	4 (Bewdley, Feckenham, Hartlebury – amendment, Kidderminster)	—	—	—
1860–1867	—	—	1 (Stourbridge)	—	5 (Bromsgrove, Bewdley – revision, Halesowen, Hanley, King's Norton)

SOURCE: *S.I.C.*, XV, West Midland Division, pp. 537–628. James Bryce's reports.

V. *Lancashire:* 73 schools were classified as being above elementary in 1866.

	1. Statute	2. Chancery	3. Trustees' Rules	4. County Court	5. Ch. Comms.
Before 1800	1 (Bolton-le-Moors)	—	—	—	—
1800–1809	—	—	—	—	—
1810–1819	1 (Wigan)	—	—	—	—
1820–1829	—	3 (Bretherton, Penwortham, Warrington)	1 (Ashton-in-Makerfield)	—	—
1830–1839	—	3 (Hawkshead, Manchester, Warton)	1 (Clitheroe)	—	—
1840–1849	1 (Warrington)	3 (Great Crosby, Kirkham, Manchester)	—	—	—
1850–1859	—	3 (Pilling, Warrington, Over Wyersdale)	2 (Bolton-le-Moors, Lancaster)	—	1 (Tunstall)
1860–1867	—	4 (Bury, Manchester, Great Marton, Standish)	1 (Clitheroe)	—	2 (Hawkshead, Great Eccleston)

SOURCE: *S.I.C.,* XVII, North-west Division, pp. 157–456. Bryce's reports.

VI. *West Riding*: 69 schools were classified as being above elementary in 1866.

	1. Statutes	2. Chancery	3. Trustees' Rules	4. County Court	5. Ch. Comms.
Before 1800	—	—	—	—	—
1800–1809	—	2 (Drax, Rishworth)	—	—	—
1810–1819	—	1 (Rishworth)	1 (Ripon)	—	—
1820–1829	—		1 (Almondsbury)	—	—
1830–1839	—		2 (Barnsley, Ripon)	—	—
1840–1849	1 (Leeds)	5 (Bingley, Drax, Giggleswick, Roystone, Skipton)	2 (Bradford, Halifax)	—	—
1850–1859	1 (Bingley)	2 (Leeds, Rishworth)	2 (Almondsbury, Batley)	—	1 (Fishlake)
1860–1867	1 (Skipton)	5 (Fockerby, Hemsworth, Otley, Sherburn, Thorne)	3 (Batley, Doncaster, Wakefield)	—	7 (Mirfield, Saddleworth, Slaidburn, Thornhill, Worsburgh, Giggleswick – 2)

SOURCE: *S.I.C.*, XVIII, pp. 17–306. Fitch's reports.

IV. *Cheshire*: 25 schools were classified as being above elementary in 1866.

	1. Statute	2. Chancery	3. Trustees' Rules	4. County Court	5. Ch. Comms.
Before 1800	1 (Macclesfield)	—	—	—	—
1800–1809	—	—	—	—	—
1810–1819	—	1 (Hargrave)	—	—	—
1820–1829	—	—	—	—	—
1830–1839	1 (Macclesfield)	—	1 (Stockport)	—	—
1840–1849	1 (Sandwich)	1 (Congleton)	1 (Bunbury)	—	—
1850–1859	—	4 (Mottram, Macclesfield, Wallasey, Witton)	—	1 (Knutsford)	1 (Lymm)
1860–1867	—	—	—	1 (Stockport)	3 (Nantwich, Caldey Grange, Darnall)

SOURCE: *S.I.C.*, XVII, North-west Division, pp. 15–107. Mr Wright's reports.

the jurisdiction over the administration of school charities, or the internal condition and administration of the grammar schools?'[47] On receiving the reply that both of these were objects of the inquiry, he said that the subject in general was one on which he had felt much anxiety, and he proceeded to enumerate some 'radical errors' in the administration of the grammar schools. Firstly, he wished to see removed by statute that 'erroneous conception' that the Church of England was the inheritor of all those foundations: Masters, he considered, need not be in holy orders.[48] Secondly, he wanted to re-establish the principle that almost all the grammar schools had been founded for the benefit of particular localities, and to this end he wanted to eradicate the recently introduced boarding element in many local schools.[49] Thirdly, he wished to see the removal by statute of Eldon's doctrine which he said confined many schools to teaching the dead languages.[50] And finally he proposed that 'useless' local charities should be converted to provide scholarships at local schools and at the Universities for deserving, able boys.[51] His evidence is the most remarkably radical set of opinions offered to the S.I.C.

The S.I.C.'s Chapter IV on charities, despite its brevity, amounts to a very potent attack upon the existing legal machinery for the maintenance and reform of endowed grammar schools, and its conclusions constitute one of the most apparently radical elements in the S.I.C. Report. Yet the opinions expressed were by no means new, since they were repetitions of notions which had been mooted officially and unofficially during the previous half-century. More particularly in the final section of the Chapter, the Commissioners openly acknowledged a heavy debt to their predecessors on the Newcastle Commission; all their main conclusions are precise echoes of statements formerly made in the 1861 Report.[52]

The Taunton Commissioners admitted that, on the subject of the law of charities, they could not 'sum up the general argument better than in the words of the Popular Education Commissioners', particularly re-emphasising the Newcastle view that 'the power of posthumous legislation exercised by a founder in framing statutes to be observed after his death is one which must in reason be limited to that period over which human foresight may be expected to extend'. But there were closer similarities between the two Reports, in relation to the management of charities, than are suggested by the S.I.C.'s quotation of this earlier judgement on the 'dead hand' of the

founder. The S.I.C.'s recommendation for the creation of new
machinery for charity reform relied strongly upon the equally
controversial but much less notorious proposals made by the
Newcastle Commission on the same subject. The earlier Commission, it could be claimed, should have confined its inquiries and
remarks to elementary education; yet once the Newcastle Commissioners entered the field of endowments they found a trail of inquiry
which led inexorably into exploring the relationship between
elementary and secondary schooling.

Bearing in mind the fundamental criterion of economy, the 1861
Commissioners expressed the opinion, 'that the Educational Charities possess powers of promoting education among all classes of the
people which are at present undeveloped, and which better organisation, more active supervision, the greater freedom of progressive
improvement and adaptation to the changing exigencies of the times
would call into action'.[53] The Newcastle Commissioners, embracing *cy près* and the interests of the poor in one flourish, noted that
the changing circumstances of society had divorced the literary
object of the founders from the charitable object, and thus had made
it possible to confine the larger charities – colleges and schools – to
the indigent. But fortunately the loss of many of these charities to the
poor had been counteracted by 'the public and private liberality
which has created and supported a great system of popular
education'. 'Middle-class education', they thought, seemed to
require special arrangements 'in the interest, not only of the middle
classes themselves, but of those with whom they are brought into
immediate relation'; in particular, foundations originally intended
to benefit the poor might be made to promote a system 'whereby the
most promising youths of those classes may from time to time be
drafted into them'. Such a system would be 'an approximation to the
founder's will'.[54]

As to the Court of Chancery the 1861 Commissioners quoted
Thomas Hare's remark that it was a tribunal 'quite unfitted for the
administration of charities'.[55] The Charity Commission, it was
acknowledged, had done useful work during its brief existence so
far, but they thought that the Privy Council was a more authoritative and respected body, particularly because of its association with
elementary education through the H.M.I.s and because it already
ratified, by Royal authority, the statutes affecting the great endowments of the Colleges at Oxford and Cambridge. The Charity

Commission ought therefore to be amalgamated with the Privy Council, since, acting independently, it was 'an authority less recognised and looked up to by the nation', and less powerful in dealing with local interests, than the Privy Council. Also, unlike the Education Department of the Privy Council, it was not constituted as a body specially equipped to deal with educational questions. Such an amalgamation of the two departments would also produce 'a saving of expense'; and the Privy Council already possessed experienced Inspectors whose action 'might easily be made to embrace . . . the endowed schools'.[56]

In the matter of small, currently useless endowments the Newcastle Commissioners thought that the extended Privy Council department ought to have the powers to consolidate two or more of these endowments, or to annex them for the use of a National or other public school. It might also be desirable that they should have the power to change the sites of schools, where necessary, and to reorganise the boards of trustees.[57] They proceeded to the conclusion that the new department's suggested powers would make possible the creation of 'a graduated system' of endowed schools connected with 'other places of popular education'.[58] This graduated system would become possible on a large scale only if a new expanded central authority were to be instituted. The Commissioners mentioned that isolated experiments in the integration of various grades of schooling had proved successful, as at King Edward's, Birmingham, and Loughborough, each of which possessed a series of classical, English and elementary schools.[59]

The complement to this new central authority would be a system of local county and borough boards. They admitted that the vision of local administrators was usually limited to their own school, and that it did not extend to 'any comprehensive scheme of improvement for endowed schools throughout the country'. Even less did it extend 'to anything like a graduated connection of school with school for the purpose of drafting promising pupils from a lower place of education to a higher'.[60] The local authorities they proposed were therefore expected to take over the administration of endowed schools only after the initial work of reform had been accomplished by the central authority, that is, by the Privy Council. This qualification of the principle of local boards was a remarkable anticipation, not of the S.I.C. recommendation, but of the more cautious creation in 1869 of the triumvirate of the Endowed Schools Commission working in the absence of the Provincial Authorities which the S.I.C. had wished to bring into being as local agencies of reform.

Historians have identified the Taunton Commission as a uniquely radical body in mid-nineteenth-century Britain. Radical it certainly was; but hardly unique. Many of its most radical proposals – root-and-branch reform of charity law, and the creation of central and local authorities for education, had been foreshadowed, not merely in public discussion, but in the recommendations of the Newcastle Commission whose reputation for innovation has been buried under the opprobrium stimulated by the subsequent policy of Payment by Results.

While the Newcastle Commissioners were interviewing their witnesses, Vice-Chancellor Page Wood gave an address to the 1859 Conference of the Social Science Association on the subject of Charitable Trusts,[61] and suggested that this was a field in which 'a general revision of the law of property is required'.[62] On the subject of *cy près* he said that 'it is impossible that any human sagacity can foresee the best mode of promoting, through all time, the welfare of the nation, or any less extensive section of the community'.[63] He believed that all posthumous charity should be 'very strictly regulated' and that 'a less expensive machinery than the Court of Chancery' was desirable. Any new regulating power should ensure that endowments were made generally available 'to the exigencies of the time'.[64] It is clear, both from this proclamation of view in a public assembly, and from the evidence which Page Wood and his colleagues gave to the S.I.C. later, that there was a considerable homogeneity of professional opinion relating to the need for wholesale equity reform, especially among the officers of the courts in which the system was administered.

At the same meeting of the S.S.A., Canon Edward Girdlestone of Bristol delivered a paper on the Charity Commission which, on his initiative, had revitalised moribund charities in that city.[65] Judicious consultation, he said, had helped to remove 'old habits and prejudices' which 'gradually gave way to a courteous representation of the solid advantages to be obtained by a different administration'.[66] Girdlestone had provided similar information at the 1856 Conference on Education in London,[67] and his successful enterprise was also acknowledged by the Newcastle Commissioners.[68] In a letter to the *Daily News* in July 1858, he had mentioned that his work in Bristol had been inspired by what Kay-Shuttleworth had written on the reform of charities, and suggested that 'the scheme which we . . . have successfully carried through' might prove useful to the New-castle Commissioners in their inquiry.[69]

Another issue which affected the status and character of the endowed schools at law was raised during the years 1859 and 1860. This was the question of conscience clauses and general eligibility for trusteeships. Lewis Dillwyn, Liberal M.P. for Swansea and, by his own estimate 'a Low Churchman', first introduced a Bill dealing with the religious issue in the endowed schools in 1859. He had hardly endeared himself to Anglicans in Parliament by his promotion of a Bill to abolish Church Rates in the same year.[70] His Endowed Schools Bill was so mutilated in committee that Dillwyn refused to own it; though the main objection to it would seem to have been that its mover was an opponent of the High Church establishment.[71] Sir Hugh Cairns and C. B. Adderley proposed in February 1860, to introduce Dillwyn's amended Bill in the Commons.[72] This pro-cedure was complicated by the introduction of a similar Bill in the Lords by Cranworth. The latter Bill had two objects: to enable the children of Dissenters to attend endowed schools, or, at least, those 'commonly called King Edward's Schools'; and to permit Dissenters to become trustees of such schools.[73]

Speaking against Cranworth's Bill, Lord Chelmsford noted that on that very evening the Archbishop of Canterbury had presented a petition from the National Society expressing great apprehension. The petition pleaded that their schools should be expressly excluded from the operation of the Bill. Chelmsford said that the term 'chari-table endowment' was not clearly defined in the Bill, and that it might later be construed to include the Society's schools aided by voluntary subscriptions.[74]

The tolerant, conciliatory character of the debate was expressed most clearly in the remarks of Lord Stanley who thought that if Dissenters came into the schools, many of them might become Anglicans. In any case, he said, they were unlikely to turn into 'bitter antagonists' of the Established Church.[75] Newcastle was anxious that 'no party spirit' should be shown over the Bill. In the light of earlier comments in this chapter on the Popular Education Commis-sion, his remarks are worth quoting, especially as they represent the views expressed before that Commission by Frederick Temple. New-castle said,

He felt the more strongly on this point, as he had been acting for the last two years as the chairman of a Commission on the subject of education, and he could assure their Lordships that if there was one thing more than another which struck him in the course of the investigation, it was that with the great bulk of the population attending schools in this country what was called the religious difficulty did not exist; and he had come to the conclusion – and, he believed, he might say for his colleagues, though they had come to no formal resolution on the subject – that if the sectarian differences of clergymen and ministers of religious denominations could be kept out of the question of schools the religious harmony would be almost co-extensive with the attendance in schools.[76]

Cranworth was obviously embarrassed by the dropping of the clauses which would have admitted Dissenters to trusteeships, for he had been induced to present his Bill 'by a number of most respectable gentlemen who were Dissenters'.[77] But he admitted that great concessions had been made. Cranworth's Act was a concilatory measure. Nevertheless it formed an important bridge between the inconsistencies of equitable jurisdiction in cases involving religious difficulties before 1860, and the more lucid principles of religious toleration in relation to the endowed schools which the S.I.C. was to enunciate. Typically the *Times* did not see the measure in quite this light. A leader of 22 March 1860 commented that, if Cranworth's or Dillwyn's original Bills had become law, the effect would have been to create a struggle in every endowment and locality in the country; the present state of affairs, with all its uncertainties, suited much better the condition of feeling on religious issues.[78] The *Times*, then, wished to let sleeping dogs lie. And the progress of the debates on the 1860 Bills in the Commons reinforced an opinion that was becoming more widely held: that the religious difficulty depended for its sustenance as a public issue, not so much upon public opinion, as upon the continuing factional strife of the clergy. A *Times* letter-writer in 1861 suggested that 'a very unfair degree of importance' had been attached to the benefactors of popular education, and especially 'to their religious views', and 'too little to those of the people themselves', according to the English principle that those who pay should rule. The writer, who signed himself 'Assistant Commissioner', regretted that the recent Newcastle Commission had not inquired thoroughly into the religious profession of parents of pupils.[79] But the failure to investigate searchingly the varied religious opinions of the middle classes, let alone those of the labouring classes, was perpetuated through the 1860s by the S.I.C. which, like its predecessor the Newcastle Commission, relied on impressionistic information about popular religious feeling in relation to schooling.

The London Livery Companies' interest in preserving their privileges has been noticed already.[80] The Companies must have become particularly anxious about the activities of the new Charity Commission since, limited as were their investigative powers, they seem to have had a predilection for inquiring into hospitals and their associated schools, with many of which the City Companies and the Corporation had close connections and they were particularly interested in the City Parochial Charities. In London, too, a proper start had been made in the reformation of local government with the establishment of the Metropolitan Board of Works in 1855.[81] A Select Committee had reported in favour of a Bill for the Reform of the City of London Corporation in 1859; but in July 1859 the Bill had been abandoned in the face of strong opposition from the City itself.[82]

Gladstone's attack upon large charities in May 1863 was part of his programme of economy, but it was also a Liberal proposal designed to re-awaken interest in the moribund character of many wealthy trusts.[83] His threat was not merely fiscal – he wished to tax charities; he also wanted to alert trustees to the reforming intentions of the Government when he declared that he was offering a compromise before the attention of Parliament was invoked 'probably for a purpose in many respects much more stringent than any to which the assent of Parliament is now invited'. He reminded the House that his old master, Peel, had promoted an unsuccessful Bill in 1845 which would have taxed charities at 6d in the pound – a proportion which came within one penny of the rate of income tax currently applied in 1863.[84] Gladstone identified as being in special need of attention the schools of Christ's Hospital, Tonbridge, Charterhouse, and Monmouth.

In the face of heated opposition Gladstone gave way; but Treasury officials continued to burrow beneath the ramparts of the trustees of hospitals and schools. A Treasury Minute of July 1863, three months after his speech, initiated an investigation of six London endowed institutions by the Charity Commission.[85] The Treasury officials noted that although it was of course 'the fiscal view of the subject' which chiefly attracted their attention, the question involved 'matters of wider interest' than simple taxation. The Government wished to discover whether, on account of their 'good husbandry', the trustees of charities should be treated any differently

from the guardians of unendowed institutions.[86] Thomas Hare was
given the task of inspecting Christ's Hospital in February 1864, and
the final reports on all six institutions were published in June 1865,
at the same time as the Taunton Assistant Commissioners were
beginning their task of inspection of endowed schools.[87]

Efforts of this kind were part of the mid-century Liberal offensive
against patronage. Other flanks of this attack are identified elsewhere
in this study, particularly in the section on examinations.[88]
Charities for the poor were easy targets for Liberal reformers, and
the hospitals and their schools were particularly vulnerable. A coherent
philosophy had been constructed which could be used to justify
the diversion of charitable benefits from the poor; and this philosophy
had been practically applied long before it became a guiding
principle for the S.I.C. and the Endowed Schools Commissioners.
Bagehot summed up the principle thus: 'Great good, no doubt,
philanthropy does, but then it also does great evil. It augments so
much vice, it multiplies so much suffering, it brings to life such great
populations to suffer and be vicious, that it is open to argument
whether it be or be not an evil to the world'.[89]

Doubts like these were commonly expressed about the effects of
benevolence; but exposure of the corruption and abuses associated
with ancient endowments was even more widespread. There were
local criticisms in abundance. For instance, in 1864, as part of his
defence of the conversion of Monmouth School (one of the charities
attacked by Gladstone) into a boarding institution 'open to the
world', a local solicitor, J. E. Powles, published a pamphlet in which
he pointed to the Monmouthshire village of Caerleon as a disgrace to
the county because of the crowds of beggars who resorted there in
order to benefit from the massive doles dispensed by the seventeenth-
century charity.[90] In the next county, Hereford, the Revd James
Fraser, inspecting schools on behalf of the Newcastle Commission,
had been told by 'a gentleman of extensive local knowledge' that the
greatest benefactor to Herefordshire would be the man who swept
away all the endowments and apple-trees: 'the one pauperise, the
other brutalise the population'.[91]

Charitable endowments were the basic materials with which the
S.I.C. had to deal: if the Commission had been denied the practical
possibility of moulding endowments into a system of middle-class
education, then their work would have lacked a substantial pattern.
In this respect the Charitable Trusts Act, 1853, and the suggestions

made by the Newcastle Commissioners provided powerful presuppositions for the recommendations of the S.I.C. But there were other elements among the antecedents of the Taunton Commission's work which were more closely related to the general question of how endowments might be made more useful, and among these the two which had the most direct bearing on the eventual progress of reform were, firstly, the traditional resistance of the great City Companies to state interference and inquiry; and, secondly, the associated problem of the largely inefficient hospital schools. The patronage system which operated in many of these schools was often in the hands of livery companies and, in particular of the City of London Corporation. Thus, the specific problem of the reform of charitable endowments merged with successive attempts of Liberal politicians and interested intellectuals and professionals to break down the last bastions of municipal privilege in local government.

The fusion of these elements in the 1860s is most precisely summed up in the career and opinions of Arthur Hobhouse, who was to play such a controversial role in the process of educational reform after 1869. The son of a Somerset squire, Hobhouse was part of that West Country group which seemed to dominate so emphatically the debate on middle-class education. He admired the honesty and diligence upon which the best examples of county government were based, and, as his biographers noted, he respected his own father for his high conception of the duties of landowners: 'He was of the type which for many generations has made the government of England by the "Country gentleman" possible'.[92] He practised at the Chancery bar, becoming a Q.C. in 1862, working particularly in the Rolls Court under Romilly. But after a prolonged illness he decided to lay aside his profitable practice and accept Russell's offer of appointment to the Charity Commission in 1866.[93] This might have marked the end of a less ambitious man's career; but for Hobhouse it was the beginning of much greater public enterprises.

As a new Charity Commissioner he was probably impressed by the searching inquiries being undertaken by Thomas Hare into the City Parochial Charities. It is suggested elsewhere in this study that Hobhouse's influence was partly responsible for City Charities being made available for William Rogers' scheme for middle-class schools in London.[94] This early aspect of his work would have closely identified him, in the minds of City trustees, with Government schemes for dismantling their privileges and patronage. It was not long before this view was substantiated by more cogent evidence.

Hobhouse was not content to remain a supine servant of what he considered to be bad charity law. In March 1868, and in May and June 1869, he gave three lectures in London on the subject of endowments and settlements of property.[95] The second of these, 'On the Authority Accorded to Founders of Endowments', dealt with the question, 'What is our present standpoint?' and was delivered at a meeting of members of the Social Science Association.[90] It consisted of a reasoned attack on J. S. Mill's more optimistic vision of the present usefulness of endowments. But Hobhouse ended with a passage which, uttered by an official lawyer, was remarkable for its stridency, political colour and candour:

> There never perhaps was an epoch when old beliefs were so extensively undermined by doubts, or when the minds of a larger number of men were empty, swept and garnished. At such epochs there happen what appear to be very sudden changes, but what are only the effects of a bold stroke of leadership, acting on minds thoroughly unsettled. It may turn out that what seems to be a solid wall of resistance will fall at the blowing of the horns. The resistance to democracy so fell on Lord Palmerston's death, and the Irish Church on the first sounding of Mr. Gladstone's trumpet-note.[97]

His final words were an exhortation to the Social Science Association, which he considered had done so much 'to force important but uninviting subjects upon public attention', to help in overthrowing 'a popular idol' and thus open one more avenue to improvement.

Such a declaration of intent could only encourage the promise of wide opposition to any scheme of legislative or executive reform with which he might later be associated. That Jowett agreed with these views is evident from a letter he addressed to Hobhouse after the second lecture. He said that he hoped the lectures were only a beginning, and that opportunities for action should be made if the course of events did not cast them in his way. 'Judging by appearances', wrote Jowett, 'there could be no better time than the present, on the eve of a Reform Parliament, and after the Report of the Schools' Commission.'[98]

The political judgement which led to Hobhouse's appointment as an Endowed Schools Commissioner in 1869 will be treated briefly later. At this juncture it is sufficient to say that his intemperance was a consummation of fifty years of frustration which had been endured by liberal reformers and enlightened equity lawyers and judges. He differed from these colleagues and predecessors in the injudicious timing of his remarks; in the fact of his being put into a position to act upon his assumptions in relation to educational endowments, and in his strong attitude to privileged corporations. But more striking than this was the way in which he openly associated his new office as Endowed Schools Commissioner with such politically delicate notions as the advance of democracy and the disestablishment of the Irish Church. George Jessel, later Solicitor-General and Master of the Rolls, told Hobhouse that he admired the sentiment, style and erudition of his lectures; 'but I do not feel at all confident that your audience admired it as much as I do'.[99] Perhaps the most interesting feature of the attack upon the archaic laws relating to charitable trusts during the first seven decades of the nineteenth century was that, from Brougham, through the Central Society, Lords Lyndhurst and Westbury, the Social Science Association, down to Arthur Hobhouse, its most consistent advocates had been the legal practitioners who operated the system. It was perhaps unfortunate for the subsequent history of secondary education in England that Authority for charitable reform was first placed in the hands of an agent in whom professional conviction often obscured political discretion.

Notes

1   Statement of Expenses incurred by the Commissioners, Treasury Return, 1846, XXV, p. 279.
2   Report of the Select Committee on Public Charities, 1835.
3   Ibid, pp. viii–ix.
4   David Owen, *English Philanthropy, 1660–1960*, Cambridge (Mass.) and London, 1964, pp. 85–6.
5   See above, Chapter IV, pp. 96–7, the Irish model for this inquiry.
6   Owen, op. cit., p. 182.
7   Nicholas Carlile, *A Concise Description of the Endowed Grammar Schools of England and Wales . . .*, I and II, London, 1818. Carlile later worked as an assistant under the Brougham Inquiry.
8   *Edinburgh Review*, XXXIX, October 1823, 'Observations on the Judges of the Court of Chancery, and the Practices and Delays complained of in that Court', pp. 247–54.
9   Ibid, p. 249.
10 *Edinburgh Review*, LXXVI, May 1823, 'Reports of cases argued and decided in the High Court of Chancery', p. 281.
11 *Quarterly Journal of Education*, I, April–October 1834, XVI, 'The Old Schools of England', p. 237.
13 Ibid, p. 239.
14 Central Society of Education, 2nd Publication, London, 1838, reprinted 1968, George Long, 'On Endowments . . . in England for the Purposes

of Education', pp. 95–6.

15   A Return of the Charitable Funds and other Property in the Possession, Order, Disposition of each Muncipal Corporation in England and Wales . . ., 4 July 1834. The section on London charities is at 339–43.

16   Report of His Majesty's Commissioners for Inquiry into the Administration and practical Operation of the Poor Laws, London, 1834, p. 362.

17   Hansard, Third Series, LII, February–March 1840, p. 1117.

18   Grammar Schools Act, 3 and 4 Victoria, cap 77, clause 1.

19   Ibid, clause IX.

20   George Griffith, *Going to Markets and Grammar Schools* . . ., London, 1870, II, p. v.

21   The English Reports, XLIX, Rolls Court II, London, 1905, Attorney-General versus Grocers' Company, p. 939.

22   Owen, op. cit., p. 249.

23   The English Reports, XXXIX, Chancery XIX, London, 1904, p. 727, 731.

24   Ibid, p. 974.

25   The English Reports, XXXVIII, Chancery XVIII, London, 1904, p. 678.

26   Ibid, p. 423.

27   The English Reports, XLVIII, Rolls Court I, London, 1904, p. 736.

28   Owen, op. cit., p. 199.

29   See below, this chapter, p. 123.

30   *Edinburgh Review*, LXXXIII, April, 1846, N. W. Senior, 'Administration of Charitable Trusts', p. 475.

31   Ibid, loc. cit.

32   Hansard, Third Series, LXXXVI, p. 736.

33   Griffith, op. cit., p. v.

34   Hansard, Third Series, XXXVII, p. 245. The Companies were Goldsmiths', Mercers', Cordwainers', Tallow Chandlers', Vintners', Armorers' and Braziers', Merchant Taylors', Clothworkers', Coopers', and Haberdashers'.

35   Ibid, pp. 1170–1.

36   Ibid, loc. cit.

37   Commission on Charities, 1849, Report of Commissioners, XX, p. 17.

38   Ibid, loc. cit.

39   Compare this with George Griffith's proposal for the supervision of endowments, below, chapter VII, p. 156.

40   Commission on Charities, 1849, Report of Commissioners, XX, p. 19.

41   16 and 17 Victoria, cap 137; 18 and 19 Victoria, cap 124; 23 and 24 Victoria, cap 136.

42   Owen, op. cit., pp. 202–3.

43   Hansard, Third Series, XXXVI, p. 743.

44   Ibid, p. 745.

45   Ibid, p. 654.

46   See below, chapter X, p. 242ff.

47   *S.I.C.*, V, p. 797.

48   Ibid, loc. cit.

49   Ibid, p. 798.
50   Ibid, pp. 798–9.
51   Ibid, p. 800.
52   The final paragraph of S.I.C. Report, chapter IV, is an extensive quotation from the Report of the Popular Education (Newcastle) Commission, I, p. 471.
53   *Popular Education Commission*, I, pp. 456–7.
54   Ibid, p. 460.
55   Ibid, p. 477.
56   Ibid, p. 475.
57   Ibid, p. 511.
58   Ibid, p. 475.
59   Ibid, p. 483.
60   Ibid, pp. 480–1.
61   *Transactions of the National Association for the Promotion of Social Science*, London, 1859, pp. 184–92.
62   Ibid, p. 185.
63   Ibid, p. 184.
64   Ibid, p. 189.
65   Ibid, pp. 257–61. See below, chapter IX, for this paper in another context.
66   Ibid, p. 259.
67   A. Hill (ed.), *Essays on Educational Subjects*, 1857.
68   *Popular Education Commission*, I, pp. 533–4.
69   PRO ED 27/1274, Colston's Hospital (Bristol) File, letter from Girdlestone to *Daily News*, 10 July 1858.
70   *Times*, 13 July 1859.
71   Hansard, Third Series, CLVI, 1860, p. 503.
72   Ibid, pp. 686–7.
73   Ibid, p. 689.
74   Ibid, p. 701.
75   Ibid, p. 1218.
76   Ibid, pp. 1223–4.
77   Ibid, p. 1226.
78   *Times*, 22 March 1860.
79   Ibid, 11 October 1861.
80   See above, chapter V.
81   Metropolis Management Act, 18 and 19 Victoria, cap 120. See also First Report from the Select Committee on Metropolitan Local Government . . . 16 April 1866; and Asa Briggs, *The Age of Improvement*, London, 1959, p. 442.
82   *Times*, Parliamentary Intelligence, 19 July 1859.
83   A. Tilney Bassett (ed.), *Gladstone's Speeches . . .*, London, 1916, 'Taxation of Charities', House of Commons, 4 May 1863, pp. 312–41.
84   Ibid, p. 314.
85   Charities, Return to an Order of the House of Commons, 19 June, 1865 . . . Correspondence between the Treasury and the Board of Inland Revenue, in August and September 1863, respecting the Exemption from

Income Tax of Rents and Dividends applied to Charitable Purposes, London, 1865. Letter of Under-Secretary, Home Office, to Charity Commission, 7 October 1863.

86   Ibid, Treasury Minute, 25 July 1863.

87   See below, chapter VIII.

88   See below, chapter VI.

89   Mrs Russell Brington (ed.), *Walter Bagehot, Works*, VIII, London, 1915, 'Physics and Politics', p. 122, quoted in Owen, op. cit., p. 167.

90   'J. E. P.', (John Endell Powles), *The Free Grammar School of William Jones at Monmouth: Statement and Suggestions*, Newport (Mon.), 1864, p. 2. (Copy in John Frost Reference Library, Newport.)

91   Popular Education Commission, I, 461.

92   L. T. Hobhouse and J. L. Hammond, *Lord Hobhouse, a Memoir*, London, 1905, I.

93   Ibid, pp. 18–19.

94   See below, chapter VIII, pp. 194–5.

95   These were published under the title, *The Dead Hand*, London, 1880.

96   Arthur Hobhouse, *The Dead Hand*, London, 1880, pp. 51–85.

97   Ibid, p. 85.

98   Quoted in Hobhouse and Hammond, op. cit., p. 31.

99   Ibid, p. 34.

CHAPTER VI

A forum for discussion, 1856–64

In the Education Department, two points may be especially noticed. The interest shown in middle-class schools afforded one of the many recent proofs that the public mind is awaking to the necessity for improving the intellectual training of all degrees of men among us; and no less striking were the facts, though almost incidentally elicited, that the religious difficulties supposed to encompass the question of an extended national education have been in some instances satisfactorily solved.

G. W. Hastings, Secretary of the Social Science Association, writing in the *First Report*, 1857.

Three main lines of ideological development have been identified in the general passage of discussion and experiment towards the establishment of the Taunton Commission: the Anglican strand, through the resurgent National Society with its diocesan boards and less formal agencies; the agricultural developments in the rural counties, more particularly in the West Country; and the attempts to reform equitable jurisdiction in relation to educational endowments. Significantly, in the first two cases, the question of endowments was largely avoided because of its legal complexity. But with the establishment of a new reforming agency, the permanent Charity Commission, in 1853, a new approach became possible which might embrace both proprietary and endowed schools in a unified system. This is not to say that the advent of the Charity Commission reduced the question of endowed schools' reform to a state of absolute simplicity; but by the mid-1850s it had become possible to conceive of the reform of the older elements in middle-class education, in conjunction with the creation of new educational agencies. In addition the elaboration of schemes for examining schools and their pupils, the new Civil Service examinations, and the first wave of reform in the old Universities provided encouragement for reformers.

In the 1850s, therefore, the middle-class debate began to develop for the first time within a broad framework. No longer were schemes merely Utopian fragments, or the unilateral experiments of individual groups of trustees, or distinct Anglican committees. Ideas were now thrown into a common area of debate. The criterion was practicability, with the important qualification of the implied need for creating an organisational structure for middle-class schooling, in relation to the 'system' of elementary education below, and the greater proprietary and public schools above.

In the writings of Thomas Arnold it is possible to see the early appearance of the broad concept of a 'National' system, which was to embrace the Universities and the public schools at the highest level, and the schools for the poor at the lowest. An additional element – foreign influence – was developed most potently by Matthew Arnold, in whose work the visionary quality of his father's ideas was transfigured by his own closer observation of foreign systems. In the late 1850s Matthew Arnold was not alone in his desire to graft on to English institutions the more symmetrical cuttings which might be culled from the Continent. Among H.M.I.s, J. D. Morell was, apart from Arnold, the most fully equipped to propose the transplantation of foreign practices and forms into England. A product of Homerton College, Glasgow University and Bonn, where he studied under Fichte,[1] he began to introduce notions of educational reform into his annual reports to the Committee of Council in the 1840s.

For the lower strata of society Morell thought there should be in every county a complete system of 'primary schools', taking culture into each village and hamlet. Next to these, 'commercial schools' were required for the larger towns, in which the arts and sciences, the elements of mathematics, and the study of modern languages would be introduced. These schools would be termed 'professional' in relation to the trading community and its specific needs. Next to these would be the high schools, in which a complete classical and scientific education should be afforded, more particularly as a preparation for the advanced studies of the Universities. Such schools ought to exist in all towns. He concluded,

> With the whole of the country divided into educational districts, the wants of each district thoroughly investigated and supplied, the proper gradations of schools established, and the whole under such management and inspection as gives no room for indolence, neglect, or inefficiency, we should come at length to something approaching the ideal we might form of what a practical system of national education, in its main provisions, ought to be.[2]

But English institutions differed widely from those of foreign states:

> ... we have institutions which are the growth of ages, which have developed themselves gradually, and which have been moulded by the spirit of the people. ... Here it is no easy matter to introduce new elements into our social life, for the new does not readily combine with the old; and if laws are prematurely enforced, a clashing of interests is the result, which impedes the working of any experiment, which has no time to grow up so as to form part and parcel of the national habits.[3]

Twelve years before the passing of the Endowed Schools Act, Morell's social and political analysis anticipated the kind of opposition such a measure might be expected to encounter.

In 1858, with Sir J. T. Coleridge in the chair, Morell read a paper, 'On the Progress of Society in England', to an audience of schoolmasters at the Society of Arts in London.[4] He believed, not only that all classes of the community should be educated, but that they should be educated 'as highly as possible'.[5] But what of the suggestion that it was useless to try to teach Latin and Greek, and the sciences, to all children? He agreed that, in attempting such a programme, 'we should stand a good chance of teaching a good deal less . . . than we do at present'. Those who could stay only a year or two at school, 'and whose circumstances in early life drive them forth to earn their bread', had to have a system of instruction adapted to this state of things. But he was idealistic enough to return to one of the themes of his 1858 report: popular education would never be truly national until a graduated series of schools existed, one rising above the other, which might form a 'regular avenue' for the diligent and gifted of all classes to rise from the very lowest form of the primary school up to the highest culture which the country could afford, as in parts of Germany and in some American states.[6]

He thought that all common objections to education were based upon the presupposition, and perhaps the wish, that society might remain always as it was, and that the lower classes should never rise to a higher position. He flatly disagreed with this, recounting his own experience of witnessing the degradation of agricultural labourers, and the squalor of the courts and cellars of Manchester and Liverpool: 'I cannot believe that this is what Providence intended to be the normal and lasting state of Christian society . . . the march of education is destined to remove the great mass of these evils', which were in themselves unnecessary.[7]

By comparison with the views of Morell and his other H.M.I.

colleagues, Matthew Arnold's opinions are now well known. His ideas about the condition of secondary education, and the possibility of its systematic improvement, were set out in detail in a series of articles he published just before the Taunton Commissioners were apointed. His opinions were a typical blend of anxiety, irony and optimism. *A French Eton* stands in a distinct historical context: its roots lay in the views he had developed while investigating French primary education on behalf of the Newcastle Commission after 1858.

Arnold saw as the question of the hour, 'Why cannot we have throughout England – as the French have throughout France – . . . schools where the children of our middle classes and professional classes may obtain', at a reasonable cost, 'an education of as good quality, with as good guarantee, social character, and the advantages for a future career in the world, as the education which French children of the corresponding class can obtain. . . .?' He quoted the extravagant claims in the newspaper advertisements for English private schools, commenting ironically, 'All this is provided by the simple, natural operation of the laws of supply and demand, without, as the *Times* beautifully says, "the fetters of endowment and the interference of the executive". Happy country! Happy middle class!'[8] Supply and demand were all very well when applied to butter; but the mass of mankind, though it knew good butter from bad, could not distinguish good teaching from bad. Securities were needed. He was sceptical about the possible success of a system based upon public subscriptions, like the Woodard schools, and not upon public grants. He considered the stream of endowment to be failing and scanty; the same situation existed in Europe, because the community had turned to the state for aid. 'It is most important to give to the establishment (of our secondary education) a wider, truly public character, and . . . only the State can do this.'[9]

But he was aware of the resistance which awaited any Government wishing to extend the range of its interference in social and educational matters. He suggested that the catch-phrase of the English middle class in the 1860s was still, 'the State had better leave things alone'. Any assistance given by the State to education was widely thought to contain elements that were 'eleemosynary, pauperising, and degrading'.[10]

Anglican, pragmatic opinions about middle-class education were represented most authoritatively by Frederick Temple who, writing

in 1856, could rely upon his first-hand knowledge of the working of
the Privy Council Education Office, of the training of teachers, and
University reform. His experience as a great headmaster of Rugby
lay in the future, and was to provide an additional dimension to his
contributions to the deliberations of the S.I.C. Temple's association
with the genesis of the 'Locals' will be described later.[11] A year
before that, he contributed to *Oxford Essays* a paper on the subject
of 'National Education'.[12] The chief interest of this lay in its char-
acterisation of the denominational controversy over elementary education; but he also remarked at length on secondary schooling. He
showed his own brand of tolerance and his scepticism about its being
accepted, when he said,

> If it were possible to find in every district men belonging to each denomi-
> nation, sufficiently interested in religious movements to be leaders in their
> respective denominations, yet sufficiently large-minded to be superior to all
> prejudices – men who were tolerant according to Coleridge's definition of
> tolerance, tolerant without being cold or indifferent – it is conceivable that
> managing committees . . . might everywhere be found. But religious leaders
> are generally quite as much attached to their own special dogma as to the
> religious spirit which they clothe in that dogma. It is possible sometimes to
> bring the representatives of two or three denominations into harmonious
> action. But everywhere to unite the officers of every denomination that
> might happen to be in a district, would be a hopeless undertaking. Above all,
> it is peculiarly difficult to unite in one bond the clergy of the Church with the
> preachers or ministers of Dissenting communities.[13]

In 1856 Temple was acutely aware of the difficulties attending the
creation of the kind of comprehensive provincial organisation which
he was to endorse ten years later as leader of the S.I.C.

He was also sceptical about the current usefulness of endowed
schools. Founded by men of ostensible religious zeal, seven hundred
of them existed; but 'if 500 were abolished tomorrow, not the
slightest ill effect would be produced on the education of the
country'. The grammar schools did not serve the upper classes: the
great public schools did that; nor did they educate the middle classes:
'the teaching which they have to offer has prevented that'. The
endowed schools were mere encumbrance. Why? 'For want of
organisation; for want of that organisation which the State, or some
equivalent centre, alone could have supplied.' Each grammar school
worked independently of the rest, shut off from 'the influence of
public opinion, with no power to adapt their statutes to the changing
requirements of the time'. Most of them, tied to Latin and Greek

teaching, had almost perished for want of something to do. They
were looking to the interference of the State as their only chance of
survival.[14]

Temple emphasised the necessity, mainly in connection with
elementary education, of making some use of endowments. A beginning had already been made by establishing the Charity Commission; but he thought that it was too limited in judicial, too weak in
administrative power: *cy près* still held the pass. But this did not
mean that there should not be a section in future educational legislation which introduced very definite relations between local authorities for elementary education and the endowed schools within the
district of each. It would be most reasonable for committees of
rate-payers to have the power of summoning the assistance of the
reformed Charity Commission, for dealing with endowments.[15] He
anticipated a Taunton recommendation when he further suggested
that endowments founded within the last fifty years ought to be
exempted from inspection. In any case the endowed schools should
be drawn into any future rate-aided system. What he recommended
in relation to central and local authorities, and the remodelling of the
Charity Commission, was later taken up by the Newcastle Commissioners.

He justified the inclusion of the middle classes within his notion of
national education by suggesting that the burden of educating
labourers' children fell very largely upon the middle classes. 'And the
middle classes will not undertake the work with any heartiness while
they feel that justice is not done to themselves.'

The middle classes do not ask for money. They are both able and willing to
bear the burden of educating their own families. And, in fact, they would not
gain much by shifting the weight on to the nation, since little of the weight
would be shifted from themselves. It might, perhaps, be expedient to provide
school-buildings for middle-class education out of the rates. But the maintenance of the schools as institutions should fall upon the parents of the
scholars. The one thing that the middle classes want, and which they cannot
get without help, is organisation. Let the schools remain self-supporting, but
let the systematic action introduced by the Government into the working of
the Elementary Schools be extended to theirs. Let inspectors visit and
examine, let exhibitions and scholarships be founded, let first-rate teachers
be distinguished, let the nation give so much money as will organise their
schools into a system – and £50,000 a year would completely do it – and the
middle classes can do the rest for themselves.[16]

It is difficult to miss how broad and various were the requirements listed by Temple in 1856; and, by contrast, how narrow was the range of elements to be contributed by the members of the middle classes themselves. Four years before Matthew Arnold, and without exclamation marks, Temple was exhorting the State to organise secondary education.

Temple was the first commentator to introduce the endowed schools as an important factor in the whole strategy of middle-class reform: 'The beginning ought to be made by remodelling the grammar schools'.[17] He assumed that these had been intended for the education of 'the whole community', but 'especially for that of the middle classes'. His definition of the group for whom he considered the schools to have been founded is classic, in the context of Victorian society and its broader assumptions; and it anticipated the ground over which the battle for grammar-school reform was to be fought after 1869: the founders had not intended their schools for the gentry, 'but rather looked to *poverty* as a special qualification for admission. The *middle classes* are thus marked out as the chief objects of the founders.'[18] He used 'poverty' as a term relative to the section of society which, by the 1850s, was collectively demanding or requiring education for their children; it did not relate to society as a whole.

Like Thomas Arnold, Temple was not convinced that classics should be retained as the core of the middle-class curriculum; though it would ever remain 'the peculiar discipline for those who are to govern others, and do not happen to possess such genius as to dispense with discipline'.[19] The Tudor founders had chosen the classics 'because there was nothing else to choose'. But the advance of English and foreign literature and 'a whole army of sciences' had changed things. The boy who left school early with some Latin might have gained part of discipline; 'but the other studies are a whole workshop of tools for the business of life'. The old grammar schools were encumbrances as long as they continued to teach only Latin and Greek; if they were reorganised they would soon be filled: '. . . in far the majority . . . the study of classics is a mere mistake'.[20]

Temple went on to suggest a model for the general organisation of the endowed schools, which foreshadowed, in some of its main items, the kind of scheme later proposed by the S.I.C. Power should be given to every district committee of rate-payers to prescribe what subjects should be taught in the local grammar schools.[21] This power would be exercised subject to the approval of the Committee of

Council, and would not extend to those schools which were linked to the Universities by scholarships. The district committees should have further power to call in inspectors from the Committee of Council to report on the schools' efficiency, and inspectors from the Charity Commission to report on the working of the statutes. He was perhaps too optimistic when he said, 'the probability is, that the trustees would be found in all cases most willing co-operators in all improvements'.[22]

He admitted that all his proposals were speculative; and that there was still opportunity for further reflection upon the subject. But for public men the time had now come for action. It was essential that some Bill should be passed to localise the resources and management of education. 'An indifferent Bill that can be carried is far better than an excellent Bill that cannot.'[23] But in the early stages of discussion about education, any proposed legislation should set out 'to impress the mind of the nation with the right view'.

The 'right view', evidently, was Temple's own. Despite his plea for further reflection, his plan for localisation and for the general re-organisation of middle-class schooling hardly altered between 1856 and the formulation of the S.I.C.'s recommendations in 1866. It can be argued that ultimately the 1869 Act was based on an 'indifferent Bill'; and that the Act, according to the Endowed Schools Commissioners in their 1872 report, did little in the way of educating the mind of the nation. It was almost as if, in 1856, Temple was preparing himself for assuming the responsibility of mapping out the future structure of secondary education, a task which did in fact fall to him in 1864.

In his 1856 essay Temple was able to gather together the main items in the discussion of middle-class education, in a form which provided the framework for the further progress of the public debate. He did so in a manner which clearly related middle-class schooling to the wider context of national education. If he had chosen to make his statement a year later he would certainly have included consideration of the Universities' Local Examinations experiment with which he became closely associated. 'National Education', with this omission, prefigured the subsequent decade of debate about middle-class education and laid down an agenda for discussion. Temple had proposed, as a result of the recent creation of the Charity Commission, the revitalisation of endowed schools, making them the nucleus of a system of secondary schooling; the development of local authorities which would act on advice from a modified and extended central authority; the construction of a 'capacity-catching machine' comprising scholarships for boys of talent in the elementary schools; the grading of schools into at least two categories: those which served the local needs of the bulk of middle-class parents, and those which had close links with the Universities; the possibility of central schools for the most talented members of the middle class; and the creation of new schools, supported by rates and voluntary subscriptions, which would fill the gaps in the existing system of endowed schools.

It is not argued here that the arguments put forward by Temple were taken up fervently by all liberal Churchmem after 1856. But Mr Kitson Clark has suggested that, from the time of Thomas Arnold, there was a numerically increasing group of influential Churchmen whose attitudes to the promotion of educational change were characterised firstly by tolerance towards other denominations, and secondly by acceptance, grudging in some cases, of the growing need to enlarge the responsibilities and duties of the State, in order to solve the problems of educational inadequacy in England and Wales.[24] The work of liberal-minded H.M.I.s, like Henry Moseley, the efforts of W. F. Hook in Leeds in the 1840s, of Richard Dawes, and a growing willingness to open formerly exclusive schools to Dissenters' children – all these factors demonstrated that a climate of opinion was being created in which members of the Established Church might develop flexible policies of educational reform. The activity of Temple and his Oxford colleagues in the 1850s provided further clear evidence of a desire to propose or accept moderate reforming plans.

In a lecture he gave in 1861, F. V. Thornton[25] expressed anxiety about the relatively declining educational position of the middle class. As they were defined by Thornton, the middle classes had fallen between two stools: the highest education was still available to them, but they had insufficient early preparation for it; the teaching of the new elementary schools was inadequate for middle-class needs. A proper primary system of education was needed, specifically for the middle class which would provide the rudiments of a liberal education – a preparation for the work of the grammar schools.

The typically liberal tone of Thornton's ideas, however, was revealed in his castigation – similar to that of Acland – of the current tendency to devise an education system according to separate castes. From this kind of separation, he said, had come the notion that the education required for each class was different in kind as well as degree:

> . . . if we could forget what we are as Englishmen, and what we should be as Christians, so far as to stamp by its early education the child of each class, and so to stereotype the separation, which is caused partly by the necessary distinction of classes and partly by pride; we should create a system of caste more fixed than that of ancient Egypt, and more degrading, because more minute, than that of modern Hindoos.[26]

He quoted at length from Arnold's 1832 letters. But he rejected Arnold's suggestion of State intervention; England, he thought, needed less 'uniformity' and a system that was 'more flexible and more independent'. Thornton's solution was a general one: it lay in the united action of the middle classes themselves. The 'missing link' in the system ought to be supplied, he said, so that Englishmen might avoid the reproach 'that free England has given a large, if not the largest share of political power to those citizens for whom alone she has provided no sound or systematic education'.[27]

It might seem possible to criticise this selection from the opinions of private individuals and public men in the late 1850s and early 1860s as being too catholic and heterogeneous. But in the first place, despite some important differences in detail, they share an optimism that something could be done on a considerable scale to solve the problem of middle-class education; and this, it is argued, was a new feature in the mid-1850s. Its novelty is accounted for mainly by the urgent need, increasingly felt, to use a broad range of educational institutions for the purpose of creating or maintaining social stability in a society where political and economic balances were constantly fluctuating, against a background of massive upheaval in Europe and Ireland. The Corn Law crisis at home, and the failure of aristocratic management in the Crimean War, provided a domestic context for the debate. But a novel feature was the possibility, after 1853, that something useful might be constructed out of the chaos of endowed grammar schools throughout the country. Previously the 'public' sector of secondary schooling – the endowments – had been left out of account. The Charity Commission, limited as were its powers, was pointing the way to simple legal solutions, so that it was now possible to conceive of a mixed system – epitomised so far chiefly in Temple's essay – wherein the old grammar schools, private and proprietary schools, and new schools with rate aid, could come together to form a system serving those parents whose children were currently excluded from the elementary system below, and from the great schools above. A second common feature was their reluctance to deal with the concepts of the middle class in a statistically accurate way. This might seem an unusual phenomenon in the great age of statistical societies; but it was characteristic also of the School Inquiry Commission itself.[28]

Thirdly, and most significantly, the renewed optimism evident in each of these contributions was modified by the underlying consciousness that the problem was intensely difficult, still buried in a dense mass of practical problems and above all prejudice. English provincial conservatism and resistance to centralisation was a counterpoint to the new possibility of general plans of reform. Lastly, by no stretch of the imagination could any of these contributors be called 'middle-class' themselves. They were members of the 'forgotten middle class':[29] not aristicrats, gentry, entrepreneurs, manufacturers; but intellectuals, professionals, clergymen. This common feature reveals another, which typifies and dominates the whole middle-class issue in mid-century: the ideology of middle-class education in all its variety emerged, not from the middle classes themselves, but from those who, above or apart from them in mid-Victorian society, could influence the course of events at national level; who had access to the makers of national policy, and who were seen to transcend, seemingly, the petty issues of provincial middle-class politics. It remains now to examine how, in the same period, these individuals came together to discuss in a truly public forum – in Associations, conferences, on Select Committees and Royal Commissions – the middle-class problem.

The impetus for revitalised discussion of the general problems of education in the 1850s came from individuals. The new force of ideas rebounded from a firm base of University reform, new administrative procedures, the reform of equitable jurisdiction and, in the field of middle-class schooling, the University Local Examinations. But the most pertinent element in the forum of debate on social and political issues was the National Association for the Promotion of Social Science which embodied a positive attempt to create a consensus over social policy. It can be seen as a mid-Victorian holding operation, a collective act of strategy performed as a means of controlling the heterogeneous radicalism of the stirring urban middle classes. It had two clear precedents: in its annual conferences at a different urban centre in turn, it imitated the British Association for the Advancement of Science; in its preoccupation with education it had grown out of a London conference on school attendance held under the aegis of Prince Albert, Kay-Shuttleworth, Frederick Temple and Henry Moseley in 1856.

The Secretary of the Social Science Association, George Hastings, wrote that in the autumn of 1856 it was suggested to Lord Brougham that he should take the lead in founding

> an association for affording to those engaged in all the various efforts now happily begun for the improvement of the people an opportunity of considering social economics as a great whole. For the ultimate success of such an undertaking, as much reliance was placed on the actual experience of social reformers as on that of *a priori* reasoning which would probably strike any thinker on the subject.[30]

From the beginning its members had two clear aims: that it should act as a powerful pressure-group for social improvement in a period of relative political inertia; and that it should attempt to bridge the gulf between the aristocratic leadership of Liberal politics at the centre and the various shades of political opinion in the growing provincial towns and cities where its annual meetings were successively held. Among the forty-three persons present at the inaugural meeting in Brougham's Grafton-street house were, as well as a number of ladies, Lord Ebrington, C. B. Adderley of Birmingham (later Vice-President of the Council), and H. J. Barton of the Northants Education Society. It was immediately decided that Education should be one of the five 'Departments' of discussion at each conference. The General Committee of 1857 read like a Parliamentary list of proponents of reform – reluctant as well as enthusiastic – from Brougham and Shaftesbury, through Russell, Pakington and Granville, to Gladstone and Ebrington. The 'professionals' on the Committee included J. S. Mill, Lyon Playfair, Ruskin, John Simon, Kay-Shuttleworth, T. D. Acland, Dawes and Charles Kingsley.

The first President of the Education Department at the conference in Birmingham in 1857 was Sir John Pakington. The names of the authors of papers at that meeting suggest that the Department's deliberations were led by a collection of Broad Churchmen and professional educationists. Pakington's address was a comprehensive review of educational problems. But he gave considerable attention to middle-class education, concentrating particularly on the lower middle class. His chief opinion was that 'there is no greater error than that of supposing that it is impossible to get the middle classes to associate with the working classes for the purpose of education'. He thought that endowments could be reorganised in order to bring the education of those two classes closer together. There ought to be local organisations which might co-operate with the 'Central Board', a re-vamped Committee of Council.[31] In his paper, the Revd J. D. Collis of Bromsgrove School, suggested that each county should have a graduated series of reformed endowed schools, the higher schools having the balanced curriculum devised by Arnold for Rugby, the lower offering 'a good practical middle-class education' for those who did not intend going on to University.[32] Giffard, Headmaster of Birmingham, sought to prove that in his town the 'religious difficulty' was no longer a hindrance to the advancement of schooling.[33] E. R. Humphreys, of Pate's School, Cheltenham, pro-posed a board of examiners for endowed schools, similar in its functions to the Inspectorate for elementary schools.[34] The subse-quent discussion stressed the need 'for some authoritative supervi-sion over the endowed schools, and for some combined action in furtherance of an improved education for the middle classes'.[35] There was some feeling against the advisability of invoking the interest of the State; but it was felt that some means of imposing unity of purpose was required.

T. D. Acland's paper at the 1859 meeting derived much of its material from his earlier contributions to the *Bath and West Jour-nal*.[36] He clearly accepted the social *status quo*, and expressed the conventional fear of the collapse of the social hierarchy as the lower orders crept up on the educational superiority of their betters. Yet these apprehensions were cloaked in the sentiment that, by improve-ments in middle-class education, 'we may augur a deeper sympathy with the feelings, and a more extended acquaintance with the wants, of the working classes, and thus look hopefully for the solution of social problems in which the welfare of England is deeply involved'.[37] At the same meeting, Canon H. G. Robinson of York, after vigorously criticising the private middle-class schools and doubting the capacity of the new 'Locals' for improving them, said that an effort ought to be made 'by the middle classes themselves': wherever a good school was lacking, they should associate together to establish one.[38] He was implying the complacency of the middle classes, in the towns as well as the countryside, about the quality of their children's schooling; and acknowledgement of this complacency was one of the main features of the transactions relating to middle-class education up to 1869.[39]

The weightiest address on the subject was given to the S.S.A. by Nassau Senior at Edinburgh in 1863.[40] Saying little that was new, he nevertheless reinforced two assumptions which were fundamental concepts. First, he described what he considered to be the constant, gradual adjustment of the English class system by means of discreet social mobility: 'The general character of the higher classes must depend on that of the new element constantly infused into them'. Unfortunately, little was known about the quality of education received by the middle classes. Since they were the most numerous group of tax-payers, middle-class men would surely soon begin to question Government spending on education in the light of the utter neglect of their own needs. Senior here took his example from rural society: 'Will the English farmer contentedly see his landlord's son educated at a highly endowed school and university, and his labourer's son educated, perhaps, still better, in a national school, to the expense of which the labourer contributes only one-third, while the farmer himself must put up with a far inferior school, and pay twenty times as much?'[41]

Senior was being speculative: the actual demands of the middle class, whether rural or urban, had not yet been canvassed, and the question of middle-class schooling was being treated, whether by Senior, Acland, Pakington or Temple, in an intuitive way, in terms of broad paternalistic judgements and proposals by an intellectual and social elite. Even after an apparently thorough investigation of middle-class schooling had been undertaken between 1864 and 1867, the general principles embodied in the S.I.C. Report were still substantially those which had been proposed in a speculative way some years before the gazetting of the Commission. The chief significance of Senior's paper, in this regard, is that it was considered by contemporaries to have been the immediate stimulus for the presentation of the Petition to Palmerston's Government in 1864, requesting the establishing of a Royal Commission, though the proposals for a petition were actually put to the 1863 S.S.A. Conference by James Heywood.[42]

The *Transactions* of the S.S.A. were, until 1867, the only anthologies of opinion on the subject. The Association played a major rôle in producing an antidote to inertia in policy-making which had characterised successive Governments, helping to create the impression that a substantial measure of agreement on formerly controversial issues was growing among people who mattered. In this connection the establishing of the Taunton Commission was the greatest single achievement of the Social Science Association.

The importance of examinations as a factor in the debate about middle-class education in the 1850s and 1860s has been established by John Roach in his extensive study.[43] This present excursion into the same field relies heavily on Professor Roach's work. His findings imply that there were two lines of development in English thinking about middle-class examinations in the period up to 1857: one remained theoretical, while the other was applied first at local, then at national level.

The first, theoretical, branch of development emanated from James Booth, in Liverpool, under the aegis of the Society of Arts.[44] As Professor Roach points out, echoes of Booth's ideas appeared ten years later in a pamphlet by Canon Richson of the Manchester Church Education Society.[45] The second line of development proved to be more profitable and permanent. The Local Examinations of Oxford and Cambridge began, not among the surging middle-class enclaves of industrial England, nor yet in the two Universities, but in the West Country, supported in principle by the Bath and West Society.[46] The 'Locals', which grew out of Lord Ebrington's Prize Scheme for farmers' sons in Devon, came under the guardianship of the Universities through T. D. Acland's enthusiasm and Temple's support in 1857. Ebrington's and Brereton's limited scheme had been rooted in rural county society; Acland and Temple, rejecting pure localism, transformed the original prize scheme by associating its principles with the University of Oxford and later with Cambridge.

Although the Local Examinations originated in the countryside, by means of the alliance between University liberals and country gentlemen enthusiasts, they were quickly taken up by men in industrial and commercial centres as a means of providing guarantees for the quality of local middle-class schooling. Professor Roach has said that the 'Locals' would achieve this object 'without infringing the middle-class love of independence' and 'without presenting problems about religious instruction or about interference in the running of a school'.[47] Two examples have been chosen to illustrate the immediacy of response to the schemes of Acland and Temple; the first of these is urban, the second rural.

The Educational Conference of June 1856, held in London, was devoted to the solution of the mid-nineteenth-century problem of early leaving in elementary education. Yet one of the most interesting papers read to it was by W. L. Sargant of Birmingham[48] on a subject not obviously related to the main theme. In the year when the 'Locals' began, Sargant was describing the enthusiasm with which the town of Birmingham had already taken up the idea of the examinations and had actively helped to bring them into being.[49] The class which Sargant thought would be most improved by the operation of the examinations was the lower middle class, whose members, 'if they are not actually the sons of mechanics, are the sons of persons just above that position'.[50] He attributed the genesis of the new project to Frederick Temple who 'agreed with his brother Inspector, the Revd H. W. Bellairs, that Birmingham should have the honour of bringing the scheme into the world', and he quoted at length a letter from Temple to Bellairs written in April 1857. Temple concluded by saying:

> The Examination should be held annually in Oxford. But an examiner should be sent down, with the same papers as were being set at the same time in Oxford, to any place where the gentry and local authorities desired it, and were willing to pay the educational expenditure incurred in hiring rooms for the examination.

A committee which had already existed in Birmingham for the object of promoting elementary education took up the 'Locals' with enthusiasm,[51] even before Oxford had formally considered the new proposals in May 1857.[52]

The general work of the Northants Middle Schools Committee in relation to the reform of endowed schools has already been considered.[53] It might have been expected that its members would immediately respond to the 'Locals' idea. At a meeting of the Committee on 7 June 1856, a resolution had been passed recommending to the Society that it should institute annual prizes for the grammar schools of the county 'to be adjudicated by some person appointed by the Society'. It is likely, though there is no direct evidence to support the proposition, that the Northants prize scheme idea was borrowed from the West of England: the connection between the Northants Secretary, H. J. Barton, and T. D. Acland, through the pages of the *Bath and West Journal*, has already been established.[54]

In July 1857, it was proposed, with Barton seconding the motion, and resolved, 'That this Committee would gladly co-operate with the Universities in carrying out the proposed scheme of Examinations for the Middle Classes'.[55] In December Barton reported that copies of the University examination regulations had been sent to the masters of the various grammar schools in the county.[56] The response was disappointing: only one of the county's endowed schools offered to take part. This reflected the complacency of the masters of such schools. Outside the county, however, Oakham expressed an interest and eventually sent candidates to the Northampton centre in 1859.[57]

The first Northants session of the 'Locals' was held in December 1859. There we only three entrants in the Senior and fourteen in the Junior division, of whom five passed, none of them with honours. However, the Committee were sanguine about the experiment: 'There can be no doubt that their very failure has proved the necessity of this probation of the middle-class education of this District and of giving it every stimulus in our power by persevering in this impartial and discriminating test. It is far better to know our shortcomings than to go groping on in self-satisfied blindness'. The examination was 'the tribunal to which all middle-class education will appeal for its character'.[58]

A letter from Acland to Barton, of 23 February 1862, contained some reflections upon the early development of the 'Locals'. He hoped that Oxford and Cambridge might allot the centres between them, to avoid duplication: 'I think the two places must work independently. Each University has a vision of its own. Oxford holds firm to absolute justice to commercial schools in which Dissenters abound'. On the question of the religious papers the Northants Committee believed that these should not form a compulsory element in the examinations. In 1864 they accepted that religious knowledge might be dropped from the requirements, but hoped that it might be replaced by an equivalent section on secular knowledge.[59]

The Committee responded to another innovatory idea at this time. Having considered the question of 'admitting females to the Local Examinations', in 1864, the Committee 'express their approval of the course and their hope that the Universities will make arrangements for carrying it into effect'.[60] At a later meeting in the same year a letter from Emily Davies was read, which stated that a petition bearing one thousand and three signatures had been sent to Cambridge in support of the admission of females to examinations. The Society resolved to petition the Syndicate themselves. Finally, in 1870 it was unanimously agreed to request that Northampton be considered one of the centres for Cambridge Local Examinations for Girls, and a Ladies' Committee was established as part of the Society. In 1874 there were thirteen female candidates.[61]

By 1864 the Northants Committee was providing a compromise between Acland's original conception of a centralised system of voluntary examinations and Ebrington's desire for county boards of examinations.[62] Among other diocesan boards, Bath and Wells had been experimenting with prize schemes for middle-class schools since the 1840s,[63] and continued to supervise the administration of the 'Locals' after 1869.[64]

The Royal Agricultural Society's interest in middle-class education has been noted earlier.[65] In 1865 the R.A.S. also actively supported the 'Locals' by offering their own prizes in connection with certain relevant subjects, like agricultural chemistry, under the Oxford and Cambridge examinations.[66]

Commenting on Jowett's proposal to open the Civil Service to competitive examination, expressed in a letter of January 1854, Frederick Temple, then Principal of Kneller Hall, wrote that he thought there was no reform which would be more likely to improve the service, 'or indirectly to promote the best kinds of education'.[67] He regarded 'the competition as the cardinal point in the plan'. The character of the examinations which Jowett proposed was accepted in principle by most of the correspondents who contributed their views in 1854, and it matched the kind of literary education which would have been acceptable to headmasters of endowed schools, like Giffard of Birmingham,[68] Vaughan of Harrow,[69] and Cotton of Marlborough.[70]

But Henry Moseley, then an H.M.I., though distinguishable from his colleagues in the Education Office by his deep interest in scientific and technical education, thought that Jowett's scheme partook too much of the idiosyncrasies of one kind of mind: it would be 'shunted upon the rail of one class of thinkers'.[71] Certainly, he said, the scheme would offer nothing to engineers, 'a class of men who seem to be taking the world in their own hands'.[72] It would surely become necessary for men of practical knowledge to be taken into the Government service. Nevertheless, Moseley envisaged the new examination having a considerable effect upon the progress of general education: 'a competition of public elementary schools and of private commercial schools would be created, greatly to the advantage of both'.

The most interesting comments on the possible effects of the Civil Service scheme came from Ireland. Charles Graves,[73] Professor of Mathematics at Trinity College, Dublin, brother-in-law of Leopold von Ranke, and soon to become a member of the Kildare Inquiry into intermediate schooling in Ireland, thought that the proposed examinations would not be democratic in tendency: but they would increase 'the influence of the intelligent and well conducted portion of the middle and working classes'.[74] In that sense they would be 'essentially conducive to the stability of our social state' by strengthening popular confidence in Government. Middle-class parents, he thought, 'would hail the prospect open to their sons of obtaining an honourable position by the exercise of their own diligence and ability'.[75] Graves, depicting himself as a man of slender influence and the father of three sons, resolved to 'direct their education in such a way that they might be fitted for the proposed competition'. He took as an instance the case of a widow with a clever son who might be receiving his education in an endowed school. Her difficulties began when his education ended. 'But if the design of the Report be realised you will make this widow's heart sing for joy'.[76] He thought that one of the reasons why the business of so many middle-class schools was conducted so languidly was that 'the influence of competition is unfelt by the masters'.[77] Ireland in particular would benefit by the examinations because it was there that patronage caused some of the worst social evils. The Irish, like most Celts, he thought, were brilliant, but lacking in application and self-reliance.[78]

Until lately, the sons of persons of the middle class in Ireland have been taught to look to the clerical, military, legal, and medical professions as their only fields of exertion; whilst agriculture, manufacture, and trade, have been at a discount. Amongst the persons who are unsuccessful in competing for appointments in the Civil Service there will be many well prepared for the pursuits I have just mentioned.[79]

Graves's evidence linked together a number of factors which were uppermost in the minds of advocates of Civil Service reform. First, he wished to improve the quality of middle-class education; secondly, he emphasised the special effects of opening up a new career for soundly educated boys; but, most important, he saw a more efficient system of middle-class schooling as a guarantee of social stability in both England and Ireland. Also, Graves, like Dr Jeune, formerly Master of King Edward's, Birmingham, thought that the opportunities created for the best pupils in the National schools would contribute to a general improvement in the quality of elementary education: 'and thus you will contribute to the improvement of every village in the country'.[80] The later acknowledgement of the effects of these examinations upon Irish education and society, at the Social Science Association meeting in Dublin, has been referred to above.[81]

The impact of the examinations upon the public mind was considerable. Addressing a public meeting called to protest against the scheme of reform for Monmouth School being undertaken by the Haberdashers' Company, Mr George, a local tradesman who had been involved for thirty years in the struggle to preserve the School's local character, spoke in defence of Latin and Greek in middle-class schooling:

> Perhaps some tradesmen and farmers would say, 'What is the use of Latin or Greek or French?' In the olden time, if a person wanted to put his son into the Civil Service he had only to do his duty on certain occasions, and then he would go to the M.P. to get an appointment; but now things were changed. A young man must know Latin and many things before he could pass the examination either for the Civil Service or to obtain a commission in the army.[82]

The S.I.C. was doubtful about the lauded effect of the Civil Service examinations upon the work of the schools. The influence of the examinations was, they thought, 'remote'.[83] Yet their final recommendations included the proposal of establishing a central Council of Examinations comprising representatives from Oxford, Cambridge and London Universities, balanced by Government appointees.[84] This idea was a neat piece of political jugglery: it blended the principle of using the Universities to guide and test the work of the schools with that of bringing in the influence of the State. Thus it seemed to avoid the kind of pure bureaucratic control of examinations from the centre which characterised the French and Prussian systems.

Notes

1   Boase, *English Biography*.
2   Minutes of the Committee of Council on Education, 1858–9, p. 513.
3   Ibid, p. 515.

4   J. D. Morell, *On the Progress of Society in England as Affected by the Advancement of National Education; read before the United Association of Schoolmasters of Great Britain, in the House of the Society of Arts, 27 December 1858*, Edinburgh and London, 1859.
5   Ibid, pp. 6–7.
6   Ibid, p. 12. This graduated series was also recommended by the Newcastle Commission. Coleridge was a member of that Commission.
7   Ibid, p. 17.
8   See G. Sutherland (ed.), *Arnold on Education*, London, 1974, p. 130.
9   Ibid, pp. 140–1.
10   Ibid, p. 144.
11   See below, p. 145.
12   Frederick Temple, 'National Education', in *Oxford Essays*, contributed by members of the University, London, 1856, pp. 218–70.
13   Ibid, p. 223.
14   Ibid, loc. cit.
15   Ibid, pp. 260–1.
16   Ibid, pp. 263–4.
17   Ibid, p. 264.
18   Ibid, loc. cit.
19   Ibid, pp. 264–5.
20   Ibid, p. 266.
21   Compare this with the proposal of George Griffith, below, chapter VII, p. 142.
22   Temple, op. cit., p. 267.
23   Ibid, loc. cit.
24   G. Kitson Clark, *Churchmen and the Condition of England*, London, 1973, p. 62ff.
25   For an earlier discussion of Thornton's ideas, see above, chapter III.
26   F. V. Thornton, *The Education of the Middle Classes in England . . . A Lecture, December 20th 1861*, London, 1862, pp. 5–6.
27   Ibid, pp. 47–8.
28   See above, chapter 1, p. 7.
29   See Harold Perkin, *The Origins of Modern English Society*, 1780–1880, London, 1972, pp. 252–70.
30   Transactions of the National Association for the Promotion of Social Science, Birmingham meeting, 1857, London, 1858; Hasting's preface, p. xxi.
31   Ibid, p. 41.
32   Ibid, 'A Few Remarks on the Foundation Schools of England, by the Revd John Day Collis, MA, . . .', pp. 122–30.
33   Ibid, 'Statistics of King Edward's Grammar Schools, Birmingham, by the Revd E. H. I. Giffard, HM, pp. 130–4.
34   Ibid, 'Examination of Endowed Schools, E. R. Humphreys', pp. 136–7.
35   Ibid, 'Survey of Middle-class Education Papers', p. 150.
36   See above, chapter II, p. 41–2.
37   Social Science Transactions, 1859, pp. 299–300.

38　Ibid, pp. 438–9. Robinson's contribution was included under 'Summary Proceedings'.

39　See below, chapter VII, for a more detailed discussion of this issue.

40　Social Science Transactions, 1863, pp. 46–72.

41　Ibid, p. 57.

42　Ibid, 'Discussions on Middle-class Education', p. 361.

43　J. P. Roach, *Public Examinations in England, 1850 to 1900*, Cambridge, 1971. See also, R. J. Montgomery, *Examinations: an account of their evolution as administrative devices in England*, London, 1965.

44　Roach, op. cit., pp. 56–8.

45　Ibid, p. 59; see above, chapter III.

46　See above, chapter II, p. 39.

47　Roach, op. cit., p. 67.

48　For further references to Sargant, see below, chapter VIII, p. 197.

49　A. Hill (ed.), op. cit., pp. 334–56.

50　Ibid, p. 335.

51　For further information about the Birmingham Educational Association, see below, Chapter X, p. 253ff.

52　Hill (ed.), op. cit., p. 338.

53　See above, Chapter III.

54　See above, Chapter II, p. 39.

55　Minutes of the Northants Middle Schools Committee, 4 July 1857.

56　Ibid, 19 December 1857.

57　Ibid, 2 April 1859.

58　Printed Report of the Middle Schools Committee, Northampton, 1859, pp. 33–4.

59　Minutes of the Northants Middle Schools Committee, 9 January 1864.

60　Ibid, 10 June 1864.

61　Annual Report of the Northants Middle Schools Committee, 1874.

62　See Roach, op. cit., p. 67.

63　See above, Chapter III, p. 60.

64　Select Committee on the Endowed Schools Acts, 1886, evidence of Archdeacon Fagan of Wells, pp. 45–6.

65　See above, Chapter II, p. 44.

66　*S.I.C.*, Minutes of Evidence, IV, evidence of Sir E. C. Kerrison, Appendix of extracts from report of the Royal Agricultural Society Education Committee, pp. 660–2.

67　Report on the Re-organization of the Civil Service, Presented to Both Houses of Parliament . . ., London, 1855, p. 32.

68　Ibid, p. 47.

69　Ibid, p. 87.

70　Ibid, p. 58.

71　Ibid, p. 39.

72　Ibid, p. 40.

73　See above, Chapter IV, p. 100. Graves delivered a paper to the S.S.A. in Dublin, 1861.

74　Civil Service Report, 1855, p. 22.

75　Ibid, p. 23.

76 Ibid, loc. cit.
77 Ibid, p. 25.
78 For a similar view of Celtic people, see Mr. Bompas's Report for the S.I.C. on Wales, S.I.C., XX.
79 Civil Service Report, 1855, p. 26.
80 Ibid, p. 51.
81 See above, Chapter IV, p. 100.
82 *Hereford Times*, 17 December 1864.
83 S.I.C., I, p. 325.
84 Ibid, p. 649.

CHAPTER VII

Unilateralism in the towns: a lack of cohesion

Chapter III showed how a number of counties, and one great conurbation, became areas in which experiments took place in the organisation of middle-class education: experiments in not only imitation but co-ordination; and they were undertaken largely by Anglicans. In trying to produce cohesive systems of secondary schooling within specific areas these unofficial local authorities were acting upon principles which were to be incorporated in the recommendations of the S.I.C. Their activities were attended by limited success. But by contrast the urban attempts to promote middle-class education were unilateral and unco-ordinated: their motivation was often arbitrary and non-educational, and the new or revived institution often owed little to earlier innovations in other similar places. Behind this urban experience of middle-class education before 1864 there was no cohesive force at work, no ostensibly shared framework of principle, and few outstanding models for imitation. To some extent these characteristics of urban experience are self-evident, and this chapter is a suitably brief survey of unilateral and mainly isolated efforts to provide education for the middle class in English towns in the period up to the Taunton Inquiry.

In 1864 George Griffith, a Kidderminster corn dealer, encouraged by the recent acceptance of a paper at the York meeting of the Social Science Association, published his *The Endowed Schools of England and Ireland*, which he dedicated to Brougham.[1] Griffith's misfortune was that he was a member of the bourgeoisie – that section of the middle class which could afford to pay the market price for the education of its children and which sustained itself by industrial and commercial enterprise. But because of his mediocre social standing, during his active career as a polemicist, from 1840 until 1870, he was never admitted to the inner circle of professional men – lawyers, headmasters and dons – and aristocrats and country gentlemen, which monopolised the debate about middle-class education. His paper at the York meeting seems largely to have been ignored by other contributors to the discussion in the Education Department of the Association. Yet in the period up to 1834, Griffith was the only truly middle-class man who consistently devoted his energy and such wealth as he had to the task of trying to co-ordinate isolated local demands for the improvement of educational provision for the children of his own class and the lower middle class.

Griffith was chiefly interested in the education of the lowest section of the middle class: the sons of artisans, tradesmen, shopkeepers, clerks, and the smaller tenant-farmers. Ironically he thus shared common ground with more socially acceptable advocates of improvement in middle-class schooling – the supporters of the National Society, the promoters of Local Examinations, and the members of the S.S.A. – in promoting particularly the cause of the lower middle class. He wrote in 1864, 'Those artisans and tradesmen are taxed to pay for the support of the Government schools', while there existed numerous schools 'from which their sons are excluded by the present system'.[2] His other published works reflect the fact that his specific inquiries and active participation were related to the endowed institutions of the English Midlands, and especially to the schools of Worcestershire, Warwickshire and Staffordshire.

He seems to have read everything written on his favourite topic. He consulted the records of all the significant proceedings relating to educational endowments, all the Parliamentary debates on the law of charitable trusts, newspaper reports of Royal Commissions and Select Committees. The product of this massive diligence, in the form of his numerous publications, is often tedious and repetitious: as a 'politician' building up a 'party' he was often forced to go over the same ground more than once. Yet as a whole his work is impressive and, at times, entertaining and strikingly perceptive. Its significance lies in its representing the only coherent attempt to create a middle-class lobby in the debate about middle-class education. On a few occasions Griffith came near to creating the pressure-group he desired: in particular he captured momentarily the support of George Ewart, M.P.; but Ewart had obsessional interests of his own and moved off along his own path.[3]

A further remarkable feature of Griffith's interest in the subject is revealed by the general title of the 1864 publication: he drew considerably on Harriet Martineau's *Daily News* articles for his extensive remarks about Ireland, describing the Kildare Report on Irish intermediate schools as 'this wonderful Report'.[4] Even when, as a corn merchant, he had visited Ireland in 1836 via stage coach and steam packet from Bristol, bearing as a gift an 84 lb Gloucester cheese for the friend of a senior partner, he could not forgo the opportunity of inspecting Waterford endowed school.

The first of his salvoes had been fired in 1852, in the form of a study of the endowed schools of his native county.[5] His general views, which seem to have developed little throughout his career, are best represented by a list of twenty-two propositions which he appended to the Preface of that volume. It is impossible now to estimate the precise weight of influence his ideas had upon the thinking of others: we know that he despatched copies of his works to members of the S.I.C. in 1865, and to Lord Brougham;[6] but whether these eminent people read them one cannot tell. The propositions, which he desired to see embodied in an Act of Parliament, deserve some consideration, bearing in mind that they were written nearly ten years before the publication of the Newcastle Report, with some of whose recommendations they had much in common.[7]

Griffith wanted the guardianship of trusts removed from the Court of Chancery. Local trustees should be elected by ratepayers. The education in endowed schools should accord with 'the wants of the locality, the requirements of the age, and the abilities of the scholars', and the pupils ought to come from the area designated by the founder and be of the class determined by him. He wanted a 'County Board', comprising one trustee from each school in the county; this would meet annually. An auditor should be appointed by the Board, and the accounts of each trust published every second year in the local newspapers. Citizens with complaints about alleged mismanagement should have access to the Board; and an appeal against the Board's decision should be lodged at Assizes. No boarders should be allowed where the ordinary funds were sufficient to support a good master. No schoolmaster should have freehold tenure of office, but ought to be removeable at six months' notice. Trustees should be allowed to sell trust property subject to ratification by the Board. Exhibitions and prizes ought to be confined to the foundation boys. 'No clergymen shall be a trustee or member of the County Board, as their parochial duties would be thereby interfered with.'[8] Griffith openly indulged his distrust of clergy, particularly of the eminent variety of the Anglican species. But he was not reluctant to make exceptions providing that they were proven victims of malpractice by superior authority, as was Robert Whiston, Master of Rochester Cathedral School.[9]

Apart from the significant omission of any reference to a central authority or to state power in any guise, his list of propositions constituted a remarkable prefiguring of the 'Provincial Boards' section of the Taunton Report. It would be unhistorical, though fascinating, to attempt a connection between his propositions and the genesis of similar ideas in the collective mind of the S.I.C.; but Temple and his colleagues either did not know of, or had forgotten the rather extraordinary wares of the Kidderminster corn dealer, for his name is not mentioned in their Report.

Griffith's career was a constant attempt to develop public interest in the question of middle-class schooling, and his efforts were not confined to writing and publication. His persistence must have embarrassed many who might otherwise have wholeheartedly supported his cause. In 1848 he had begun to take an interest in the case of Kidderminster Free School and conducted a fierce campaign against the admission of boarders.[10] He became involved in the affairs of Bromsgrove Grammar School and addressed a meeting in the town in January 1852. He also communicated with the Charity Commissioners over Kidderminster School.[11] Later his interest turned to a defence of local rights in Repton School.[12] His first adventure on a wider stage occurred when he was invited to address a meeting on the subject of educational endowments at Manchester in January 1852. He was introduced to the meeting as an authority of the Grammar Schools of England.[13] James Heywood was present and supplied a complement to Griffith's proposals, suggesting that it was desirable that a Ministry of Public Instruction should be appointed, 'or some central authority'.[14] The meeting resolved that a petition be sent to Parliament regretting that so many of the endowed schools of the country were being turned over to the education of the 'upper classes', against the wishes of the founders.[15] Nothing came of this meeting, however, in terms of widespread, concerted action. Heywood's interest in middle-class education did not develop further: he might have assumed an authoritative leadership of a middle-class party on the issue, but his only subsequent contribution was his brief participation in discussions at the Social Science Association.[16]

Addressing a question to Granville in the Lords at the time of the Social Science meeting in 1864, Brougham reminded the House of the improvement in elementary schooling which had been accomplished in consequence of the 1833 Treasury Grant. 'But for the middle classes no such improvement had been made, and their schools might be in the worst hands both as to the master's capacity for teaching, and as to his character.' The same applied to schoolmistresses; and about the education of girls Brougham expressed particular concern on this occasion.[17] It must be admitted, however, that despite his huge reputation in the field of national education, Brougham failed to generate support or interest on the question of middle-class schooling.

Two bodies served as private co-ordinating agencies in the 1840s and 1850s. The first was the College of Preceptors which had been founded in 1846 'for the purpose of promoting sound learning, and of advancing the interests of education, more especially among the middle class'. Its current secretary, J. Robson, was in fact the first witness called by the S.I.C. in 1865.[18] But the Commission did not favour the work of the College, and were of the opinion that it was characterised by a distinct lack of rigour. The second body was a pressure-group born at the same time as the S.I.C., the Association for Promoting Scholastic Registration. An offshoot of the College of Preceptors, it devoted its energies to winning support for the registration of schoolmasters, according to the model already provided by physicians in the Medical Registration Act of 1858.[19] Both the Association and the College, though they were ostensibly fighting for greater securities and guarantees for middle-class parents, were basically self-interested bodies trying to achieve professional status for private schoolmasters.

The true thrust of any middle-class demand for improved education, it might be thought, should be found in the motives for establishing new schools in provincial towns in the period up to 1864. Perhaps there were links between those institutions, or at least similarities of purpose which can be characterised clearly. But evidence in support of this proposition is hard to find.

Hazelwood School, in Birmingham, has conveniently occupied a central position in discussions about the existence of a philosophy of middle-class education in the early nineteenth century.[20] In its Historical Sketch the Spens Committee, referring to Hazelwood and its successor, Bruce Castle, Tottenham, spoke of 'the breadth of the curriculum and the arrangements for self-government' and 'the influence of Pestalozzi', noting the publicity the school received in an article by de Quincey for the *London Magazine* in 1834.[21] Yet two points need to be made about Hazelwood: firstly, that its direct influence upon other institutions seems to have been minimal; secondly, that its innovatory features have been distorted or overemphasised.

P. W. Bartrip, in his study of the career of Matthew Davenport Hill, son of the founder of Hazelwood, has attempted a radical revision of interpretations of the school's importance in the history of curriculum development.[22] Although the school began in 1802, the innovations which have been attributed to it emerged only as the conduct of the institution fell more and more into the hands of Thomas Hill's sons, Matthew, who took charge of teaching and the curriculum, and Rowland, who looked after disciple and administration. The revised estimate propounded by Bartrip consists largely of his modification of long-held opinions about the modernity of the Hazelwood curriculum. Thomas Hill's original aim had been to develop a school which, in contrast to the public schools, would prepare its pupils for commercial life. General science was taught, as were instrumental music, modern languages and gymnastics; and the school had what was probably the first central heating system in an educational establishment since the Roman exodus from Britain.[23]

But Bartrip argues that the Hills' work was more important for its method than for the content of the curriculum. In fact he makes a powerful case for Hazelwood's reversion to a more conventional curricular position in the 1820s. Matthew's and Rowland's reforms were born of a desire to make it 'a thoroughly good school': they became dissatisfied with its character after visiting a school where 'the boys were immoral but in instruction, especially in Latin, . . . were far in advance of ours'. Accordingly their first improvement was Matthew's taking over the teaching of Latin.[24] Their 'regression' to a policy in which Latin held a central position in school studies was in part a reflection of the Hills' social insecurity as a family. Matthew and Rowland each subsequently enjoyed considerable pre-eminence in other fields, but both were aware of their father's lower middle-class origins in Kidderminster; and Rowland was particularly conscious, when he held Government office, of the comparative inadequacies of his own education. He felt that his father had encouraged originality at the expense of breadth and depth of knowledge; and in his seventy-second year he contemplated entering Cambridge as a student, only to find that he could not financially afford such a venture. Bartrip says that 'as an idealist Rowland championed the sciences', but 'as a pragmatist he supported the classics'. He found, particularly through his direct experience of the world outside Hazelwood, that the classics were, for a man of his aspirations, the truly 'useful' discipline, not the sciences. He certainly found this to be true of his period at the Post Office.[25] It is perhaps significant that 'Science' was not mentioned in the later editions of Matthew's *Public Education*, the work which first attracted public attention to the school.[26]

In an important sense Hazelwood might be seen as the end of one phase in the development of education in England, almost as a dying fall. It is certainly difficult now to view it as a beginning. De Fellenberg and Pestalozzi were forerunners of the Hills, and the publication of Bentham's *Chrestomathia* preceded the plans of Matthew Hill by two years. Matthew contended in later life that the school was original and owed little to such foreign founding fathers of the new education. But his protests seem akin to those of Robert Owen in a similar circumstance. It has been suggested that the Hills read and synthesised the writings of Bell, Lancaster and others.[27] The truly radical aspect of Hazelwood seems to have consisted in the democratic form of its pupil-government, and the absence, after 1816, of corporal punishment.

Despite previous references to foreign reformers, Hazelwood lies at the end of a distinctively English radical tradition in education. It owed much to the Calvinist upbringing of Thomas Hill and, through Joseph Priestley's influence upon Hill, to the dissenting academies of the eighteenth century. If there was ever any co-ordination of ideas about middle-class education before 1864, it should be sought in the tradition of the dissenting academies. In particular the most striking unity of purpose and interrelationship occurred during the heyday of Unitarian activity at Warrington, Hackney, Manchester and Exeter.[28] Joseph Priestley had been a pupil at Daventry. While he was tutor at Warrington in 1765 he published a treatise on education which exercised wide influence over his contemporaries. C. G. Hey, in another study of Hazelwood, has emphasised the significance of Priestley's encouragement of the teaching of science.[29] Yet even in 1765 Priestley was careful to say that 'a tradesman', though he had no direct use for Latin, would benefit by acquaintanceship with that language, though his composition should be in English; and he laid chief emphasis upon History in the curriculum. He wrote in 1765,

> It seems to be a defect in our present system of public education, that a proper course of studies is not provided for gentlemen who are designed to fill the principal stations of active life, as distinct from those which are adapted to the learned professions. We have hardly any medium between an education for the counting-house, consisting of writing, arithmetic, and merchants' accounts, and a method of instruction in the abstract sciences; so that we have nothing liberal that is worth the attention of gentlemen whose views neither of these two opposite plans may suit.[30]

The new articles of learning which Priestley proposed were various aspects of History, in particular English History and Constitutional History.[31] The great purpose of education, in his view, was 'to inculcate such principles and lead to such habits as will enable men to pass with integrity and honour through life, and to be inflexibly just, benevolent, and good'.[32]

Two principal features emerge from the writings of Priestley: firstly, that he clearly prefigured the educational proposals of the Utilitarians who took from him much inspiration.[33] Secondly, it is evident that he accepted, certainly in the passage quoted above, that provision for a barren 'commercial' instruction existed already, and that it was in the 1760s a feature of the work of private academies which was taken for granted. Also he wished ideally to raise this 'instruction' to the level of a truly liberal education. It was with Priestley, in fact, that the notion of a 'useful education' became part of the common currency in relation to middle-class schooling. 'Useful' was a characteristically Utilitarian term: the Charity Commissioners employed it as late as the 1850s and 1860s in their schemes for the reform of a handful of schools. In this sense they stood in the Priestley tradition. To quote one example, the Charity Commissioners' scheme for Moulton School in Devon referred to the governors' right to authorise the provision of 'a sound religious, moral, and useful education'.[34] This triple conjunction would surely have warmed Priestley's heart. The Courts of Equity also took the term into use, and a petition to the Rolls Court from the inhabitants of Brentford in 1833 begged that the instruction in their Grammar School should be made 'more useful and practical, and better suited to the wants of the inhabitants'.[35]

Nicholas Hans' judgement is that all movements for educational reform in the nineteenth century can be traced back to men and institutions of the eighteenth century: the Mechanics' Institutes, the 'Arnoldian' public schools, and the Infant School movement all had their roots before 1800. The work of the Benthamites and of Brougham and his circle, Hans contends, should be seen, not as innovations, but as consummations. 'The modernisation', he says, 'of the curriculum in the grammar schools, at Oxford and Cambridge . . . was started in the eighteenth century.'[36] The essential feature of the process of change which Hans characterises was the interpersonal transmission of ideas, achieved accidentally in most cases, and along the flow of a general philosophical current. Within that process there seems to have been no institutional coherence which can be seen as a systematic alternative to the local and national associations which have been identified in an earlier chapter.[37] It is argued here that the cohesiveness and power of the philosophical radicals' propositions in the 1820s, and their attack upon an outmoded system of schooling, were idealistic, and that they never thoroughly penetrated the new institutions for middle-class education which were being established in the second quarter of the nineteenth century.

The development of new institutions in the 1820s has been traced elsewhere and requires little further elucidation for the purposes of the present study.[38] But it is necessary to put forward certain exemplary cases for consideration. One of the most influential figures discussed by Hans was John Clarke, Master of Hull Grammar School between 1720 and 1733. Clarke's *Essay upon Education*, published in 1770, owed much to the writings of John Locke, and in it he demonstrated his opposition to the prevailing methods of teaching Latin. He introduced English as the medium for teaching Latin at Hull.[39] It was with this in mind that Clarke published also his many English translations of Latin school texts.[40] For Clarke, Latin remained an important intellectual key; but his principal object was 'to have education less concerned with words than things, with real or "practical" knowledge'.[41]

Neither Clarke nor his immediate successor, however, seem to have enjoyed the success in practical terms which his writings anticipated.[42] Under a headmaster appointed in 1811 the classics at Hull became 'only one among many subjects' and the curriculum was widely extended 'to meet the new demand' from the local middle classes for an 'English' education. John Lawson, the historian of Hull education, mentions the town of Beverley as another example of this kind of development.[43] The problem for schools like Hull was that, though they might make alterations of this kind, they remained two-man schools with, at the most, perhaps sixty pupils. By the 1830s the town had a population of 60,000: a single grammar school with an average endowment could not cater for the demand for education among the middle classes of such a community. It must have been similarly the case in many early nineteenth-century towns, therefore, that the creation of new schools was not so much an implied criticism of the curriculum of an ancient institution as an expression of the need for more school accommodation with a reasonable guarantee of efficient teaching. This new demand among the professional people, as distinct from the bourgeoisie, could be served by the growing public schools.

The first wave of proprietary schools seemed initially to provide this guarantee. In Hull the movement for the creation of the Hull and East Riding Proprietary School began in February 1836. But, as Lawson says, 'almost immediately it provided a clash of sectarian interests'. The result was that one group – Anglican and conservative – set up Kingston College; the other – Liberal and largely dissenting – founded Hull College, which was officially unsectarian. Each school company had a capital of £5,000 in £25 shares, with roughly the same number of staff, similar fees, and predominantly day-boy population.[44] Both colleges were in financial difficulties by the mid-1840s, though both managed to totter on as private schools under their original headmasters. In a significant way the experience which Lawson describes at Hull reveals the fundamental problem of internal strife in provincial communities which operated against the possibility of a general middle-class movement in support of either national reform or interrelated local activity over a certain urban area. Though the Leicester Proprietary School, which had attempted to combine 'a sound classical education with those subjects which more especially qualify for the pursuit of an active commercial life', seemed to represent a rather more united front than the colleges in Hull, the collapse of the Leicester School has been attributed to the lack of adequate support from among the nonconformists of the district.[45] In the Leicester case, too, the master was reduced to setting up his own private school in the town.

The fortunes of middle-class schools in Sheffield in the second quarter of the nineteenth century illustrate the potency of this sectarian controversy, but also introduce another element into the

discussion of middle-class demand: the direct influence of Thomas
Arnold upon the establishing of new institutions. Arnold's letters to
the *Sheffield Courant* in 1832[46] seem to have inspired local activity
in the West Riding; and in this sector of the provinces, it can be
argued, his opinions were empirically at least as potent as the theoretical propositions of the philosophical radicals. The Sheffield
Collegiate School, which opened in 1836, seems to have been the
direct result of Arnold's admonition to the middle classes. An Anglican institution, it enjoyed the patronage of Lord Wharncliffe, a
member of the local aristocracy and later a proponent of the reform
of laws relating to charitable trusts.[47] In his speech at a commemor-
ation dinner in 1852, Wharncliffe on two occasions quoted from
Arnold's Sheffield letters. Before denying that, in the early 1850s,
Sheffield's nonconformist citizens had anything to fear from an
Anglican institution, Wharncliffe said, 'to suppose that a person
about to begin in any of the active occupations of this world can be
worse off for a high and liberal education, is a libel upon the human
mind'.[48]

W. H. G. Armytage, in a brief survey of Sheffield education, has
dated the inception of the Collegiate School to 1834. He notes the
immediate eruption of sectarian rivalry, and the retort of the nonconformists in the town which took the form of the creation of the
Wesleyan Proprietary School in March 1837. Despite the 1852
celebrations, neither school was ever financially secure, and stability
in local secondary education was ensured only after 1870 with the
establishment of higher grade schools and the revival of the moribund grammar school.[49]

The first meeting of the Sheffield Collegiate sponsors took place in
September 1834.[50] Wakefield had already established its educational precedence in South Yorkshire, for its West Riding Proprietary School opened on 6 August 1834. At Wakefield the first meeting
to inaugurate the School was on 10 May 1832. Nowhere in the
proceedings of the Committee of Proprietors is Arnold's name mentioned; but since the Sheffield letters had been published in the
previous month, it is not too flattering a proposition to suggest that
his influence may also have activated Anglicans at Wakefield.[51]
Plainly, however, the proprietors, led by Earl Fitzwilliam, were
aware of other similar institutions recently founded, as they
admitted, in 'the South of England and in Edinburgh', for middle-
class persons 'of limited means'. Just as at Sheffield the Wakefield

School set out to provide a broad curriculum based upon the classics, but including science and modern languages 'because of the increasing importance of our commercial and manufacturing interests'.[52] In a West Riding context it is almost possible to treat the Proprietary School as an early anticipation of the county schools inspired by Fortescue and Brereton, since it was supported by gentlemen from Halifax, Oulton, Huddersfield and Bradford, with a clutch of local clergy, presided over by Fitzwilliam.[53]

In Lancashire, apart from the Manchester Society's commercial schools, there were two new institutions which went some way towards providing healthier examples of urban middle-class enterprise in education: the College and the Institute at Liverpool. According to the estimate of one ancient citizen of the town, Liverpool was the natural home of the English bourgeoisie in the first half of the nineteenth century:

> We have never loved brilliancy from our hearts in Liverpool. We have tolerated it at times for the sake of other qualities by which it has been accompanied, but were also anxious to get rid of it as soon as possible. Liverpool looks upon able and clever men as Athens looked upon Aristides. Mediocrity suits our temper best.[54]

Lord Derby's more obsequious remarks in 1863 have been quoted earlier.[55]

Seaforth became the fashionable residential district for the merchant aristocracy of Liverpool early in the century. In an Anglican private school there, built with John Gladstone's money, the Vicar prepared W. E. Gladstone for Eton and A. P. Stanley for Rugby.[56] Unlike Manchester, Liverpool had no considerable endowed school, and the first modern educational initiatives were directed towards the provision of adult education. The Unitarians were a strong group in the community, and it was from the influence of a small clique of radical intellectuals, led by William Roscoe, that the adult movement sprang. The Athenaeum with its reference library was founded in 1799, and the Public News and Coffee Room with its library began three years later. Inspired by a similar project in London the Royal Institution School opened in 1819.[57] In its early days the Institution School gave evidence of a stunning tolerance which must have alarmed some of its nonconformist promoters: in 1820 the pupils organised a 'King and Country' demonstration through the town. Although some of Gladstone's cousins attended the school, it was never very prosperous: in the period up to its closure in 1892 the

largest number of pupils at any time was seventy.[58] However, the
S.I.C. Report depicted it as a classical school with a strong mathematical side; and the list of its honours at Oxford and Cambridge
between 1847 and 1868 was impressive.[59]

The most striking of the Liverpool schools, despite its name, had
little to do with the Royal Institution. The Liverpool Institute School,
or, more properly, Schools, began in 1835. According to Wainwright, the Institute owed its inspiration to similar schools in New
York, and it originated in the Liverpool Mechanics' Institute and
Apprentices' Library which had opened earlier the same year. It soon
began to flourish under its first great headmaster, W. B. Hodgson,
who had received his own schooling and higher education in Scotland. When he resigned in 1849 there were two schools for boys: the
High School, 'to afford a good education suitable for the sons of
professional men, merchants, etc.; those forming the upper side of
the middle classes'; and the Commercial School 'to afford a good
education for the sons of small tradesmen, clerks, etc.; those forming
the lower side of the middle classes'.[60] In addition Hodgson had set
on foot in 1844 a school for girls, associated with the Institute, but
called the Blackburne House Girls' School, providing a middle-class
education at moderate expense.[61] These schools, in relation to the
middle classes of Liverpool, must have been truly comprehensive for,
in 1849, the whole institution had 1,650 pupils, including eight
evening classes of 400 pupils. There was a library of 15,000 volumes,
a sculpture gallery; and each week there were public lectures
attended by 1,200 persons. The teaching staff numbered between
sixty and seventy.[62] The Institute was probably the most remarkable
school of its day in the 1840s. There were no religious tests for entry.

In the late 1830s political upheavals in Liverpool and a new thrust
towards middle-class schooling by the National Society seem to have
combined to encourage the creation of another middle-class school.
James Murphy has described the sequence of events which led to the
adoption of the Irish National system in the elementary schools
which were in the care of the Corporation.[63] The impetus for this
crucial change was the landslide victory of the Whigs in the local
elections of 1835. The reform of the Corporation's schools was part
of the policy of general social reform. The immediate Anglican
antidote to this 'mixed' system came in 1836 when the local Anglican
clergy, led by the Revd Hugh M'Neile, opened rival schools. With
the return to power of the Tories in 1840 the 'mixed' policy was

reversed. The brief period of reform, however, had seen the port of Liverpool develop its own sense of civic importance and the town create briefly the most remarkable hierarchy of educational institutions in England.

The precise source of the idea of forming an Anglican middle-class school in Liverpool at this time is unknown. But since the meeting at which the idea was announced was attended by M'Neile and took place in July 1839, it could be assumed that a powerful group of Anglican clergy in the town were taking their lead directly from the National Society's new programme and from the declared policy of the diocese of Chester which was one of the Society's most dynamic agents.[64] The circular composed at the July meeting was signed by M'Neile and by Robertson Gladstone, the brother of W. E. and the member of the family designated to stay and manage the business.[65] The others were a mixture of clergy, merchants and brokers.

The task of preparing the first prospectus for the School was given to John Gregory Jones who was to remain Secretary to the Governors for fifty years. He wrote, in 1839,

> It is impossible to contemplate without alarm the evils which the exclusion of the word of God from the studies of youth, or its introduction under degrading restrictions, is calculated to entail upon the rising generation. . . . The children of the middle classes, upon the character of whose training the fate of this mighty empire must essentially depend, are still exposed to the risk of imbibing latitudinarianism, if not infidel opinions, in the schools.[66]

The proprietors announced a school for the education of 'the Commercial, Trading and Working Classes'. The Bishop of Chester agreed to become the School's first Visitor. W. E. Gladstone, burdened with his notoriety as the author of the recently published *Church and State*, disturbed the even progress towards the School's opening by complaining that the stipulation that masters ought to be 'orthodox, Trinitarian Protestants' might let in Quakers and Baptists. As a result the rules were revised and, at his insistence, it was decided that at any time three-quarters of the governing body had to be Anglican.[67] The initial, rather troubling, problem of financing the School was solved by Lord Stanley's accepting the office of Patron. In his speech at the opening in 1840 he hoped that similar schools would be established 'throughout the great towns of this vast Empire', schools with the faith of the Established Church at their core.[68]

The extraordinary tripartite pattern of this School was not

formulated until a later stage. Originally the College was constituted as two day schools (on the pattern of the earlier Institute and evidently in direct competition with it), an evening school, and a hall for popular lectures. But as its advantages became apparent to the wealthier middle-class inhabitants, the upper school was divided into two – a high school and a commercial school; while the lower remained separate.[69] The S.I.C. Report therefore described the School in the following terms: an upper school affording 'a liberal education', consisting of a classical and a modern division; a middle school furnishing 'a complete commercial education'; and a lower school providing 'a practical education for the trading classes'. The description continued,

> Designed to supply at a moderate expense to three classes of society a sound education based upon the principles of the Church of England. Three schools entirely distinct, one not being limited to be preparatory for the other.[70]

The Liverpool College thus prefigured the Taunton 'grades', but without the blessing of a 'ladder' system.

The experience of Liverpool in fashioning its own middle-class provision was characterised by a unique moment of unanimity in a mixed community. But by the end of the 1830s the town had fallen into line with the sectarian polarisation which seems to have been common to the development of proprietary schools in other parts of the North of England. One item in the terminology of the discussion of middle-class education in Liverpool, however, deserves attention. Stanley had spoken of 'the might of Empire', and this expression reflected the port's intimate involvement in the second phase of England's great commercial expansion. More acutely than any other urban population, with the exception of London, Liverpool at this time felt the need for efficient middle-class education as a presupposition for the maintenance of mercantile supremacy, though this kind of consideration has already been noted in connection with the work of the Manchester Church Education Society.[71] The imperial emphasis was developed in 1846 by James Booth, who had considerable experience of education at another point on the western seaboard: he was the former Principal of the short-lived Bristol College and later Vice-Principal of Liverpool College.[72] Booth postulated that England's rôle in the world, as the centre of Empire, was the end to which education should be raised. In a passage which may have reflected Liverpool's recently having shaken off the bonds of conscience in abandoning her connections with the slave trade, he said,

> Let us now consolidate and Christianise; and although our path might have been hitherto tracked by blood and human suffering, perhaps unavoidably, let us exhibit to them power, not as it has been to them ever exhibited, under the aspect of fierce rapacity and unrelenting cruelty . . . but rather tempered with mercy, dispensing happiness, announcing the glad tidings of the Gospel, with the adjustments of industry and the blessings of education.[73]

Despite the uniqueness of Liverpool among provincial towns, in its ability to sustain the continued development of three considerable schools throughout most of the nineteenth century, it still represents the main weaknesses of the unilateral, almost parochial character of middle-class education in its development in urban communities. 'Development', wherever it occurred, was isolated. There may have been a discrete process of interchange and cross-reference of ideas; but the urban proprietary schools of the first half of the century exhibited none of the characteristic features of a system. Indeed it can be argued that the principles which underlay urban, commercial middle-class education were themselves commercial and competitive, and therefore implied unilateral, rather than co-operative, effort. Uniting influences were often at work at the inception of a school: Wakefield, Sheffield, and to some extent Liverpool demonstrate the operation of outside influences at first. But the subsequent working of each school remained independent. It might be a subject for further research to prove the significance of the movement of masters among this category of town schools and of the patterns of common practice which may have resulted from such movement. Nevertheless, the mutual imitations and common features of curricula and teaching did not constitute a system.

The middle-class proprietary schools of the northern and midland towns were the creations of prominent citizens, most often leaders of religious communities, not of municipal corporations. In London, on the other hand, in the 1830s one of the most famous of nineteenth-century schools was founded; and the City of London School, well known for its curriculum innovation, was established by the ancient Corporation of the City. Sidney Webb described the government of the City in the early nineteenth century as a blend of intense democracy, radicalism, laziness, lavishness of hospitality, and mediocrity.[74] In 1833 Francis Place characterised the coping-stone of London City government, the Court of Aldermen, as '. . . old men – no, old women, gossiping, guzzling, drinking, cheating, old chandler's shop women, elected for life, and thus in the Corporate capacity made into a little world of their own, for the advantage of which they manage, not legislate'.[75]

Webb could find no appraisal of the Corporation of London so apt as de Tocqueville's carefully weighed judgement upon the government of France between 1830 and 1848:

> The dominating spirit of that government . . . was the spirit characteristic of the trading Middle Class; a spirit active and assiduous; always narrow; often corrupt; occasionally, through vanity or egotism, insolent, but by temperament, timid; mediocre and moderate in all things except in the enjoyment of physical indulgence; a spirit which when combined with the spirit of the manual working wage-earners and the spirit of the aristocracy, may achieve marvels; but which, taken alone, inevitably produces a government without elevation and without quality.[76]

But soon after the Court of Aldermen, or rather, their representatives in Parliament, had exempted the City from the Police Act of 1829, and while they were holding at bay the inquiries of the Government into the working of their Corporation, they became involved in the creation of an extraordinary School. Webb noted that the Corporation had not made up for its supineness about sanitation or prisons, about the River or the Docks, by any display of enterprise in providing for religion, education, or public recreation, still less for science or art; but he did refer, in a footnote, to the establishment of the City of London School in 1835.[77]

The proposal to found a 'City of London Corporation School' came from the Board of Governors of the London Workhouse who had been constituted in 1662 as the Lord Mayor, Aldermen, and fifty-two citizens elected by the Common Council of the City.[78] In 1829 the Corporation had obtained an Act for disposing of the workhouse and vesting the government of its school in the Lord Mayor, Aldermen, and not less than sixty citizens, with power to add, as governors for life in the manner of Christ's Hospital, all who should become subscribers to a certain amount. Donations were offered, by fifty-two prospective governors, amounting to £1,208 10s 0d. The Corporation also promised £2,000 for the building of the school.[79] But when the Commissioners investigating muncipal corporations entered the City, the Corporation changed its policy. The founding of the School was then seen as a means of keeping the Commissioners at bay, a strategy repeated by the Grocers' Company in the early 1870s in the face of the Endowed Schools Commissioners. The Headmaster of the City of London School, the Revd G. F. Mortimer, giving evidence much later to the S.I.C., described the passage of events thus: 'The Commissioners of Charities coming into the City, the present Lord Mayor, (in 1865), then Alderman Hale, called attention to the application of Carpenter's Charity, and brought forward a Bill in Parliament with their concurrence and with the concurrence of the Corporation, for establishing a school to be called the City of London School'.[80] Lord Brougham and the Earl of Shaftesbury were on the Lords' Committee which reported on the London Bill in July 1834.[81] Carpenter's Charity, which had been founded for the gratuitous instruction of four poor boys in the City, and which then had an income of £900 p.a., was incorporated into the endowment for funding the new School.[82] But the most interesting feature of the 1834 Act was that the new School was intended to provide, not an education for the poor according to Bell's system, as had been initially proposed in 1829, but 'a liberal education for the sons of freemen and householders of two years' residence'. The stipulation about the education of four poor boys was to be incorporated into the new scheme as a sop to the founder of the £900 charity.[83]

The curriculum of the new School was broad and innovatory. It included, in addition to English, Greek and Latin, the teaching of French, German, Italian, Mathematics and Natural Philosophy, Ancient and Modern History, Chemistry, Geography and Bookkeeping.[84] But the historian of the School has written that the two greatest nineteenth-century headmasters, Mortimer and Abbott, 'sublimated the economic pressure of the interests of commerce, which demanded an alternative to the monopoly of education by the classics'. The alternative which they provided was the teaching of modern subjects 'at a level hitherto unknown'.[85]

It is interesting that the founders of the School appointed T. R. Key, then headmaster of University College School, as a curriculum consultant.[86] He had in 1832 become the first Master of the U.C.S. which was perhaps the most 'liberal' of all the early nineteenth-century foundations. Key told the S.I.C. in 1865 that religious teaching was absolutely excluded from U.C.S., since its pupils included one Hindu, several Parsees, fifty Jews, dissenters of all classes, Unitarians, a few Roman Catholics, and 'a large number of Church of England'.[87]

Unity and uniformity of purpose and method were lacking in urban middle-class education before 1864. A kind of cement for the separate units of schools and colleges was provided for the first time in the 1850s by two kinds of examination: those for the Civil Service, and the 'Locals'.[88] But the question of examinations as a unifying force directs attention to another related area which was not considered to be truly a part of middle-class education before 1864. In 1851 the Society of Arts, in an effort to revive the flagging fortunes of the mechanics' institutes, which were then as isolated and unco-ordinated as the grammar and proprietary schools, took up a proposal of Harry Chester and, with the help of James Booth, set up a union of institutes and published a prospectus of examinations, the first of which took place in 1856.[89]

The Society of Arts and the Science of Art Department examinations were taken up by the local unions of mechanics' institutes which developed in the 1850s, and helped to stress the need for a connection between the education of the lower middle classes and preparation for particular trades. Prominent among the new unions were those of Yorkshire, Lancashire and Cheshire.[90] In a later chapter it will be shown that the Yorkshire Union developed a parallel branch in the form of the Yorkshire Board of Education, based upon Leeds.[91] The Yorkshire Board was to be the first instance of inter-urban co-operation in the general fields of middle-class education, though it shared generic characteristics with rural county bodies. Like the Northants Committee its activities covered almost the whole field of local educational provision. The 1868 Annual Report of the Board dealt with elementary and middle-class education and with night schools and mechanics' institutes. It is significant, in the light of earlier examples of sectarian dichotomies, that the Yorkshire Board possessed as Vice-presidents, on the one hand, Edward Baines, W. E. Forster, Titus Salt, James Hole, A. J. Mundella and J. Stansfeld, and on the other Canon Bird of Ripon, Canon Robinson of York (soon to become an Endowed Schools Commissioner), J. G. Fitch and Colonel Akroyd. Four of its patrons were the Duke of Devonshire, Earl Fitzwilliam, Lord Wharncliffe and Lord Ripon. The President was Lord Frederick Cavendish, brother-in-law of Lord Lyttelton, Chief Endowed Schools Commissioner.[92]

The most remarkable instance of urban co-operation, however, though it too was only temporary, occurred in Birmingham partly as a result of the town's reaction to the visit of T. H. Green on behalf of the S.I.C. in 1865 and 1866.[93] In 1867 George Dixon was, according to one commentator, 'probably the most popular man in Birmingham'.[94] In February 1867, as a consequence of the work of the Free Grammar School Association, which had been set up in opposition to the conservative governors of King Edward's School, Dixon invited to his home a number of prominent people, all with known interests in education and sympathetic to ideas of reform. Most of them were local industrialists and businessmen, but there were also Anglican clergy like Dr Miller and the Revd Yorke, and leading Dissenters. In addition a former collaborator in schemes of middle-class education in the town, Frederick Temple, then the presiding genius of the Taunton Commission, and T. H. Green were present.[95] The result of this informal meeting was the founding a few weeks later of the Birmingham Education Society. Its chief aim had little to do with middle-class education: the members were agreed upon the need to use a local rate for the promotion and extension of popular education. But the leading protagonists represented a kind of denominational and political unity of purpose at local level unrivalled elsewhere. Dixon became President; Dale, the leading Dissenter, and Yorke, a prominent Anglican, were Vice-presidents, and Jesse Collings became Honorary Secretary.[96]

Yet even this instance of urban co-operation may have owed some of its impetus to events and persons outside the commercial community of Birmingham. In their Third Report for 1864 the Children's Employment Commissioners had noted with approval the work of the Birmingham Educational Association.[97] In particular they had considered the Association's 'inquiry into the state of education of the children of the working classes, as affected by the demand for labour and by other causes'. The Association had been founded in 1857 for the purpose of promoting 'education in general' in the town, and, with the special initiatives of C. B. Adderley and W. L. Sargant,[98] had established a prize scheme to encourage regular attendance at elementary schools. It was, in the words of the 1864 Commissioners, 'presided over and supported by a body of noblemen, members of Parliament, clergymen, manufacturers, and other gentlemen interested in the district'. Among these were Lord Lyttelton, Sir John Pakington, and Adderley.[99] But the 1864 Report noted that the class affected by the prize scheme for attendance was 'different from the mass of those whom I found and examined in factories and workplaces'. One of the aims of the Association was 'to furnish to the community a means of expressing an opinion on the various educational measures that may be proposed for consideration, either in Parliament or elsewhere'.[100] The statistical section of the Association was managed by the local manufacturer and former pupil of Hazelwood, W. L. Sargant. The Secretary was John Thackray Bunce, who had also been Secretary of one of the sections of the 1857 Educational Conference in London.[101]

The Educational Conference of 1857 and the Birmingham Educational Association not only epitomised the intensity of the educational initiatives which were being taken in Birmingham, but also reflected the co-operation which existed in the town between the leading families of the surrounding counties and the active members of the manufacturing and commercial classes in Birmingham. Attending the 1857 Conference in London were Pakington, George Dawson, Dr Miller and Lord Calthorpe.[102]

The family of Lord Calthorpe, in its relations with Birmingham, has recently been used as an example of the continuing influence of local, traditional landowners upon the political and social evolution of Victorian provincial cities.[103] The Calthorpes were one of a number of county families near Birmingham which exemplified the rôle which the landed interest could still play in urban politics and society in the mid-nineteenth century. Yet none of the celebrated historians of Birmingham has had anything to say about aristocratic influence in that period. David Cannadine has written that 'Conservative interest has always been less alluring to the historian than Attwood or Chamberlain'.[104] The inert nature of Birmingham government in the 1850s and early 1860s meant that the solution of local social problems – the provision of education, the elimination of poverty, the very making of the town itself – was a matter of private rather than muncipal enterprise. Therefore local landowners with property near the old town, like Calthorpe, Adderley and Lords Lyttelton, Dudley and Dartmouth, were almost inevitably invited by middle-class men to preside over schemes of local improvement. As Cannadine says, 'the habit of deference towards them had not yet died'. In the 1850s and 1860s 'there was not so much a power vacuum in the town as a status vacuum', for the filling of which the local aristocracy and gentry were well suited.[105]

The movement from deference to sturdy independence in

Birmingham can be exemplified by two public statements. The first took the form of a petition to Calthorpe from his middle-class Edgbaston tenants in 1862, in which they expressed their 'high approbation of the great benefits which you have, by your example and your influence, conferred upon this neighbourhood'.[106] This was signed by future 'radicals' like George Dixon, Robert Martineau and John Jaffray. The second was made by Chamberlain in a speech to the Town Council in 1875 after the Radicals had assumed real power in urban affairs: he said, 'All private effort, all individual philanthropy, sinks into insignificance compared with the organised power of a great representative assembly like this'.[107] It is possible to argue that before 1870, in matters relating to education, the great urban centres were not organised internally for dealing with the provision of schooling or its reform. Much less was there evidence of co-operation among localities in relation to middle-class education. One of the most important components of the watershed which divided the 'old' urban politics from the 'new' was, in addition to the 1870 Elementary Education Bill, the Endowed Schools Act of 1869 which appointed as one of its three Commissioners Lord Lyttelton who exemplified as a Whig the intrusion of aristocratic centralised authority into urban localities which had hitherto been largely indifferent to the possibility of providing efficient schooling for the sons and daughters of the middle classes.

It is fair to say that the chief mode in which the middle classes generally expressed their interest in middle-class schooling was not that of a great national association, like the Social Science Association or the National Society, but the independent private or proprietary school, whose response to market forces suited the temper of their attitude to the provision of a socially exclusive education for their children.

Notes

1   G. Griffith, *The Endowed Schools of England and Ireland, Their Past, Present and Future*, London and Stourbridge, 1864. For a description of the York sessions of the Social Science Association, see above, Chapter VIII, p. 185.
2   Ibid, p. 32.
3   See W. A. Mumford, *William Ewart, MP, 1798–1869: Portrait of a Radical*, London, 1960.
4   Griffith, op. cit., p. 34–5.

5   G. Griffith, *The Free Schools of Worcestershire and their Fulfilment*, London, 1852.

6   G. Griffith, *Going to Markets and Grammar Schools*, II, p. 295ff.

7   The preface containing the Proposition is dated '1 November 1852, Kidderminster'; *Free Schools of Worcestershire . . .*, p. xiv.

8   Griffith, *Free Schools of Worcestershire . . .*, p. xxiii–xiv.

9   For the Rochester Cathedral School Case, see Griffith, *Going to Markets . . .*, II, pp. 486–7.

10   Ibid, p. 268.

11   PRO ED 27/5407, Kidderminster Free School File, letter from Griffith to Charity Commission, 9 April 1860. He was interviewed by Commissioner Hill on 10 May 1860, in London.

12   Griffith, *Going to Markets . . .*, II, pp. 453–5.

13   Ibid, p. 455.

14   Ibid, p. 456.

15   Ibid, p. 457.

16   At the 1863 Edinburgh Conference of the Social Science Association, Heywood contributed briefly to the discussion on middle-class education; at the 1859 Conference, seconded by Archdeacon Fearon of Loughborough, he moved a resolution for the co-ordination of local examination committees.

17   Hansard, Third Series, 27 Victoria, 1864, CLXXV, 27 May, p. 697.

18   See below, Chapter VIII.

19   *S.I.C.*, V, Deputation from Scholastic Registration Association, pp. 203–4.

20   See Brian Simon, Studies in the History of Education, London, 1960 edition, pp. 82–4.

21   P. W. Bartrip, *The Career of Matthew Davenport Hill, with special reference to his place in penal and educational movements in mid-nineteenth century England*, unpublished Ph.D. thesis, University of Wales, 1975.

22   Ibid, p. 18.

23   Ibid, p. 29.

24   Ibid, p. 18.

25   Ibid, p. 37.

26   M. D. Hill, *Public Education*, London, 1822 and 1825 editions.

27   J. L. Dobson, 'Thomas Wright Hill and the School at Hill Top', *Durham Research Review*, 1959, II, p. 3.

28   J. W. Ashley Smith, *The Birth of Modern Education*, London, 1954, p. 152.

29   C. G. Hey, *The History of Hazelwood School, Birmingham*, unpublished M.A.(ed.) thesis, University of Wales, 1954, pp. 129–130.

30   J. Priestley, 'Essay on the Course of Liberal Education for Civil and Active Life (1765)' in *Works*, XXIV, p. 7.

31   Ibid, p. 8.

32   J. Priestley, 'Observations on Education (1778)', in *Works*, XXV, p. 6.

33   Simon, op. cit., p. 120.

34   First Report of the Charity Commissioners, 1856, p. 29.

35 *The English Reports*, XXXIX, Chancery XIX, 1904, p. 727.
36 N. Hans, *New Trends in English Education in the Eighteenth Century*, London, 1957, p. 209.
37 See above, Chapter III.
38 Simon, op. cit., pp. 115–17.
39 Hans, op. cit., p. 41.
40 J. Lawson, *A Town Grammar School through Three Centuries*, Oxford, 1963, p. 146.
41 Ibid, p. 147.
42 Ibid, pp. 189–90.
43 Ibid, p. 191.
44 Ibid, pp. 198–9.
45 A. Temple Patterson, *Radical Leicester*, Leicester, 1954, p. 243.
46 See above, Chapter I, p. 13–18.
47 See above, Chapter V, p. 109. Wharncliffe was a member of the temporary 1849 Charity Commission.
48 ——, *The Sheffield Collegiate School, a Commemorative Brochure*, London, 1852, p. 32.
49 W. H. G. Armytage, 'Education in Sheffield', in D. L. Linton (ed), *Sheffield and its Region, a Scientific and Historical Survey*, published for the British Association, Sheffield, 1956, p. 204.
50 Ibid, loc. cit.
51 ——, *Proceedings at the Opening of the West Riding Proprietary School . . .*, London and Wakefield, 1834, pp. 61–2.
52 Ibid, p. 32.
53 Ibid, p. 65.
54 Revd James Aspinall, writing in 1852, quoted in D. Wainwright, *Liverpool Gentlemen, A History of Liverpool College*, London, 1960, p. 8.
55 See above, Chapter I, pp. 11–12.
56 S. G. Checkland, *The Gladstones, A Family Biography*, London, 1974, p. 211.
57 A. T. Brown, *The Royal Institution School, Liverpool*, Liverpool, 1924, p. 25.
58 Wainwright, op. cit., p. 21.
59 S.I.C., XVII, pp. 588–90.
60 Ibid, p. 591, 596.
61 Ibid, p. 621.
62 S.I.C., V, evidence of W. B. Hodgson, I.
63 J. Murphy, *The Great Experiment, The Religious Problem in English Education*, Liverpool, 1959, p. 106.
64 See above, Chapter III, p. 69.
65 Wainwright, op. cit., p. 26.
66 Quoted in Wainwright, op. cit., p. 29.
67 Ibid, p. 30.
68 Quoted in Wainwright, op. cit., p. 33.
69 Ibid, p. 40.
70 S.I.C., XVII, p. 574.

71 See above, Chapter III, p. 67.

72 For a brief account of Bristol College, as a precursor of Clifton College, see O. F. Christie, *A History of Clifton College*, Bristol, 1935, p. 2.

73 J. Booth, *Education and Educational Institutions considered with reference to the Industrial Professions and the Present Aspects of Society*, London, 1846, pp. 75–6.

74 S. and B. Webb, *English Local Government from the Revolution to the Muncipal Corporations Act: Part II, The Manor and the Borough*, 1908, p. 688–92.

75 Quoted in S. and B. Webb, op. cit., p. 669.

76 Ibid, p. 692.

77 Ibid, pp. 691–2.

78 *Second Report of the Commissioners appointed to Inquire into the Municipal Corporations Act in England and Wales: London and Southwark, London Companies, 25 April 1837*, p. 187. NB: A. C. Douglas Smith, *The City of London School*, Oxford, second edition, 1963, p. 47, gives its date of origin as 1830.

79 *Second Report . . . 1837*, loc. cit.

80 *S.I.C.*, IV, p. 359.

81 Douglas Smith, op. cit., p. 67.

82 *Second Report . . . 1837*, loc. cit.

83 Ibid, loc. cit.

84 Douglas Smith, op. cit., p. 57.

85 Ibid, p. 68.

86 Ibid, p. 67. See also, *S.I.C.*, IV, p. 313.

87 *S.I.C.*, IV, pp. 315–16.

88 See above, Chapter VI, p. 145.

89 Roach, op. cit., p. 62.

90 G. W. Roderick and M. D. Stephens, *Education and Industry in the Nineteenth Century*, London, 1978, p. 58.

91 See below, Chapter IX, p. 202; *Annual Report of the Yorkshire Board of Education for the Year 1868*, Leeds, 1869, II.

92 *Annual Report . . . Yorkshire Board . . . 1868*, pp. 3–4.

93 See below, Chapter VIII, p. 197ff.

94 G. Kenrick, 'George Dixon' in J. H. Muirhead (ed.), *Nine Famous Birmingham Men*, Birmingham, 1909, p. 53.

95 A. F. Taylor, *Birmingham and the Movement for National Education*, unpublished Ph.D. thesis, University of Leicester, 1964, pp. 27–8.

96 Ibid, p. 32.

97 Children's Employment Commission, Third Report, 1864, p. 154.

98 For Sargant, see above, Chapter VI, p. 133; and below, Chapter 00.

99 Children's Employment Commission . . . 1864, loc. cit.

100 Ibid, loc. cit.

101 Hill (ed.), op. cit., p. viii.

102 Ibid, p. 369.

103 D. Cannadine, 'The Calthorpe Family and Birmingham, 1810–1910', *Historical Journal*, XVIII, 1975, pp. 725–60.

104 Ibid, p. 727.

105 Ibid, p. 731.
106 Quoted in Cannadine, op. cit., p. 740.
107 *Birmingham Daily Post*, 10 November 1875.

CHAPTER VIII

The Schools Inquiry Commissioners at work

How ridiculous it will seem in years to come appointing a lot of squires and a stray lord or two to gather promiscuous evidence on an intricate professional question, and sum up, and pronounce infallible judgement on it. However, this is the English panacea now – this witches' cauldron – and small hopes it gives.

Edward Thring, Headmaster of Uppingham School.

On 18 June 1864, a deputation from the Social Science Association met Lord Palmerston 'to represent the expediency of issuing a Royal Commission to inquire into the grammar schools and other endowed schools in the United Kingdom not yet reported upon and generally into the state of education of the middle classes'.[1] A tantalising insight into the discussions which preceded the Petition was given by the Bishop of Gloucester and Bristol when he distributed the prizes for the Oxford 'Locals' at Bath later in 1864. He admitted that he had had the honour of being present at Earl Fortescue's when the subject was first discussed. 'He would not say that the result of that meeting was the present Commission (the S.I.C.), but some of those present in the room formed part of the deputation that waited on the Prime Minister.'[2]

The compilers of the Petition quoted lengthily from Presidential Addresses to the S.S.A. In 1857 Pakington had said, 'It is the respectable tradesman, the small farmer, the clerk, and the men of that description who know not where to go to get education for their children, and who, practically speaking, pay very dearly for a bad article'. Sir John Shaw-Lefevre, in 1861, drawing on his experience as a moderator for the new Civil Service entrance examinations, had said, 'When the examination extends to English composition, or history, the performance of some candidates is poor beyond belief, and we are under the necessity of keeping the standard very low, in order to prevent the inconvenience which would arise from indiscriminate rejection'.

Her Majesty's Commission was issued on 28 December 1864, The *Times* took a continuous interest in preparations for its appointment, reporting at length a speech of Granville at the presentation of Oxford 'Locals' prizes in London in November. The Lord President had spent the previous three months composing the new

Commission and determining its terms of reference, and he devoted a major portion of this November speech to considering the views of three leading figures closely associated with the Education Department Henry Moseley, Matthew Arnold and Robert Lowe.

Moseley's opinions on curriculum reform, based on his experience in building up the Bristol Trade School for artisans, were rather too 'practical' for Granville's taste: abandoning 'a smattering of Latin' for 'instruction somewhat of a scientific character' was very radical. 'I believe', said Granville,

> that as long as the study of a certain class of subjects is held to be necessary for the higher classes, a large number of the middle classes will certainly require and insist that the same sort of education, though perhaps in a shorter and cheaper form, should be given to their sons, in order that they may be able, not to maintain, but to improve upon the social position of their fathers.

He dismissed 'Professor' Arnold's preoccupation with State interference on the French model: '. . . while state interference with middle-class education continues to be utterly distasteful to both the aristocracy and the middle classes, it would be perfectly Utopian for any Government or individual to attempt to introduce such a system'. This judgement had probably helped to disqualify Arnold as a potential Commissioner, and relegated him to an assistant-commissionship on the Continent, which was surely, in Granville's view, his métier.[3]

Granville does not now rank high among Victorian politicians. Personally lethargic, he was a survivor, and a leading engineer of precarious continuance of rickety coalitions in the 1850s and 1860s. In 1864 he was engaged in the task of preventing middle-class education becoming a topic which might destroy the delicate balance and compromises which dogged party politics. Despite his affection for Lowe, therefore, he felt constrained to be critical even of him:' . . . while Professor Arnold is perhaps a little too constructive, Mr Lowe is, in some respects, a little too destructive'. He agreed with Lowe's dismissal of state interference; but he did not wholly accept his notion of the inherent evil of endowments: '. . . it must be owned that it is to endowments that we of all classes owe a great deal of the education we have obtained'.

It is unlikely, however, that Granville had concerned himself much with the issues of middle-class schooling before 1864 and he consequently relied heavily on the advice of others in his task of assembling the Commission. Choosing its members was evidently still partly a matter of patronage, but of a kind quite different from the warm-blooded nepotism and corruption which had been features of the pre-Reform era. Although the favoured candidates were still chosen from those who mattered in society, the influence of College tutors, among others, had been added to country-house contacts, family ties and the recommendations of amateur enthusiasm. Aristocrats still took the leading places; yet to their conventional disinterestedness were now added interesting 'crotchets' and enlightened opinions. The aristocratic element in the Taunton Commission was able to display considerable inquisitorial expertise and took the trouble to be well informed. Also, party, and a wide variety of allegiances had to be seen to be equitably represented. Two elements – one old, the other new – had to be given prominent places. The older, because the S.I.C. was to be so closely concerned with endowments, was the group of 'technicians' of the law of charitable uses; the more recent was Dissent, of which a representative could hardly have been omitted from this Commission, any more than from the Newcastle Commission in 1858.

Of Granville's advisers, Bruce, judging by the written correspondence, seems to have been the most continuously influential, partly because of his soundness, but mainly because of his position as the minister currently responsible for education in the Commons. He wrote initially to Granville expressing his puzzlement about defining terms of reference. 'What is a middle-class school? . . . if by a middle-class school are understood schools for the sons of tradesmen, farmers, and in which classics are *not* taught, the result will be that vast numbers of endowed and other schools, much, and in some cases, chiefly, frequented by the middle classes, will be excluded from the inquiry, and probably no schools need investigation more than these'.[4] He recommended Granville's taking further advice from Brougham and Fortescue. Later, he resolved his own answer into the formula, 'to inquire into the State of Middle-class Education in England and Wales, and into the application of endowments designed to promote it'.[5] It is clear that he, at least, now foresaw the S.I.C.'s central preoccupation with endowments and their future use.

In a letter attempting, perhaps, to be diplomatic, Temple warned Granville against the dangers of invoking the demon of State intervention.[6] Bruce remarked ironically, 'Perhaps he (Temple) dreads the influence of Mat. Arnold's pamphlet on Middle-class Education on the President's mind'.[7] Temple was responsible for recommending the name of the man who became the influential Secretary to the Commission, and later an Endowed Schools Commissioner, H. J. Roby, who was then an assistant master at Dulwich and had formerly been Secretary to the Cambridge Local Examination Syndicate.[8] Temple tried to appear reluctant to serve himself, but did not succeed.[9] He also offered Acland's name, a choice endorsed by Acland's old friend, Gladstone; and he further proposed Taunton as Chairman,[10] though Granville's personal choice would have been the ailing Lord Overstone, formerly Peel's economic helpmeet, Samuel Loyd Jones.

Lyttelton, who had recently attended all 127 meetings of the Clarendon Commission, was also reluctant to serve. His letter must be one of the funniest to pass between two public men in the nineteenth century.[11] Clarendon, he said, had been a conscientious Chairman on the Public Schools Commission, though his grasp of the subject had been limited. 'He seemed to have a very unoriginal mind. . . . Gladstone once told me that his forte was to put other people's ideas into good English.' Lord Devon, he thought, would make an admirable Chairman; he knew a great deal about the subject through his work for the Devon County School. 'He can laugh sometimes, but a joke you might as well expect from an old bellwether or Newfoundland dog.' Northcote was 'the ablest and most serviceable of the lot', but 'he is devoured by political ambition, and if your rickety Government tumbles to pieces, he becomes Chancellor of the Exchequer, and exit'. Lyttelton presumed Granville had asked Fortescue to serve: '. . . he is a great authority on the matter. But I doubt if he would act, nor is it much to be wished, for our excellent friend is a pre-eminent bore, and his nervous laugh alone would drive any Commissioners mad'. 'Tom Acland' was also an authority; 'but he is crotchety'.

Lowe seems at first to have been willing to serve,[12] but when he discovered who were possibly to be his colleagues, he retreated: '. . . the list . . . is quite enough to satisfy me that I could be of no use'. He said he never liked entering such a body 'without having some hope of managing it'. The only man for whom he had any respect was Temple, 'and he could not attend regularly, and is a parson after all, a very material point when you come to deal with the appropriation of endowments'. Forster 'is not the least to be trusted in Church and Education matters, and wants education himself. Northcote is a hypocrite, Lyttelton a bigot'.

The most surprising omission from consideration was the name of Nathaniel Woodard whose impressive trio of schools in Sussex had just been completed, with help from Lyttelton, Gladstone and Granville, among many other prominent persons. His omission is perhaps explained by the tight hold which the Liberals and moderates of the S.S.A. held over the 'official' approach to the question of middle-class schooling. Woodard, despite his successes, was eccentric to the main stream of thinking in the 1860s. H. G. Robinson, in a paper to the S.S.A. in 1864, said that Woodard's schools owed their existence to 'the spirit of zealous churchmanship'; around them there floated 'something of High Church atmosphere' which would alienate general sympathy.[13] Woodard's extreme doctrinal position would always limit the range, if not the quantity, of support for his schools.

For Granville and Bruce the Social Science Association conference at York in September 1864, provided a timely opportunity for putting their own evolving conclusions in a wide perspective. Granville despatched Bruce to York, and the conference attracted most of the ideologues and pragmatists of middle-class education, who perhaps imagined that they might make an influential contribution before the veil of the Taunton Commission descended. No thoroughly original views were expressed but Robinson's paper was a useful moderate survey of current ideas. Though it might not lead to the establishing of any great system of education, he thought the S.I.C. would at least 'bring together a variety of important facts, supply some valuable suggestions, and awaken increased attention throughout the country'.[14] The 'natural course of things' and private enterprise had both failed, and the time had come for external stimulus, without the complication of Government control.[15] He favoured the combination of a variety of plans, so that different groups would not be alienated. Of current schemes he most preferred Fortescue's in Devon and hoped that soon all populous counties would have similar schools of their own. His reasoning here summarised the whole feeling of the rural movement: 'It seems desirable that in each case the movement should originate with the great proprietors and leading persons in the counties. The co-operation of such men will give soundness and stability to the undertaking, and will tend to attract the notice and secure the confidence of the public'. He thought the founding of district committees or county boards might be the first step, and recommended the amalgamation where that might be judged necessary, despite possible problems with jealousy about local privileges. But Robinson's idea of State action was clearly different from Matthew Arnold's: in Robinson's plan, the State would have been left, after its initial foray into reform, with simply the role of inspection.

After 1869 Robinson was to become the blandest of the three Endowed Schools Commissioners; though it can be argued that, in his quieter way, he was the most successful. His 1864 paper at York was hardly a piece of ideological dynamite – except for the absence of tender feeling for local privileges – but its lack of novelty should not be allowed to conceal the perceptive nature of his summary of the main issues. His career as a national figure in education began with the York meeting. He was for a measure of State intervention; he wanted registration, inspection and certification; he wished to tone down the denominational issue in middle-class schooling; he was in favour of grading schools, according to a national, though county-based pattern; he favoured the county principle and the idea of a county board based upon an existing local social hierarchy; and he was willing to see endowments reformed, amalgamated, or diverted to more appropriate uses.

It is impossible now to know whether Granville ever studied Robinson's paper. But it is evident that at York, or soon after, Bruce and Robinson became closely acquainted; for when, in 1869, Robinson came south to take up his appointment under the Endowed Schools Act, Bruce, rejecting 'Rugby without Temple' for his son, William, sent him to Harrow to lodge in Robinson's house there as a day boy.[16]

The discussion of the papers on middle-class education at York was started by H. S. Thompson, experimental farmer and prominent member of the Royal Agricultural Society, who entertained Bruce as his guest during the conference.[17] Thompson thought it was 'hopeless' to try to educate the middle classes in one type of school. He gave as an instance 'the agricultural classes, with whom I am best acquainted'. There was a vast difference between the tenant-farmer who had £50,000 and another who farmed single-handed. Endowments, originally created for the poorest, should now be used in 'a form which would be more effective for the education of the middle classes', to counteract the aid given by the State for the schooling of the poor. The endowments ought to be supervised by a 'local board' composed of 'men of high character and station' who would guarantee the quality of the education and the character of each school. In his contribution, Northcote also stressed a suspicion of centralisation: the system ought to remain various and 'as free as possible'.[18]

Bruce had almost the last word. He hoped that reactionary 'localising influences' might disappear and knew that, 'as the Government faithfully reflects the opinion of intelligent men throughout the country, there is no fear that the Government will interfere more largely than it does now with the education of the middle classes, unless it is the expressed desire of the middle classes that the Government should do so'.[19]

The York meeting seemed to represent a consensus of view which rested on the belief that whatever action might be taken should be a development of the provincial and voluntary initiative which had been undertaken in the previous two decades: the activities of county committees and groups of provincial gentry and aristocrats. There was also the feeling that the middle classes themselves could not yet be trusted to find a solution for their own problems: the making of the master-plan would still be left to those who truly mattered in mid-Victorian society. Underlying all was a distaste for the prospect of State intervention, qualified by a reluctant admission that it might have to be accepted as a necessary evil. The discussion also confirmed that the lower-middle class was considered to be the category of most urgent concern, though the metaphors and instances in the discussion were still taken largely from the rural county society which they knew best.

By the close of 1864 Granville and Bruce – in consultation with Lyttelton and Temple, having sounded out opinions at the S.S.A., by looking at the Kildare Report, and by ignoring Matthew Arnold – had determined the beginning of the Royal Commission's main lines of inquiry. As far as it is possible to judge, they chose Commissioners in accordance with their proposed lines of inquiry. It might have been considered, therefore, that the Commission would give priority to the possibility of reforming the endowed schools; that it would have considerable investigative powers, on the models of Newcastle and Clarendon, without being able to intrude too rudely upon the private sector; that it would at least consider the question of *cy près*; that it would look closely at the needs of the lower-middle classes; that it would review present and possible future arrangements for examination and inspection; and that it would consider again the proposal for a graded system of linked schools first officially mooted by the Newcastle Commission. It must be presumed, therefore, that at this stage the judicious antipathy of the Lord President and his servants towards State action was strictly limited. They accepted the proposition that central government might make temporary incursions, by legislation or recommendation, and by setting up new or revised legal machinery, into the field of middle-class education. But in 1864 this 'intervention' was acceptable only as a means of dealing summarily with abuses; it would not include the much more dangerous idea, so closely akin to Matthew Arnold's extremism, that there should be a central authority and provincial boards for controlling specifically middle-class education. And yet, as has been shown, these very controversial notions – later adopted by the Taunton Commission – might be considered logical extensions of the proposals made in the Newcastle Report and the informal practices already adopted by county and diocesan committees.

Henry, Baron Taunton, could be called the conscientious captain of the West Country team of Commissioners.[20] By contrast with men of energy, like Temple, or of ambition, like Northcote, he must have seemed an ideally grave Chairman. Lord Stanley could contribute high intellect and Tory principle tinged with Liberal sentiment. Of him one of his biographers wrote, 'No politician of his time retained so remarkably, amid party conflicts, the power of judging questions from all their sides; of balancing, judiciously, opposing considerations; of looking beyond the passions and interests of the hour'.[21] Northcote was a careerist with an informed, intelligent interest in all kinds of education. Lyttelton was, in two senses at least, a joker; called a bigot by Lowe, in 1864 he still seemed to show signs of intransigence over the Church's interests.

Temple was feared and respected by those around him. His involvement, with Jowett among others, in recent religious controversy, only served to emphasise the liberal character of his approaches to a wide range of issues; and his experience in education as practitioner, theorist and administrator, along with his immense capacity for hard work, made it certain that his contribution to the S.I.C. discussions would carry great weight. Dr Hook of Chichester shared with Temple a willingness to take into account the other point of view, and he knew at first hand the life, and particularly the educational needs, of a great industrial city through his mission to Leeds thirty years earlier.

T. D. Acland's work for the Local Examinations alone should have guaranteed him a place on the Commission. Having voted for Repeal as a Tory, he had begun to emerge from the political wilderness in the early 1860s. He no longer tied himself tightly to the carriage of the National Society. Like Lyttelton he had reached a turning-point in his thinking on religious and political issues in 1864. He was as much an educational expert as any of the other members of the S.I.C., and his commitment to promoting the well-being of the rural economy was manifest.

Among the remaining members, Edward Baines took his place as Lyttelton's statutory Dissenter; though the acerbity of his recent attacks upon Establishment opinions in the *Nonconformist* must have suggested that he was unlikely to make as reasonable a contribution to the S.I.C. as Miall had to Newcastle. Yet Baines was also about to experience a *volte face*. It would be inaccurate to say that he was changed simply by his working on the S.I.C.; but it is certainly true that his ideas about education were considerably modified by that experience and by other events in the years from 1864 to 1867.[22]

W. E. Forster, as the son-in-law of Thomas and the brother-in-law of Matthew, had sufficient credentials for his appointment, and these were qualified, favourably, by his own former links with Nonconformity. As a Liberal M.P. for Bradford, with Baines, he supplied a brand of refined urban radicalism which complemented the 'gentry' and predominantly county associations of other leading members of the Commission.

The remaining members have left shallower marks upon the record of mid-Victorian public affairs. Yet each must have had a distinctive rôle assigned to him. Peter Erle was qualified by his technical experience as Chief Charity Commissioner.[23] His evidence and advice to the Newcastle Commission on the possibility of finding solutions to equity problems reinforced arguments in favour of his appointment; though it should be added that the recommendations of that Commission seemed to have been almost controversially radical in relation to endowments. Dr. John Storrar represented the education lobby of the medical profession and, perhaps obliquely, the educational interests of other learned professions.[24] Finally, the Revd A. W. Thorold, the Commission's leading nonentity, counted among his achievements the holding of fashionable livings in London and his marriage to Lord Taunton's niece.[25]

Terms of reference

The working papers of the Taunton Commission no longer exist.[26] But a graphic picture of its labours can be pieced together from private papers and memoirs of leading participants. The *Times* provides a comprehensive list of each of its meetings. The first took place on 24 January 1865, at 2 Victoria Street, Westminster, with nine further discussions through February and March. The first assistant commissioners were appointed on 2 April.[27] D. R. Fearon was to investigate London; H. A. Gifford was given Surrey and Sussex; C. H. Stanton, Devon and Somerset with Bristol; T. H. Green, Stafford and Warwick; J. L. Hammond, Norfolk and Northumberland; J. G. Fitch, the West Riding; James Bryce, Lancashire; H. M. Bompas, parts of Wales. Matthew Arnold was to investigate secondary education in selected parts of Europe, the Revd James Fraser, parts of Canada and the United States. Initially, the S.I.C. was following the selective pattern adopted by the Newcastle Commission after 1858.

Bryce and Green, young Oxford Fellows, welcomed the opportunity to move in the world of public affairs. If the territories they were encountering were not absolutely new to them, they were certainly approaching them by a novel route. Bryce wrote to his friend and fellow-historian, Edward Freeman, in March 1865:

Manchester is a much more agreeable place than I had supposed: not as dirty as London: the people rough, but straightforward and hearty; society, it is true, overridden by wealth, but that wealth employed in a bold, generous way. Politically there seems to be very little stir ... the merchants ... represent a state of society and a framework of notions so unlike what we have in the South of England.[28]

The instructions to assistant commissioners had been issued in March. The grammar schools in the light of continuing debate over *cy près*, were to be examined to ascertain their general condition, and to find whether they were fulfilling the founders' intentions, with particular reference to the class of children they had wished to benefit. The proprietary schools, rapidly gaining public favour, were to be examined with a view to the possibility of some of their features being appropriated to the grammar schools. Private schools were too numerous to be inspected individually; but specimen examples in the 'county towns' ought to be looked at.[29] The assistant commissioners were also expected to examine the balance of the curriculum in each school. Girls' education 'did not fall so largely within the province of the Commission as that of boys'. But it seemed to the Commissioners necessary that the public might wish to be presented with information about its condition sufficient to provide a basis for subsequent discussion. Parents' opinions were to be canvassed on such topics as subjects of instruction, vocational training, the cost of a sound education, the juxtaposition of social classes in one school, and on day and boarding education.[30] It was considered that these inquiries could be completed within six months, and that reports would be submitted two months later.

However, a year later, in March 1866, the *Times* reported that the S.I.C. was extending its inquiries beyond the selected districts to cover all the grammar schools in the country.[31] No public explanation was offered; but it could be assumed that this change was brought about by the Commissioners' desire to consider in greater detail the proposals for creating local or provincial authorities which they had received from a number of witnesses by this time. It was at this point, too, that they requested written evidence, on the subject of the advisability of trying to construct local authorities, from selected witnesses.

Quite early in their proceedings the Commissioners must have tabulated a list of witnesses grouped in relation to distinct educational issues. Acland wrote to his wife, early in 1865: 'Eleven Commissioners. Lord Stanley alone absent in consequence of especial business, but he means to be a regular attendant. We are likely, I think, to work harmoniously and honestly. I have already had to take some part in settling the course, but I try not to talk too much'.[32] 'The course' can be traced through the sequence of witnesses' evidence recorded in Volumes IV and V of the S.I.C. Report. Acland's influence was surely felt, since the first batch of twenty-one witnesses to be called was connected with examinations, one of his 'crotchets'. The next group was the headmasters, and they were followed by a select clutch of Parliamentarians including Lowe and Pakington.

On 27 June the Commissioners changed gear and, taking up the question of large endowments recently raised by Gladstone, devoted two days' questioning to the largest endowment of all, Christ's Hospital. At a time when the policy of 'Payment by Results' was being carried out, a charity school whose chief master received £600 per annum was an anomaly which seemed to call for the redistributive action of the central government. Gladstone's celebrated speech on

Charities[33] to the Commons in 1863 had been an antecedent of the S.I.C.'s special interest in over-wealthy and unsupervised educational trusts. The Commission was to incorporate the results of this interest in a chapter of its main Report entitled 'Eight of the Largest Endowments', whose author was Gladstone's brother-in-law, Lyttelton.

Christ's Hospital figured in another category which the Commissioners identified, the hospital schools. In attempting to reform these institutions after 1869 the Endowed Schools Commissioners met their most virulent and well-organised opposition. Basing its judgement on the reports of assistant commissioners, the S.I.C. considered that hospital endowments 'now act largely, though indirectly, in discouragement of education, and they are applied very frequently to the relief of classes of persons who could hardly have been regarded by the founders as within the immediate purview of their intentions'. Therefore, entry to such schools ought to be by means of 'good entrance examinations' which would benefit children of the lower-middle class.[34]

A further distinct group of witnesses gave evidence on the curriculum. For instance the Commissioners heard from the Revd J. R. Bryce about courses of studies in Scottish schools and at the Belfast Academy.[35] The most powerful advocacy of the claims of science, however, came in the form of a report from the British Association's Dundee Conference of 1867, prepared by a Committee including Joseph Payne and Professors Huxley and Tyndall.[36] But despite their claiming 'the existence of a general and even a national desire to facilitate the acquisition of some scientific knowledge by boys at our public and other schools', they had to admit the serious difficulties attending the introduction of science into middle-class schools. The final recommendations of the S.I.C. on the curriculum were, in fact, of a neutral kind: such questions as 'whether the boys should learn botany or experimental physics, or the rudiments of chemistry' were best left, the Commissioners thought, to the headmasters and governors of each school.[37] There was no clear prescription for the secondary curriculum in the S.I.C. Report.

Quite late in the sequence of hearings, the Commissioners summoned twelve witnesses for the purpose of receiving evidence about female education, though Roby, as Secretary, had replied to a numerously supported petition on the subject as early as February 1865.[38] Acland was impressed by the female witnesses: 'Our ladies gave excellent evidence . . . some of the best we have had yet, calm, clear, modest, yet thoroughly knowing what they were about'.[39] As might have been expected, the most impressive were Miss Davies and Miss Buss. But even in this field a West County bias asserted itself, with witnesses from Taunton and Frome. Mark Pattison, drawing on his experience as a College Tutor for men, gave the female cause its final filip when he said 'whereas you had in some measure to drive boys to make them learn, the girls come to you and want to learn'.[40] The immediate consequence of the work of the ladies' pressure-groups was that Lyttelton was given the task of composing a separate chapter of the main Report dealing exclusively with girls' education. The S.I.C. finally recommended, with some caution 'wherever in the administration (of endowments) it shall be found possible to admit Girls' schools to a direct and substantial participation in them, we conceive that, with a few modifications, they may be done'.[41]

Another group of witnesses spoke of the claims of the county as an administrative unit for the organisation of middle-class schooling. The Commissioners interviewed Fortescue and Brereton (even summoning R. D. Gould, architect of the Devon County School), Kerrison, the chief promoter of the Suffolk County School, H. S. Thompson, and William Torr, a farmer on a large scale in Lincolnshire and 'much connected with the Royal Agricultural Society'. Torr's evidence is interesting chiefly for three reasons. Firstly, he was the only farmer who spoke to the S.I.C., but in this respect he qualified probably because of the exceptional size of his holding. Secondly, his notion of an appropriate education for farmers' sons included Latin, omitted French, and would have touched upon the elements of chemistry and botany.[42] Thirdly, he was clearly in favour of making educational distinctions in the rural middle class: the smaller tenant-farmers' sons would remain at school only till 14; sons of men like himself till 16.[43] In a pragmatic way he was providing confirmation of the Commissioners' age-limits and their curricula for second- and third-grade schools.

The Chancery witnesses were also a coherent group.[44] They included not only the Lord Chancellor and the Attorney-General, but Kay–Shuttleworth and Lingen, formerly and currently at the Education Department. In addition to reinforcing general principles which had been widely acknowledged before 1865, these witnesses informed the Commissioners about specific cases of legal abuse. This was specially true of Thomas Hare who, as an Inspector of Charities,

was then involved in arguments with the City of London Corporation about the conversion of charitable bequests to more beneficial
uses.[45]

In this multitude of witnesses only two were summoned who may
be said to have represented the middle-class clientele of local schools.
Yet throughout the main Report of the S.I.C., and the reports of
assistant commissioners, there was constant reliance upon the opinions of unidentified parents about their requirements for schooling.
Mr Edmund Edmunds, a Rugby ironmonger and a member of the
Farmers' Club, was invited probably because of his indirect associations with Temple and Acland. He was exceptional in that he had
addressed the Club, in February 1865, on the subject of middle-class
education when he had suggested that farmers ought to be interested
in the subject since they were 'the largest class following any one
profession or business in England'.[46] His interest was matched by his
knowledge, for he spoke of West Buckland, the Surrey County
School, the Harpur Commercial Schools at Bedford, and
Woodard's, Hurstpierpoint.[47] He thought that the better-off
tradesman's feeling that Latin was 'a waste of time' was 'every day
dying away': 'if you only take a book like Caesar, and take any of
those long sentences, and make a boy carry in his mind, from the
beginning to the end of it, you have done a great deal, you have
brought the boy to think more than you could in any other way'.[48]
How Temple and Acland must have relished this statement of opinion. The other lower-middle class witness was William Barham,
probably a builder, from Lambeth, but he was accompanied by his
Rector, the formidable Robert Gregory, a prop of the National
Society and devout supporter of Woodard. Barham's occupation
might have accounted for his view that Euclid was a more necessary
part of the curriculum than chemistry.[49]

Apart from these two witnesses, the Commissioners themselves
relied on largely impressionistic evidence about the texture of
middle-class life. T. H. Green, in his assistant commissioner's report,
described a 'typical' commercial family thus, with perhaps his Tem-
perance opinions peeping through: 'The father, probably, spends the
evening with his friends at some place of social resort; the mother is
tired with household cares, and if she had the will, has not often
sufficient elementary knowledge to overlook the studies of a small
boy'.[50]

Parallel activity

The period when the S.I.C. was taking evidence was not a 'close season' for experiments and further developments in middle-class education: the years 1864–7 were a time of feverishly executed innovations, most of which fall into one of two broad categories. Firstly, there were those events which constituted a process of abreaction – attempts to clear the decks before the Government declared an interest in reform. Secondly, there were experiments which may have been directly encouraged by the inquiries of the Commission.

The reactions of the Established Church to the work of the Commission were various. Bishop Ellicott of Gloucester, a conservative by nature, had looked forward hopefully to the start of the inquiry: he expected it to be 'thoroughly probing, but considerate'.[51] Yet there must have been many among clergy and laity who regarded the genesis of the Taunton Commission as an event whose consequences might jeopardise the strong connections between the Church and the endowed schools. In the recent past, Lewis Dillwyn's Endowed Schools Bill, which would have opened the schools to a denominationally mixed clientele, had been fiercely debated and rejected in favour of a much blander measure. The Church Defence Institution had been established in 1859, at the same time as Dillwyn's Bill, as a bastion against the forces of Disestablishment, and the personnel of the Institution overlapped the membership of the National Society in the 1860s. Lyttelton, Redesdale and Harrowby were leading supporters of both at the beginning of the decade.[52] The heyday of the Institution, as a kind of English political Inquisition, was to come in the early 1870s with the founding of its journal, *The National Church*, and the accompanying attack on the Endowed Schools Commissioners.

The National Society's revived interest in middle-class schooling began, two months before the first meeting of the S.I.C., in November 1864. A sub-committee was appointed 'to consider and report whether the Society can assist and if so how best in promoting the Education of the Children of the Poor just above those who usually attend the National Schools'. This echoed the S.I.C.'s and the S.S.A.'s special concern for the educational well-being of the lower-middle class. The Revd Robert Gregory[53] was the most active promoter of the new cause and elaborated the Society's aims in a pamphlet published in December 1864.[54] But the funds allocated to the sub-committee were never adequate, and most of its grants to schools and parishes were trivial. Nevertheless, its limited activities reflect the anxiety felt by some prominent members of the Society about the prospect of a liberal programme of reform emerging from the S.I.C., while, in a broader context, they demonstrated that the initiative was moving away from narrow sectional interests into the hands of tolerant groups with wider bases of support.

It could be argued that the single most active promoter of new middle-class schools in the mid-Victorian era was the Revd William Rogers, who is now remembered chiefly for his soubriquet, 'Hang Theology'. Recently a member of the Newcastle Commission, a friend of Northcote, Hobhouse, Gladstone and Pakington, and a trustee of Dulwich, one of the largest charities, Rogers created a system of schools in the parishes he served in London. His last great educational campaign began in November 1865, with a great meeting of bankers, merchants and tycoons in the City of London, for the purpose of establishing a middle-class school which would produce candidates fit to be clerks in the great metropolitan houses.[55] In the Chair was the Lord Mayor, Alderman Hale, who deplored the lack of efficient middle-class schools in the City. The audience included members of the Livery Companies who had so far managed to defend their corporate wealth from the curiosity of central government. When he asked for financial support for the proposed school, Rogers used blackmail: something was brewing, he said: 'Perhaps the Attorney-General has got some grand scheme, or the Chancellor of the Exchequer something grander'. By this piece of irony he played on the fears of the Company men and City trustees about Government intervention in their charitable affairs, and was consequently able to raise a subscription of £50,000 within a month of the first meeting. Less than a year later, the new school opened on a site off the City Road. It was to serve the lower-middle class. Presiding at the opening, the new Lord Mayor said he thought hexameters 'were of little use in warehouses, counting houses, or entering rooms'. For those places a sound practical education was required, to fit boys 'for that position in life which they were likely to occupy'. Rogers had created a school for Cratchits. Challenged to state his religious views, in relation to the origins of his financial support, he replied, 'Away with theological questions and away with economical; let us begin . . . .'.

The efforts of Gregory and Rogers, though mutually exclusive, were independent responses to the Government's setting up the S.I.C. At the same time there were instances of unilateral reactions in institutions and corporations. A number of schools were rapidly transformed, independently of each other, between 1864 and 1868: Giggleswick, Saddleworth and Wakefield in the West Riding;[56] Maldon, Felsted, Chigwell and Grays Thurrock in Essex;[57] Taunton College (of which Lord Taunton was President) and Martock in Somerset,[58] Bromsgrove and Kinver (Lyttelton was a trustee of both), Bewdley, and King's Norton in Worcestershire and Staffordshire.[59]

But the most notable instance of this independent reform in the 1860s was at Monmouth. Gladstone had already implied the Government's intention to investigate Monmouth School,[60] and it was soon to figure as one of the eight great endowments specially noted by the S.I.C. Its governors were the Court and Wardens of the Haberdashers' Company. In 1832 the trust income had been a comfortable £779; but by 1867 it had risen to a massive £3,000, as a result of the incursions of railway companies on to trust property in south London. Mr Bompas, the S.I.C.'s assistant commissioner, noted in 1867 that the pupils were still 'principally the sons of labourers and small tradesmen', with very few children of local professional people. The school was confined to local boys, except for a few who boarded out.[61] Gladstone's threatening remarks in 1863 probably prompted the Haberdashers to renew their interest, and they asked for permission to make building extensions. The Master of the Company laid the foundation stone in June 1864.

While Granville was publicly discussing the forthcoming Royal Commission, in November 1864, the townspeople of Monmouth received notice of a visit by Thomas Hare, Inspector of Charities. The Company evidently intended to forestall any external attempts to reform 'their' School. In February 1868, the final Charity Commission scheme for a boarding school of large proportions at Monmouth was published.[62] When, in 1870, the Endowed Schools Commissioners found what had happened at Monmouth, their Assistant Secretary, D. C. Richmond, told the Haberdashers that the new Commissioners 'are plainly bound by the purport of the Endowed Schools Act (1869) to give a general effect to the recommendations of the Schools Inquiry Report. That Report contains many important enunciations of general principles with which the new (Charity

Commission) scheme of the Company, though carefully and in many respects liberally framed, does not in all respects accord".[63] But, with one bound, the Company had released its wealthy School from the threat of probable reform by central government. In the process the town and county of Monmouth were largely deprived of the benefits of one of the richest educational trusts in the country.

Constructing recommendations

In making its recommendations the S.I.C. relied primarily on the reports prepared by assistant commissioners. Of these, T. H. Green's on Birmingham, Staffordshire and Warwickshire, are perhaps the most striking examples. Green was an Oxford philosopher formally encountering public affairs for the first time, and he reacted healthily to the challenge cast down in Birmingham, a city about to reach its Radical simmering-point, yet a centre also of conventional Anglican sentiment. His work in the Midland counties put him in touch with the equally chaotic, inefficient work of middle-class schooling in hamlets, towns and villages. His investigation usually began with a visit to the master of the school; then, 'having conciliated him as much as possible', he would decide upon a day when he might review the teaching. Afterwards he might interview trustees and parents.[64]

Green's visit to Birmingham had been anticipated by at least one leading citizen. William Lucas Sargant was a local gunsmith who had made a small fortune selling weaponry in colonial Africa. A pupil at Hazelwood School in the 1820s, he was a friend of Matthew Davenport Hill and became the first Liberal 'outsider' to penetrate the closed Anglican corporation of trustees of King Edward's School in the town.[65] He had already earned a wide reputation through his statistic surveys[66] and by his contribution to the 1856 Educational Conference in London.[67] He heralded the arrival of the assistant commissioner by starting an entertainingly acrimonious exchange of views with Lord Lyttelton in the local press, the substance of which he later published.[68] In the course of this correspondence Sargant warned Green, albeit indirectly, that a 'fanciful or prejudiced or perverse' assistant commissioner could do great mischief in a place like Birmingham. The substance of Sargant's opinions comprised a classic argument for local interests against impersonal interference by a central authority. However, whether intentionally or not, Green gained the confidence of middle-class Birmingham citizens.

He hob nobbed with the local press and was willing to 'poke into back-shops and small manufactories'.[69]

In addition to Green's report on Birmingham the S.I.C. received evidence from eight witnesses who were members of the reforming 'Free Grammar School Association',[70] from three of the trustees of King Edward's School, and from the headmaster, Charles Evans, who had taught Green at Rugby School.[71] The Association had been formed in June 1865, that is, after Green began his local inquiries; so once again, the S.I.C. seems to have been responsible for promoting new activity.[72] Among its powerful members were Sargant, George Dixon and M. D. Hill. They thought the curriculum was too classical, that the commercial element ought to be expanded, and that the schools of the foundation ought to be much enlarged, with, if necessary, higher fees.[73]

In his report on the School Green showed no special favour towards Evans. He thought that the government of the School ought to be more obviously representative of a broad range of interests in the town, though he had been unable to find any cases of gross injustice by the Anglican trustees towards local Dissenters, who patronised the School in large numbers.[74] Similar opinions about the waning problem of Dissent were offered by witnesses before the S.I.C.[75] and these reinforced Temple's earlier remark to the Newcastle Commission that, in elementary schools, the religious difficulty 'hardly exists at all in the minds of the parents'.[76] Green judiciously congratulated the inhabitants of Birmingham: '. . . it was a great advantage to me to meet with so much intelligent opinion on education'.

Green's General Report on the counties covered a wider range of issues. He divided the endowed schools into two classes: those which did or did not profess to give an education higher than that provided in elementary schools for the poor. His short way for dealing with defects in provision and in the curriculum of the grammar schools was to suggest that, in relation to most of their pupils, the grammar schools had hardly begun their task, since most of the boys left before they had acquired even the elements of a liberal education.[77] English, French, and occasionally German were the main subjects of an 'English' curriculum and seemed to be attractive to middle-class parents below the professional level; but, for Green, they were 'comparatively poor' as instruments of a liberal education.[78] It was impossible for the smaller grammar schools to operate alternative systems of education alongside their classical departments.[79]

The 'commercial' parents had, in most cases, received only a brief education themselves. Consequently their educational aspirations for their children were often limited. Dissenters were sometimes discouraged from envisaging an advanced schooling for their children because of the restrictions which still applied to University entry.[80] For these and other reasons there was little evidence of a mixing of classes in the grammar schools of the area. The only school he had found which satisfactorily mingled social classes was Loughborough Grammar School.[81]

Green showed that within the region there were large numbers of the population with no endowed school close to their homes, particularly in the iron and pottery district of north Staffordshire. In the Black Country there were four schools with a total of 1,500 pupils serving a population of about 800,000. Yet even in that area market forces had not created a sufficient supply of private and proprietary schools.[82] In the countryside the farmers only rarely sent their sons to local grammar schools; usually they patronised inferior private schools in the smaller towns.[83] The grammar schools would 'kill' such educationally impoverished private institutions even though they continued teaching Latin; even Green's recipe was simple:

> The means of reconciling the opposite wants of classical and commercial education are to be found . . . (1) in the exaction of larger amounts of elementary knowledge at entrance to the grammar schools than is now required at best, (2) in such postponement of Greek as would render it possible, without trenching on time given to Latin, to secure that the average boy should be perfect in arithmetic, and able to write English correctly by the age of 14 at latest. After that age a bifurcation might be allowed either, where the staff is strong enough, at the grammar school itself, or at the upper schools to be founded for the purpose. This plan . . . I believe to be the only one by which commercial requirement can be satisfied and at the same time the way kept open to higher learning, without sacrificing the great advantage of uniformity of system. The words 'arithmetic' and 'Latin' should be graven on the heart of every grammar school master. The one represents the primary condition of popularity with the commercial class; the other the wicket-gate through which must pass every boy, not endowed with special gifts or the subject of uncovenanted mercies, who is to attain an appreciation of anything high and remote in the intellectual world.[84]

In his final summary Green suggested that, where appropriate, two small and otherwise useless endowments might be amalgamated; though he thought that local gentry and farmers would often resent the conversion of endowments from elementary to middle-class education.[85] He also foresaw the allied accusation of injustice to the poor:

> Education is thought to be an affair of classes, and all classes above the poor, it is said, can afford to pay for the teaching suitable to them. It is not yet a recognised idea, that educational endowments can be so worked as in some degree to efface demarcations of class, to give a freedom of self-elevation in the social scale other than that given by money, and keep 'the career open to talents'.[86]

The poor were thought to be interested only in primary education, and since this was not yet supported wholly or largely by taxation, it was seen to be the one proper educational object of charitable bequests. 'For a single man to be found having views about better education for the middle class a hundred may be found having views about the education of the poor.'

He also proposed a grading of schools according to a two-tier pattern. The similarities between his scheme and Evans's advice to the S.I.C. suggest that there might have been some collusion.[87] Green wanted one high school to be created in each of the counties of Warwick and Stafford. Exhibitions for county boys ought to be available at £25 a year. The schools would provide competition for bright boys and 'would make it possible to simplify the work of the smaller grammar schools and remove the educationally unsound division of schools into classical and commercial departments'.

After the grammar-school system had been 'fairly put on its legs' by the action of the central authority, there would be the question of whether the trustees should be left alone or whether 'county boards' should be established. Green saw advantages in the latter. It might bring the grammar schools more systematically into relation with the elementary schools, which might then be seen by the farmers as useful for the education of their sons; and it would certainly facilitate the reapportioning of endowments (though, presumably, he saw this as a function of the central authority).[88]

At all times Green attempted to be pragmatic, basing his judgements on what he had seen for himself. But there can be little doubt that he took counsel from Temple with whose views he was in accord on every important issue. In May 1877, Green gave a lecture on the grading of secondary schools to the Birmingham Teachers' Association, in which he said, clearly referring to Temple:

> There was no statesman for whom it was worthwhile, or who had the

leisure if he had the inclination, to push the scheme for reorganising our superior education through in detail. The head that conceived could not also command the hand to execute it. The fortune of English public life has always been celebrated for putting the round man in the square hole, and, in this case, having excluded the author of the scheme in question from the possibility of becoming a minister of education, it made him a bishop in the most backward corner of England.[89]

Green was wrong in assuming that Temple had been pushed unwillingly into Exeter by Gladstone in 1869:[90] Temple had also been offered Bath and Wells, Oxford and Manchester; but his West-Country association prevailed. Nevertheless, he was correct in identifying Temple as the 'author' of the Report of the Schools Inquiry Commission.

The S.I.C. heard the last of its witnesses in July 1866.[91] Temple had attended thirty-five of the sixty-eight meetings at which the Commission had taken evidence.[92] His absences are accounted for by the competing demands of his headship of Rugby. But he missed none of the remaining fifty-seven meetings which were devoted to the stern business of drafting the Report. H. J. Roby seems to have been aware that, while no one 'could have been more willing to listen to the suggestions of others', Temple still strongly adhered to his own views as published in 'Oxford Essays' in 1856.[93] He outlined his draft plan of discussion to Acland in September 1866:

> In regard to our recommendations, I think we have two things to do: to organise what we have got, i.e. the endowed schools; and to create what we have not got, a system of schools for the lower middle class. . . . In doing the first we ought to do something about the second. But not all. And my idea is that *Rates* should supply and keep in repair the *Buildings* where Endowments were not at hand to do so.[94]

These remarks sound fresh and radical; but they came directly from Temple's 1856 essay.

The Commissioners who took part in the discussion of recommendations were a rather more select group than those originally chosen. Erle, Storrar and Thorold were hardly ever present at later meetings; Northcote and Stanley ceased to appear when they took office under Disraeli in July 1866.[95] Baines attended regularly till the end.[96] Temple's dominating presence was not always grave: Acland told his wife, 'we have a great deal of fun. . . . I am always coming down on the Head Master; he takes it very well'.[97] It seems that, as a general rule, the leading Commissioners – Temple, Taunton,

Lyttelton and Acland – each prepared papers on topics allocated by Temple. Eventually Acland wrote parts of Chapter III of the Report, on the local distribution of endowments; Lyttelton wrote the chapters on Girls' Education and the great endowments. But the bulk of the Report, including Chapter VII which stated the recommendations, was the work of Temple, with Roby's assistance.[98] In helping Roby with Chapter II, he wrote continuously for thirty-six hours, 'having tea brought to him at intervals and the printer's devil in constant attendance'.[99] The manic-depressive Lyttelton evidently enjoyed his 'high' on completing his chapters. In a *jeu d'esprit* to his wife, he wrote:

Births: At Carlton Terrace, on July 11th, after a painful and protracted labour, Lord Lyttelton of a child on Girls' Schools. Friends at a distance will be glad to hear that this long expected event has taken place and that parent and child are charming well.

The infant chapter has a strong likeness in features and deportment to its parent. It is uproarious – squalls incessantly – and hopes to make much noise in the world.[100]

Temple's position as *primus inter pares* might have caused some problems. But his acquaintanceships, even friendships, with the others can be traced back well before 1864. And though he and Baines appeared to share little in common, the latter stuck to his overseer's task, attending five of the last seven meetings of the Commission. But Temple had long been in favour of conscience clauses, which must have helped to make his views more congenial to Baines, who may be said to have experienced a change of heart himself in 1866, so that, in the following year, partly as a result of the findings of the Manchester and Salford Educational Aid Society, he and Miall acknowledged that the idea of a national system of elementary education was now acceptable to them, on certain terms.[101]

Acland and Lyttelton, in accepting the religious recommendations of the Report, had moved to a new position from slightly different directions. Both had kept pace with Gladstone's movement from his 'Church and State' posture of 1838. In 1855 Lyttelton still staunchly supported the principle of a system of Church schools: the separation of secular and religious elements was then anathema to him,[102] and, since his 1855 statement was reprinted unchanged in 1864, it can be assumed that his views remained the same. In name, at least, Acland and Lyttelton had supported the new National Society initiatives in 1865.[103] Though there is no direct evidence, it seems likely that Lyttelton's 'conversion' by 1866 was partly the result of his talk with Temple on the S.I.C. And the convoluted style of the Appendix to the S.I.C. Report, in which Lyttelton announced his acceptance in principle of conscience clauses suggests that his decision had been reached after a severe struggle with his own conscience.

Acland shared in Lyttleton's change of mind and pronounced his new views in privately-circulated printed pamphlets. He wrote:

I am not one of those who entertain the opinion that the National Society has done its work, and that its services are no longer required by the Church. The functions of the State in the Education of the Nation are becoming every day more clearly recognised: probably at no distant period they will be much expanded. The legitimate claims of all ranks and denominations to some share in the advantages of public institutions will no longer be resisted. The Church of the Nation may ere long have greater need than now for united voluntary action, and for some metropolitan centre for its internal organisation.[104]

In a letter to the Bishops, in May 1867, before the publication of the Report, Acland declared his belief in 'absolute liberty in teaching' and 'absolute right of withdrawal' from religious teaching in schools.[105]

The deliberations of 1866 led directly to the recommendations of 1867. Between 29 February and 4 March 1868, the *Times* published a three-part summary of the Report. The only comment was a somewhat negative congratulation to the Commissioners on having accomplished such a massive task so succinctly.[106] The final article ended with a quotation from the Report:

We believe that schools, above most other institutions, require thorough concert among themselves for their requisite efficiency; but there is in this country neither organisation nor supervision, nor even effective tests to distinguish the incompetent from the truly successful; and we cannot but regard this state of things as alike unjust to all good schools and schoolmasters, and discreditable and injurious to the country itself.[107]

The final recommendations[108] represent the immediate application of Temple's analytical and synthetical skills to an immense problem. But they also mark a point of consummation in the process of a debate which had been conducted since the early years of the century. It is possible, with some accurancy, to place each of the recommendations in a particular context of development. W. L.

Burns' comment, that the Report was 'infinitely more radical than anything that has come to pass in the interval' since its publication, misleadingly suggests that there were radically novel elements in what the Commissioners proposed. But they produced few new ideas. The novelty of the Report lay in the proposal that a Government ought to act upon its recommendations. It was, as Burns also says, 'a remarkable radical–collectivist document'.[109] But most of its ideas had a long history in theory and even in practice.

The notion of creating a central authority was rooted in a series of suggestions dating back, in Britain, to the remarkable Irish Report of 1791,[110] and to the Irish Schools Act of 1813; to Arnold's exhortations of 1832, and, more recently, to the Newcastle Commission's demand for an Education Department with enlarged powers of supervision. The provincial or county boards proposal had some non-educational precedents, but could be seen as a reproduction of similar agencies suggested for Ireland and, more importantly, as an equitable modification of the diocesan and county boards which had been working intermittently in some parts of the country since 1838. The Newcastle Commission had also suggested local and county borough boards, and it is surprising that the S.I.C.'s similar proposal has been consistently interpreted as a radical innovation despite that recent precedent. The tripartite grading of middle-class schools suggested by the S.I.C. lay at the end of a chain of ideas which can be traced back to the agriculturists in the earliest years of the century, and to a series of experiments which had the Sussex schools of Woodard and the Liverpool Collegiate Institution as their chief exemplars. The involvement of the Universities in the proposed Examinations Council owed much to the increasingly successful incursions of Oxford and Cambridge into the field of middle-class examinations. The attack upon *cy près* which the S.I.C. wished to mount was the fulfilment of a strategy which had been gathering since, once again, the Irish Act, 1813, and which had grown through the Charity Commissions of 1818 to 1853. Here, too, Newcastle had supplied a strong precedent.

Edward Thring's judgement on the S.I.C., quoted at the head of this chapter, may seem rather uncharitable, especially because of his earlier friendship and co-operation with Acland. Yet his comments nicely point up Burns' more balanced description of the Commissioners as 'men substantially representative of upper- and upper-middle-class Liberalism'.[111] In 1864 Temple had expressed to

Granville his anxiety about the West Country bias of the list of names he was proposing; and the nucleus of this western group represented, in a liberal way, the fertility of the rural counties as a seedbed for reform in the territory of middle-class education. They were essentially men of the English landed interest whose experience of affairs was based on their traditional influence in county society, though they were extraordinary members of that society because they were trying to come to terms with elements of stress and change within it. Despite their relative ignorance of life in large urban communities outside London, they had acquired a new characteristic which separated them from the conservative traditions of the countryside in which their wealth was largely founded: they were men of the post-Northcote-Trevelyan era; men of what John Roach has called 'the new world' of Jowett, in which University education was seen primarily as a preparation for effective public service,[112] in very much the same way as the Inns of Court had been seen as a preparation for public life in the counties in the sixteenth century.

Yet these new men seem to have avoided, in a self-conscious way, the issue of technical education, which they might have taken as a synonym in the 1860s for lower-middle-class education in the larger towns. In their recommendations they touched upon the subject only once in the main text: 'Nor do we think any better or wiser encouragement could be given out of the endowments to the technical education, for which there is at present an earnest demand, than to permit the holders of exhibitions to take them to technical schools'.[113] But even this remark applied to the higher grades of technical education, in the schools of mining and engineering.

It could be said that there was no member of the S.I.C. who was capable of writing, or who had any inclination to write, an informed paragraph on the subject of technical education. Their failure to discuss the subject is nevertheless surprising in the light of the heavy emphasis they placed on the need to provide appropriate schools for the lower-middle classes. The only oral evidence they received on the subject came almost accidentally from Henry Moseley who had been called to give evidence in his capacity as an examiner. Moseley's Bristol Trade School was at this time a unique experiment in curriculum innovation and vocational training.[114] It is ironic that one of the most successful schemes later published by the Endowed Schools Commission under the 1869 Act was the re-working of the inefficient trusts in Keighley for the purpose of setting up a similar trade school.[115] The S.I.C. seems to have been unaware of the 'so earnest' demand for technical education until a late stage in their proceedings. Despite letters which were received in 1866 and 1867 from P. le Neve Foster of the Society of Arts, on education in France, and from J. C. Buckmaster on science education, the S.I.C. seems not to have wished to be informed on the subject.[116]

This underlines the significance of the rural concept of middle-class education which was central to the Commission's presuppositions. It can also be seen as foreshadowing the deeper division which was to be engineered between technical and secondary education in the early years of the Board of Education after 1899.

Notes

1 *Times*, 20 June 1864. The Petition referred to "the United Kingdom", i.e., it was intended to include Scotland and Ireland.
2 Ibid, 25 November 1864.
3 Ibid, 17 November 1864.
4 Ibid, 20 June 1864.
5 PRO. Granville Papers, Bruce to Granville, 6 August 1864.
6 Ibid, Temple to Granville, 11 August 1864.
7 Ibid, Bruce to Granville, 17 September 1864.
8 Ibid, Temple to Granville, 11 August 1864.
9 Ibid, Temple to Granville, 15 August 1864.
10 Ibid, loc. cit.
11 This is partially quoted in Lord Edmond Fitzmaurice, *The Life of Lord Granville, 1815–91*, London, 1905, p. 434.
12 Granville Papers, Lowe to Granville, 17 October 1864.
13 Canon H. G. Robinson, 'Suggestions for the Improvement of Middle-class Education', *Transactions of the National Association for the Promotion of Social Science, York meeting of 1864*, London, 1864, p. 371.
14 Ibid, p. 367.
15 Ibid, p. 370.
16 ——, *Letters of the Rt Hon. Henry Austin Bruce, Lord Aberdare of Duffryn*, Oxford, privately printed, London, 1902, I, pp. 290–1.
17 H. S. Thompson, of Kirby Hall, Yorks. (1809–1874); Trinity College, Cambridge; studied under Charles Darwin. Extensive agricultural tours, "following the example of Arthur Young". Experimented as agricultural chemist. Eighteen papers published in the Royal Agricultural Society Journal. (D.N.B.)
18 Social Science Transactions, 1864, p. 455.
19 Ibid, pp. 463–4.
20 D.N.B.
21 T. H. Sanderson and E. S. Roscoe, *Speeches and Addresses of Edward Henry, XVth Earl of Derby*, prefatory memoir by W. E. Lecky, London, 1894.

22 See below, p. 202.
23 See above, Chapter V, p. 110.
24 John Storrar, MD (1811–1886). Member of Senate of London University, 1859–88; represented London University on General Medical Council, 1858–86.
25 Anthony Wilson Thorold (1825–95), rector of St Giles in the Fields, London, 1856–67; chaplain of Curzon Chapel, Mayfair, 1868–9; vicar of St Pancras, 1869–74; member of London School Board, 1870–4. Bishop of Rochester from 1877. Married Emily, daughter of John Labouchere, 1865.
26 See P. Gordon, 'Some Sources for the History of the Endowed Schools Commission', *British Journal of Educational Studies*, XIV, 1965–6, p. 59ff.
27 *Times*, 3 April 1865.
28 Bodleian Library, Oxford, Bryce MSS, 9/72, letter to Freeman, 22 May 1865.
29 S.I.C., II, Instructions, Circulars, Correspondence, I, pp. 123–6.
30 Ibid, p. 125.
31 *Times*, 26 March 1866.
32 Acland, op. cit., p. 231, letter from Acland, 24 January 1865.
33 See above, Chapter V, p. 123.
34 S.I.C., I, p. 215.
35 S.I.C., V, pp. 862–85.
36 S.I.C., II, pp. 215–30.
37 S.I.C., I, p. 584.
38 *Cornhill Magazine*, X, July–December 1864, p. 549ff, 'Middle-class Education in England: Girls'.
39 Acland, op. cit., pp. 257–8, letter of T. D. Acland to his wife, 30 November 1865.
40 S.I.C., V, p. 952.
41 S.I.C., I, pp. 607–8.
42 S.I.C., V, p. 324.
43 Ibid, p. 325.
44 These were, James Hill (Charity Commissioner); Vice-Chancellor Sir William Page Wood; Thomas Hare (Inspector of Charities); R. R. W. Lingen; John Wickens (Junior Counsel to the Crown in Equity); J. P. Fearon; and the Master of the Rolls, Lord Romilly.
45 See below, this chapter, p. 196, for Hare's involvement in the affairs of Monmouth School.
46 'Middle-class Education', taken from the *Journal of the Farmers' Club*, February 1865, p. 3. (Copy in D.E.S. Library.)
47 Ibid, pp. 5–6.
48 S.I.C., V, p. 487.
49 Ibid, p. 609.
50 S.I.C., VIII, p. 169.
51 *Times*, 25 November 1864. Some Liberals found Ellicott's views on social questions appalling: Granville once asked, 'Is he really such a fool as he seems?' (Quoted in G. Kitson Clark, Churchmen and the Condition of

England,' p. 249.)
52 *National Church*, July, 1873, p. 189.
53 See above, Note 24.
54 National Society, General Minutes (Church House, Westminster), 10 November 1865.
55 *Times*, 8 November 1865.
56 *S.I.C.*, XVIII, p. 193, 238, 287.
57 *S.I.C.*, XIII, p. 72, 56, 30, 64.
58 *S.I.C.*, XIV, p. 236, 227.
59 *S.I.C.*, XV, p. 541, 537, 596.
60 Ibid, p. 419.
61 *S.I.C.*, XX, p. 538.
62 PRO ED 27/6612, Monmouth File, Charity Commission papers.
63 PRO ED 27/6617, Monmouth File, 11 February 1870.
64 R. L. Nettleship, *Memoir of Thomas Hill Green*, 1906, p. 73.
65 Hey, op. cit., pp. 267–8.
66 W. B. Stephens, 'Illiteracy and Schooling in the Provincial Towns, 1640–1870', in D. Reeder (ed.), *Urban Education in the Nineteenth Century*, London, 1977, pp. 30–1.
67 W. L. Sargant, 'On the Proposed Middle-class Examinations as a Means of Stimulating the Education of the Lower Classes', in Hill, op. cit., p. 334ff.
68 W. L. Sargant, Lord Lyttelton and Mr William Lucas Sargant on the Education of Birmingham and on Commissions of Inquiry, Birmingham, 1865.
69 Nettleship, op. cit., p. 61.
70 *S.I.C.*, V, Appendices A to D, p. 1006, 1023.
71 Ibid, pp. 957–1006.
72 *Birmingham Daily Post*, 26 May and 31 May 1865.
73 *S.I.C.*, V, p. 1010.
74 *S.I.C.*, VIII, pp. 93–4.
75 *S.I.C.*, IV, evidence of Howson, Principal of Liverpool Collegiate Institution, pp. 291–2.
76 Popular Education Commission, 1861, VI, p. 338.
77 *S.I.C.*, VIII, p. 149.
78 Ibid, p. 150, 186, 204.
79 Ibid, p. 153.
80 Ibid, p. 172.
81 Ibid, p. 162. See also Green's Report on Loughborough Grammar School in *S.I.C.*, XVI, pp. 58–62.
82 *S.I.C.*, VIII, p. 166.
83 Ibid, p. 170.
84 Ibid, p. 191.
85 Ibid, p. 232.
86 Ibid, loc. cit.
87 Ibid, pp. 232–3.
88 *S.I.C.*, VIII p. 226.
89 Ibid, p. 234.

90   R. L. Nettleship (ed.), *Works of Thomas Hill Green*, III, London, 188, p. vi; the paper is at pp. 387–412.
91   E. G. Sandford (ed.), *Memoir of Archbishop Temple by Seven Friends*, London, 1905, p. 273.
92   *S.I.C.*, V, p. 1006.
93   H. J. Roby, 'The Schools Inquiry Commission', in Sandford, *Memoir . . .*, p. 136.
94   Acland, op. cit., p. 262, letter of Temple to Acland, 12 September 1866.
95   Sandford, *Memoir . . .*, p. 134, 137.
96   Information about attendance is taken from the *Times* for the two quarters, October–December 1866, and January–March 1867.
97   Acland, op. cit., p. 265, letter to his wife, 1867 (otherwise undated).
98   All the information about the apportioning of chapter-writing is taken from Roby's contribution to Sandford, *Memoir . . .*, p. 135.
99   Ibid, pp. 135–6.
100   Quoted in B. Askwith, *The Lytteltons, A Family Chronicle of the Nineteenth Century*, London, 1975, pp. 154–5.
101   See Kitson Clark, op. cit., pp. 135–6.
102   Lord Lyttelton, *Ephemera*, London, 1864, p. 117.
103   See above, this Chapter, p. 194.
104   BM, Gladstone Papers, BM Addl. MSS, 44608, printed letter from Acland, 19 February 1868.
105   Ibid, printed letter, 23 May 1867.
106   *Times*, 2 March 1868.
107   Ibid, 4 March 1868.
108   See above, Chapter I.
109   Burns, op. cit., p. 202, 201.
110   See above, Chapter IV, p. 97.
111   Burns, op. cit., p. 201.
112   J. Roach, 'Victorian Universities . . .', *British Journal of Educational Studies*, III, 2, December 1959, p. 148.
113   *S.I.C.*, I, pp. 602–3. There is also a brief footnote, at p. 86 in I, which refers to the Report of the British Association for the Advancement of Science Committee.
114   *S.I.C.*, IV, pp. 198–210.
115   See below, Chapter IX, p. 220.
116   *S.I.C.*, II, p. 89, 81.

Response: the work of the Endowed Schools Commission

The most striking feature of the passage of the Endowed Schools Bill was the general passivity with which it was accepted by members of both Houses of Parliament. The reform of endowed schools at that time, as in 1864–5 when the S.I.C. had begun its work, was not a contentious issue, and did not seem about to become a 'party' question. It has already been noted that two leading members of the 1866 Derby administration, Stanley and Northcote, withheld their signatures from the Report, not because they disapproved of any of its recommendations, but because they did not wish to commit the new Conservative administration to indirect support for the Report in principle.[1] But it is often forgotten that the first Endowed Schools Act, which received the Royal Assent in June 1868, was passed by Disraeli's government.[2]

The preparation of the 1868 Act had been set on foot by Taunton in the Lords. In April he had asked the Lord President of the Council, Marlborough, whether the Government intended tackling the basic problem of limiting endowed-school headmasters' freehold tenure, which was a hindrance to any future programme of reform in the schools: a bill of a single clause, he said, would suffice.[3] Marlborough agreed that 'no new interests should be created pending legislation on this subject' (of endowed schools)', and he reported that he had communicated with the Home Secretary, Gathorne Hardy, with a view to introducing a bill which would limit the future interests of headmasters newly appointed, 'so that Parliament might be left free to deal with the matter in the next session'. He promised that such a measure would be prepared at once.[4] There were no further debates on what became the 1868 Act. It is therefore fair to say that a sequence of events which led to the creation of a measure whose implementation caused so much controversy, was officially initiated by a Conservative Government. A little over six years later, the next

Tory administration was to stanch trouble by amending the 1869 Endowed Schools Act.[5]

When Forster introduced the Liberal Endowed Schools Bill in February 1869, he reminded the Commons that the Report of the S.I.C. had been unanimously endorsed by the Commissioners, 'gentlemen of different political and religious opinions'.[6] Despite Tory complaints about the haste of the First Reading stage, the Bill passed smoothly through Parliament. It was the least controversial Bill, in its passage, of all Gladstone's administration. Forster was careful to establish that it embodied no threat to 'good' endowed schools, though he mentioned no schools as examples of good or bad. It was the intention of the Government 'to introduce good management' into the schools.[7] The Bill provided for the appointment of three Endowed Schools Commissioners though it did not name them. They would undertake the necessary work of reform and would, for the moment, bypass the obstructions of the Court of Chancery and the dilatoriness of the Charity Commission. The new Commissioners, he said, would be 'under the greatest sense of responsibility to local and public interests. Public opinion is, after all, the best check in this country'.[8] Forster expressed his own predisposition towards Provincial Boards, as outlined by the S.I.C., as the ideal reforming agency 'if we could find such a constituency as we required'.[9] He also regretted the omission from the Bill of provision for an inspection agency and for rate-aided secondary schools.[10] Nevertheless, it is worth reflecting on the fact that he was speaking only a year before the passage of another Bill, also introduced by him, which provided for the wholesale financing of elementary education from the rates. Also, in July 1869, a Select Committee reported upon 'County Financial Arrangements', recording its desire that local rating in counties should be placed upon a more representative footing.[11] Part II of the 1869 Bill, which would have appointed a Council of Examinations, was dropped at the Committee stage, in the interests of expediency.

It is important to reconstruct accurately the sequence of decisions which comprised the drafting of the Endowed Schools Bill, which involved the omission of a number of the most interesting of the S.I.C.'s proposals. The brief for Cabinet discussion was prepared by Roby, formerly Secretary of the S.I.C., in the month when Gladstone took office.[12] His memorandum followed closely the S.I.C.'s analysis of existing school provision and their suggestions for reform. It already contained some interesting deviations from the Report's proposals. In the second section, headed 'The Remedies proposed by the Commissioners', Roby outlined the need to substitute for the action of Chancery 'the action of Commissioners with the tacit consent of Parliament'; an arrangement similar to those earlier made in connection with the Oxford University Act and the Public Schools Act. Also, the section entitled 'Machinery Suggested by the Commissioners' stressed that it was important for the work to be done quickly and simultaneously; that the needs and wishes of each locality should be fully considered and local opinions heard; and that the work of reform should be undertaken by 'Commissioners or Provincial Boards'. The 'or' in the last proposal suggests that a preliminary discussion had taken place at which the S.I.C.'s uncompromising recommendation of local boards had been modified to produce a clear alternative. This decision was probably Forster's, since he had not taken part in the final drafting of S.I.C. recommendations and was currently taking into account the findings of the Committee on County Financial Arrangements.[13]

The generally bland acceptance of the new Act is partly explained by the greater controversies which encompassed other measures passing through Parliament in the first years of Gladstone's administration. The Irish Church Bill was introduced on 1 March 1869, between the First and Second Readings of Forster's measure. The first Irish Land Act became law in 1870; and a year later the University Tests Act was passed. All these measures contained revolutionary implications and, for the time being, attracted the main fire of opposition. So initially the Endowed Schools Act escaped controversy, even though it contained contentious items such as the reform of endowments, the competitive principle in the allocation of charity money, the destruction of Church monopoly, conscience clauses, and the temporary interference of the central government in local affairs. By 1874, however, the Endowed Schools Act lay in ruins, the victim, it has been suggested, of vast and various opposition.

In another respect the terms of the Act were an elaborate skein of concealment. The possible interpretations of the Act were infinite, for while no reference was made in it to the work of the S.I.C., it was implicit in its clauses that the three reforming Commissioners would be expected to use the Taunton Report as a major point of reference when they came to prepare schemes for schools. The powers of the

Commissioners were therefore potentially immense. They could override *cy près*; they could augment and amalgamate trusts, move schools, and apply non-educational endowments to education. It was their duty to prepare schemes which could include the appointment of entirely new governing bodies. They could decide that the master of a school need not be in holy orders, and they could apply part or the whole of an endowment to girls' education.

Much depended, therefore, on who the Commissioners would be, and the Government refused to announce their names until the day after the Bill became law, on 2 August 1869. Lyttelton, Hobhouse and Robinson, with their Secretary, Roby, held their first meeting on the day their names were published.[14] The appointment of Lyttelton seems to have been Gladstone's doing. In June Lyttelton had written to the Prime Minister that he was 'very flattered by the wish of the Government that I should be First Commissioner', but that he had to refuse since he would find it difficult to treat the most urgent issues – perhaps he had Birmingham in view – with a mind 'free from previous conclusions'. He quoted Charles Evans, Headmaster of Birmingham, as saying that he hoped the new Commissioners would be 'persons free from bias or appearance of such'.[15] Any doubts which might have been entertained about this new agency by potential opponents must have been confirmed as soon as Arthur Hobhouse's name was announced. The conjunction of Hobhouse and Lyttelton may have convinced at least a few that the Liberal Government had printed a licence for iconoclasm.

Yet it can be argued that the opposition to the working of the Act, though pressing after August 1869, was not overwhelming; that the Commission achieved a great deal during a short span of time – in the first instance they were granted only three years in which to accomplish such a massive task; that opposition, when it came, was stage-managed, rather than spontaneous; that the Commissioners were given assistance of a remarkable kind and quantity; and finally that the abolition of the triumvirate, and its replacement by an extended Charity Commission, was immediately caused by an attempt to deal with a clash of relationships within the Tory Party which had little to do with educational issues.

The Commissioners worked efficiently and strictly within the terms of the Act. Each Commissioner had an assistant, and Roby became first Secretary. Lyttelton dealt with his home ground, the Midlands, assisted by C. H. Stanton; Hobhouse covered his own

West Country, with J. G. Fitch; and Robinson worked the area he knew best, the North of England, with D. R. Fearon.[16] All three assistant commissioners had served the S.I.C. in a similar capacity. The Commission did not purse its work inflexibly, and their plan of regional apportionment was distorted by the need, or their desire, to deal with hospital schools at an early stage, with the largest endowments, and with points of definition raised by Forster's Elementary Act after 1870.[17]

In 1870, before concerted opposition had begun to reveal itself, Lyttelton wrote to Gladstone of his 'excellent and most able Mr Hobhouse' who was 'strongly anti-ecclesiastical'; Robinson was equally able, and though 'not exactly anti-ecclesiastical . . . 'somewhat latitudinarian and Erastian'.[18] As their work advanced they were criticised by Dissenters for being an Anglican clique, and by the party which published the *National Church* as despoilers of Church institutions.

Preliminary instructions to assistant commissioners were outlined in Paper F. Firstly they should arrange private consultations with local governors,[19] who should be informed of the heads under which a scheme would be drafted: the constitution of the governing body, the scope of the School, whether day or boarding, ages of scholars, limits of fees, the course of study, exhibitions, and headmaster's stipend. Paper F also established the authority of the S.I.C. Report for much of what the Commissioners had to do: '. . . the Commissioners have accordingly taken the recommendations of the Report as their principal guides on those points on which the Act itself does not speak'.[20] This was one of the most controversial factors in their proceedings. It was their duty to consult the S.I.C. Report 'to see how far and in what mode these principles are applicable to the actually existing state of facts, and to devise the best methods of applying them in each case'. The Act did not mention the tripartite grading of schools, a characteristic it shared with the 1944 Education Act. Yet the Commissioners affirmed in Paper F their clear intention of grading schools.[21] They anticipated that cases where they would wish to transfer a school to another locality would be rare. For their opponents on the Tory–Anglican side, the most unwarranted principle which the Commissioners applied was that 'there should be no gratuitous education except as the reward of merit'. Members of the Church Defence Institution and others translated this into the more succinct and politically telling 'Robbery of the Poor'.

The assistant commissioners' modes of working were determined partly by local circumstances; and among these were the accidental personal contacts which they already had in certain areas. In October 1869, the annual meeting of the Social Science Association was held in Bristol.[22] One of the papers given in the middle-class section was by Joshua Fitch. It dealt with the Educational Council in the Endowed Schools Bill.[23] It was read several months after the Bill had been divided in Committee, and with hindsight it can be said that Fitch was, in this case, espousing a lost cause. However, one of those there to hear him was John Percival, sometime assistant at Rugby under Temple, and, on Temple's recommendation, Charles Evans' successor as Headmaster of Clifton College.[24]

In the following year at the Newcastle conference of the S.S.A. Percival himself presented a very remarkable paper entitled 'By What Means Can a Direct Connection be Established between the Elementary and Secondary Schools and the Universities?'[25] He acknowledged that England was passing through 'a period of unusual activity' in educational matters, and he thought that the most interesting current question related, not to any particular branch, but to '. . . the organising of our whole system, and the co-ordering of different grades, so that forces now wasting may be economised, and the national life, which was never in greater danger of splitting into sections, may be bound closer together by this most effective of all bonds'.[26] The achievement of this end, he said, would be facilitated by the appointment of 'a Minister of Education', with responsibility for every grade, rather like von Humboldt sixty-two years before in Prussia. The elementary schools might be linked to middle-class schools by exhibitions. But the most pressing problem of alienation, as he saw it, lay in the comparative absence of communication between the Universities and the secondary schools. The men who frequented the Universities were not those 'who are directing the life of Liverpool, Manchester, Newcastle, Bristol, or Birmingham', but the sons of country gentlemen, or men destined for certain professions. This was a question which touched the business class very sensitively, for it behoved them to remember 'that even in business they may fall behind if they, as a class, get separated from the highest culture'.[27]

In its context Percival's paper must stand as a document containing evidence of great vision and liberal determination. In his own career at Clifton he embodied, so far as he was able, the implementation of the kind of principle he was recommending at Newcastle. His educational interests ran widely. He gave his own first school a reputation for scholarship. He established, in one of the poorer parishes of Bristol, the Clifton College Ragged School in which Clifton boys taught as a species of social service.[28] When Bristol seemed likely to create a School Board after 1870 he offered himself as a candidate, and overrode the objections of the College Council in achieving his aim, on the condition that he never became Chairman. Also, Percival might be seen as the leader of an influential group of Churchmen-educationists all of whom were resident in Bristol during the twenty years 1860 to 1880.[29]

O. F. Christie, in his history of Clifton College records one master's memory of Percival: 'he would "stand out on the Downs and hear Bristol" as a prophet might listen to the sounds of a great city'.[30] A letter which he wrote to Fitch, who was assistant commissioner for Bristol schemes, might well have been prompted by one of these moments of solitary reflection. It was dated 27 March 1870, six months before the Newcastle paper. He said that the proposal he was going to make was based on a recent suggestion which Fitch had made to him, perhaps during informal conversation at the Bristol conference. He wished that Clifton might be incorporated into the 'general scheme for the endowments of Bristol'.[31] He presented a brief description of the College's statutes and more tellingly of its financial position: 'Our income depends entirely upon the charges for tuition' (always a weakness in an 'independent' school). He realised that Bristol, after the City of London, was the most wealthily endowed muncipality in the kingdom. His plan was that some local charity money might be used for the incorporation of Clifton as an endowed school, as had happened in the town of Taunton by a scheme of the Charity Commissioners.[32] The College would then stand as the first-grade school for the City; the Grammar School, also by this time a healthy institution, would become the second-grade school; and the hospital schools, led by Colston's, would provide the bases for a system of third-grade elementary schools. He thought that the College Council would have no objection to the proposal. He was perhaps optimistic when he said that such a suggestion emanating from him might arouse 'some local jealousy', whereas anything proposed by the Commissioners would be accepted 'as the wish of a higher power, against which some may perhaps reserve the privilege of grumbling, but to which they know they must submit'.

Since the original suggestion seems to have come from Fitch it is hardly surprising that he took it up wholeheartedly in his communication with Hobhouse, his senior colleague, while admitting that Percival 'would like to see some element of permanence introduced into the Constitution (of the College) through the work of the Commission'.[33] By November, however, the proposal was shelved. It is not clear what precisely led Fitch and Hobhouse to this decision. But it seems that information about the 'secret' scheme had been leaked to Caldicott, the Headmaster of the Grammar School, who naturally saw Clifton as a rival rather than a hierarchically superior institution.[34]

There can be little doubt but that the Fitch–Percival proposal soured the rest of the long negotiations over Bristol charities, the final scheme for which came before Parliament in 1875.[35] Fitch's task at Bristol was immense; and there are grounds for suggesting that the final schemes for the City's schools comprised the greatest triumph of all for the Endowed Schools Commission. Yet the early passage of events of dealing with difficult local issues by means of local professional contacts points up the danger inherent in the Commissioners' autocratic manner of working a public Act. Fitch acted high-mindedly, yet on his own terms, and, at first, with incomplete knowledge of the feelings of the middle classes in Bristol.

The problems facing Fitch in Bristol can be contrasted markedly with the smoothness of the process of reform undertaken by the Commissioners in Yorkshire. Canon Robinson dealt with the northern area, assisted by Fearon. Of all the Commissioners' regional activities those in Yorkshire were by far the most successful. Reflecting in 1873 on his experience in the county, Robinson could say that, perhaps due to his previous occupation in the area,[36] the work in the West Riding had been completed quickly.[37] Before this first phase of northern reform had ended a county committee had come into being which helped with the changes in the West and North Ridings.

This was the Yorkshire Education Society, with the Archbishop as President, supported by the Bishop of Ripon and ten local M.P.s, and noblemen like the Duke of Devonshire and Lord Zetland. As well as helping with reform schemes for local schools, this *ad hoc* body favoured setting up a 'county' school. The immediate inspiration for founding the Yorkshire Society had been the publication, early in 1870, of the S.I.C. volume containing Fitch's reports on Yorkshire

endowed and proprietary schools. On 18 January a meeting was held
in Leeds, with Wharncliffe in the chair, to discuss local aspects of the
middle-class problem.[38] Referring to the report of 'the Revd Mr
Fitch' (sic), Wharncliffe noted that he had drawn attention to the
inadequacy of the majority of the people as judges of what good
middle-class education should be. He remarked that if the south of
England could provide itself with public schools for the middle
classes, then so could a wealthy area like Yorkshire. He mentioned
especially Suffolk, where 'an intimate friend of his', Kerrison,[39] had
been one of the most active promoters of the new county school at
Framlingham. The Dean of York and the Vicar of Leeds seconded his
proposal that a middle-class boarding school should be started in
Yorkshire. Within a day land had been offered and £650 subscribed.[40]

There was another body active in the West Riding, the Yorkshire
Board of Education.[41] Its members helped Robinson towards the
greatest single achievement of the Endowed Schools Commission in
the county. In 1872 D. R. Fearon published an article entitled 'An
Educational Experiment in Yorkshire'.[42] He began by posing four
questions of current interest: how to found in a manufacturing town
a system of secondary education for boys adapted to special local
needs; how to ensure that the 'intelligent and careful members of the
working classes' were able to obtain a share in this education for
their sons; how to reform an old and decayed endowment so as to
'popularise', without wasting, its resources; and finally how to
extend to girls the benefits of such an endowment. All these things, he
said, had recently been achieved at Keighley under the aegis of the
Endowed Schools Commissioners.[43]

In 1867 the Mechanics' Institute at Keighley was in a depressed
condition and the managers had begun to press for the construction
of a new building, also hoping to extend its work to the 'provision of
scientific and technical instruction.'[44] They believed that such
instruction would enable English skilled workers to compete more
favourably with their foreign counterparts.[45] While they were delib-
erating, the Yorkshire Board of Education 'gave to their proposals a
definite shape and a support which was very valuable'. Fearon
described the Board as 'a voluntary association of Yorkshire
noblemen, country gentlemen, and manufacturers' whose rôle could
be defined as the doing of educational work in the county which was
not being done by any other body. 'Their work is the work of

educational initiative – a most valuable work in a busy county, and one which a local body is particularly fitted to perform.'

The models for the Keighley enterprise were largely foreign. Fearon mentioned La Martinière at Lyons and the Turgot School in Paris. The new building had been started in 1869; but meanwhile 'a new force had come into action, which disturbed all the calculations of the promoters'. This was the Endowed Schools Commission. The Commissioners' first concern was for the two ancient endowments in Keighley, Drake's and Tonson's, which together had an income of £300. Early in 1870 Robinson informed the men of Keighley that their local endowments were to be reorganised. The promoters of the work there at once opened negotiations with the Commissioners.[46]

Robinson was enthusiastic about a possible amalgamation of interests in the town. But he was also aware of the necessity for treading carefully, since he knew there was a marked local division between radical and conservative interests. His advice to Fearon on the conduct of his business at Keighley showed the value of his long experience of education and politics in the West Riding:

> The rector of Keighly is a man of some ability and a gentleman. He is unobtrusively High Church, not much in rapport with the great body of his parishioners, somewhat old, not likely to sympathise with any bold reform. . . . All churchmen are in favour of the Trade School idea except the rector . . . He has a curate . . . who was once a pupil of mine at York Training College, a superior sort of man in his way, able, I imagine, to tell you something of the mind and temper of the place, and to suggest suitable persons for interviewing. Another old York pupil of mine is a rising trades- man and active churchwarden. . . . I can confidently recommend him as a man knowing K. well. Call on him and the curate using my name. Mr Laycock for whom I enclose a note is agent to the Duke of Devonshire. He is a leading Methodist and can get you the views of that party.[47]

It is clear, however, that when Fearon visited Keighley he soon became attached to advice from one particular source. The informa- tion about the recent events at the Mechanics' Institute he obtained, through H. H. Sayles, Secretary to the Yorkshire Board, from Swire Smith, a wealthy woollen manufacturer, leader of the technical education movement in the West Riding and later to be a member of the Royal Commission on Technical Instruction.[48] Smith met Fearon in May 1870, and conducted him round the new building with Sayles. Later in the same month Fearon put to them 'my proposition for converting the Grammar School into a girls' school and subsidising the Trade School'. In spite of two protest meetings organised by the conservatives, Robinson accepted Fearon's suggestion in principle the following month.[49]

In the Autumn of 1870 the Keighley scheme became law. The buildings were opened by the Duke of Devonshire, and the guest-list included Robinson, Lord Frederick Cavendish (President of the Yorkshire Board), Forster, Henry Cole, Baines, Fearon, Bernhard Samuelson, C. S. Roundell and Sayles.[50] It is interesting that the 1875 Report of the Mechanics' Institute suggested that the founders of the institution had in 1870 'begun to consider the organising of a Trade School after the model of the one which was established at Bristol', and that Moseley's model had come to their attention through the agency of Sayles. But the final achievement of this objective, the Report stated, 'had been made possible by Mr Forster's scheme for the reorganisation of the secondary schools of the kingdom'.[51]

The Keighley scheme was remarkable for a variety of reasons. With the exception of the Bristol Trade School, which was part of the Merchant Venturers' scheme for that City,[52] Keighley was unique. The scheme also pointed up a moral for the draftsmen of the 1869 Act, in that its smooth completion had been the result of a combination of initiative in the town, of promotion and guidance from a 'county' body, and of objective yet sympathetic direction by agents of central government. More remarkable still was the fact that the 'county' body seems to have represented the interests of divergent political groups. The events at Keighley showed that such practical co-operation was possible. The only weak element in this convergence of interests lay in the relative impotence of the local charities and the complacency of their guardians. Nevertheless the success of the scheme raises the hypothetical question of what might have happened in a number of other localities if the reforming agencies defined in the 1869 Bill had included strong local elements.

The Yorkshire Board shared many of the characteristics of the 'county' associations and committees described earlier.[53] Some of the county associations remained active in the field of secondary education after 1869 and in general demonstrated their intention of trying to co-operate with the Endowed Schools Commission when its agents visited their localities. The *ad hoc* Yorkshire Society was therefore not alone.

The appointment of Frederick Temple to the vacant see of Exeter has been adjudged one of the most controversial acts of Tait's tenure of Canterbury.[54] Temple was not intimidated by the reaction to his appointment within his new diocese; and he had old friends and allies among the local laity, like Acland, Fortescue, Northcote and Taunton. Opposing him stood Dean Boyd, a truculent defender of Exeter charities and of the interests of the City against those of the county of Devon.

At Exeter in October 1870, a county meeting was called to consider the application of the Endowed Schools Act to Devonshire. Lord Devon, who had been considered by Granville as a possible chairman for the S.I.C. moved the first resolution: 'That, in considering the most expedient mode of employing educational endowments available in the county, it was necessary, while paying due regard to local wants, to take into consideration the requirements of the county generally'.[55] His resolution contained the fundamental feature of the programmes of this and other county association: the desire to supersede petty local conservatism, and to introduce a comprehensive element into the county's view of its own educational needs. He ended his speech by hoping that the county would 'co-operate with the Commissioners, (giving them) an assistance which he believed would be welcomed by the Commissioners themselves'.

Bishop Temple proposed the second resolution, which was appropriately more technical: 'That the educational organisation of the county, so far as endowed schools are concerned, should consist of schools of different grades, so connected together by Exhibitions as that the progress of the deserving scholar from a school of a lower grade to one of a higher grade may be provided for and facilitated'. He then expansively explained the principles on which his resolution was based. This, as will be found in each of the county examples to be discussed, was an essential part of the 'county committee' process, perhaps in the long term the most important part: that members of the ruling hierarchy, who had connections with the conduct of national affairs, should explain and interpret the policy of the Government in their localities. At a rather late stage, the middle classes were being 'educated' in relation to the schooling of their children. Sir John Coleridge seconded Temple, saying that 'this was no place to discuss the Act'. Their duty was 'to carry out its principles'; the Commissioners would be sure to benefit from 'the assistance of a body of gentlemen who would represent on this question the general opinion of the best intelligence in this county'.

Stafford Northcote moved the third resolution and also besought his neighbours to 'proceed in the spirit of the Act'. They were in the process of founding a national system of education, and it ought to be possible to bring endowments within their system. His farming analogy probably impressed his audience, though it was hardly elegant:

> They should look upon these endowments in the same way as they now did on the acts of those who in former days sank a large amount of money in drainage of their own estates. Now, recognising the importance of drainage, they were desirous of constructing great arterial drains throughout the country, with which these isolated drains should be brought into connection, to the advantage both of the country at large, and the separate estates.

Northcote's main contribution to the meeting lay in his proposal that, while Devonshire endowments were not separately very profitable, the county's resources ought to be treated as an aggregate; and that the Commissioners should be approached according to that principle. In addition he stressed the need to provide for female education by means of endowments.

J. W. Walrond moved the appointment of a committee which would include all the noblemen, trustees of schools, and the leading gentry of the county. He was warmly supported by the final speaker, Joshua Fitch, who said that the Commissioners would be only too glad to co-operate with such a committee; but that it would have to be constituted in a manner which would prove acceptable to those who would eventually administer the schools. He touched upon the question of the Commissioners' large powers, but assured the meeting that they had no intention of attempting to 'make a clean sweep of all the endowments in one common fund and distribute them equally throughout the country'. A committee was chosen and the meeting adjourned.

In Devonshire it is clear that Temple, with Northcote's authoritative assistance, was adopting the rôle of advocate for the Endowed Schools Commission. He knew his territory well, and it seems that he was anticipating resistance which might arise, particularly in Exeter. For in February 1870, he had addressed the anniversary meeting of the Exeter Grammar School.[56] Northcote, a trustee, was unable to attend. Temple devoted his good-humoured speech to a lucid description of the intended work of the Commission, and in particular to the checks on its powers at Committee of Council and Parliamentary level. 'As it has been remarked', he said, 'there is nothing to prevent the Commissioners from turning a boys' school in

Devonshire into a girls' school in Lancashire.'[57] However, he did not think 'that they have the power of turning you all into girls'. Their powers had to be great and wide-ranging because there was no formula by which the Act could have expressed the needs of each town: this had to be left to the discretion of the Commissioners in consultation with the inhabitants. He thought that Exeter would have a grammar school 'in some shape or other'.

He also tendered advice to the Commissioners. In July 1870, he wrote to them because he understood that the Exeter Town Council had requested an early visit from Fitch. Temple thought that there was a strong reason 'why the two western counties should be dealt with early'. Devon and Cornwall, he said, should be treated together; likewise Somerset and Dorset. 'Moreover I think . . . there is a very strong desire indeed in Devon and Cornwall to take up the reorganisation of schools vigorously, and I should decidedly advise that that desire should be encouraged by immediate action.'[58] Roby replied that as yet the Commissioners had no precise plans for those areas; in fact their preoccupations lay elsewhere.[59]

The separation of Exeter from the county in the negotiations with the Commissioners became clear when the Town Council appointed a committee to represent Town interests. A meeting of this committee was held in April 1871, at which Fitch and Temple were present.[60] The Bishop attended with the special purpose of counteracting expressions of narrow local opinion. He warned the meeting that 'any place pursuing the selfish policy of thinking of itself without any reference to the outside world would in the end lose a great deal more than it gained'. He reminded Exeter of its status as county town and said that its citizens should never forget 'the rights and still less the duties of a county town'. The Dean of Exeter spoke on behalf of Town interests. He said that the County Committee contained members much more influential than those representing the City; and it therefore became the City Committee 'to make a bold and determined stand for the interests of the City'. The question as he saw it was one of finance: Exeter should not be 'swamped in the county of Devon', losing her patrimony by seeing it absorbed in the coffers of the county.

In May 1871, the City Committee published its scheme which required that City charities should be treated separately from those of the county.[61] In the following month Fitch sent an extensive report on the Exeter schools to the Commission.[62] In July Lyttelton

received a four-page document headed, 'Recommendations which
the Devon County Committee on Educational Endowments propose
to submit to the Endowed Schools Commissioners'.[63] The main
principle of the County Committee had been 'to make the educational endowments and institutions of the county useful to the
whole of it' and 'to do this as far as may be without removing them
from the places where they actually stand'. It had been found,
however, 'that the latter aim must sometimes give way to the former'. Wherever a community was felt able to support a day school,
the Committee had avoided the controversial tendency to accept the
principle of allowing boarding pupils.

Three 'great educational centres' had been identified in the county:
Exeter, Tiverton and Crediton. These already had University connections. To these ought to be added Plymouth which was as well
endowed as the others, but at present mainly for elementary education. The first three towns should therefore be able to maintain
first-grade schools, and Crediton should have a first-grade girls'
school. This and the boys' school at Tiverton ought to have accommodation for boarders. The Committee went into considerable
detail over the provision of second- and third-grade boarding and
day schools, and their decisions were founded upon the practical
availability of existing endowments in various areas of the county.
They also established the principles on which educational endowments should be made to serve the needs of 'deserving boys' from the
elementary schools. 'Until the Legislature has provided a system of
examinations' for the three grades of schools, the best examiners for
scholarships and exhibitions, they thought, would be the headmasters of schools of the first and second grades.

Fortescue played a leading part in the meetings of the Devon
Committee, while safeguarding the interests of his County School.
He wrote to Brereton in March 1871, giving details of the county
scheme which he had helped to prepare. He noted that the Duke of
Bedford had promised land on which to relocate Kelly College, at
Tavistock, and said that he himself had guided the Committee away
from a proposal to establish another middle-class boys' school which
would have competed with West Buckland. He wrote, 'the Commissioners are likely to be much influenced, and rightly so, by our
County Committee. . . . We owe much to our good Bishop in bringing and keeping (the County Committee) together so well'.[64]

Eventually, despite all these plans, the county's trusts were settled independently of each other. Exeter's scheme, for instance, was finally adopted in 1873.[65] But the experience of Devonshire nevertheless emphasises the persistence of the 'county' idea in the minds of both the official and unofficial agents of the Endowed Schools Commission, and in the policy of the traditional leaders of county society. There is little doubt but that Temple remained a guiding force in the affairs of Exeter, despite its local pride and prejudice. In a printed letter which he addressed to the Mayor in February 1872, he propounded the principle of grading middle-class schools in the City, and defended the Commissioners' proposals against the common imputation that they wished to deprive the poor of their traditional sources of aid for elementary education. In 1905 Michael Sadler produced his 'Report of the Secondary and Higher Education in Exeter' in which he pointed out that the City had a higher proportion of boys and girls attending secondary schools than any other city in the country. He concluded that this was due 'in no small measure to the educational improvements which were carried out in Exeter about thirty years ago, largely under the influence of Dr Temple'.[66]

In October 1869, the *Gloucester Journal* carried reports on two conferences held lately at Bristol. The first, the Social Science Congress, has been referred to already.[67] The second, held a fortnight later, was the conference of the Gloucester diocese at which a leading paper in the section on 'Middle-class Education' was presented by Earl Ducie, the Lord Lieutenant of the county, whose father had been a member of the 1849 Commission on Charities, one of the founders of the Royal Agricultural College at Cirencester, and President of the Royal Society of Agriculture.[68] Ducie was a Liberal until he abandoned Gladstone over Home Rule in 1886, and he was a close friend of Lyttelton. It is perhaps interesting that, of the 14,500 acres owned by the family in 1883, one acre, worth £122 p.a., was in the centre of Manchester. This partly explains why Ducie's father had been a contributor to the funds of the Manchester Church Education Society during the 1840s.[69]

In his paper on middle-class education Ducie addressed himself to 'its present condition and its requirements in this county'.[70] He was not interested in the section of the middle class which sent its sons to Cheltenham, Marlborough or Clifton; but rather in those who oscillated between the better elementary schools and the private schools. He evidently hoped for much from the 1869 Act, but warned that 'local prejudices, vested interests, and obstructiveness of ordinary parochial type' would be encountered before it could be fully applied. Like Temple and Northcote in Devon, he took it upon himself to interpret for a local audience the main principles of the Act and also provided a detailed summary of the S.I.C. reports on Gloucestershire endowed schools.

Mr Holland, speaking second to Ducie, supported his proposal for a 'County College', but thought that a 'County Board, made up of those gentlemen in the county who had an interest in the subject, and with representatives from the different endowments', would supply a useful agency for surveying local needs and making appropriate plans. The County Board suggestion was taken by one of Gloucestershire's Liberal M.P.s, S. S. Dickinson: he thought such a Board might co-ordinate the administration of both elementary and secondary education. Ducie returned to the debate on his paper, hoping that such proposals, coming from an Anglican conference, would not antagonise Nonconformity in the county. Canon J. P. Norris of Bristol spoke in favour of spreading the boarding-school idea and argued for a better system of female education. Percival of Clifton proposed boarding schools for rural areas and day schools for the towns.

The local prejudices of which Ducie had been aware soon set themselves to work. In a letter entitled, 'The Late Conference', J. P. Heane, a Gloucester city councillor, lent his support in the press to the Mayor of Gloucester's opposition to the county proposal, referring to the county-school idea as 'a sort of Great Eastern ship'.[71] On the other hand, Dickinson contributed a most useful conciliatory letter to the debate. He felt sure that the Commissioners would exercise what he called ironically their "despotic powers" with good sense; and he went on, 'It seems in every way desirable that the trustees of the various schools . . . within a compact area such as a county offers, should consult with each other and with the Commissioners to agree upon some system of reorganisation and rearranging the existing schools of the county, so as, in the language of the Act, 'to render them most conducive to education'.[72] Dickinson could speak authoritatively on the language of the Act since he had sat beside Forster when the Minister introduced the 1869 Bill to the Commons. In further letters he tried to inform the public about the S.I.C.'s recommendations.[73]

An immediate result of the Diocesan conference occurred in the form of a meeting of county trustees in November 1869, at the Shire

Hall, convened by Ducie. The Bishop was present, as was Moseley, representing Bristol trustees. Ducie declared that he had been persuaded to drop his county-school idea and to adopt instead a plan of 'judicious reform' of existing schools.[74] He said that, although the Act had made no provision for creating provincial boards, the Commissioners would welcome any help that may be offered locally. 'I have the authority of Lord Lyttelton for saying than anything we submit to them will receive due consideration.' It might be difficult to produce immediately 'any perfect or synthetical scheme'; but no doubt representatives of the county could 'contribute to the edifice of the future'. The Bishop proposed the first resolution: 'That it is desirable for the educational endowments of the county . . . to be organised in such a manner as, while having due regard to the educational interests of the localities in which they are situated, to provide for the educational wants of the county at large'. Allowing for slight adjustments of wording, this was precisely the sentiment expressed in the later resolution of the Devon County Committee.[75] Dickinson, seconding the Bishop's resolution, hoped that Bristol might be included, largely, it might be presumed, because of its immense wealth of endowment. But he uttered the first anticipation of separation by saying that, even without Bristol, the county had a population of 300,000.

Mr Whitcomb, speaking for the trustees of the Crypt School, Gloucester, which was being worked under a Chancery Scheme of 1860, defended its integrity against any possible future meddling by the Commissioners. But Curtis Hayward, supporter of Industrial Schools and trustee of Cheltenham College, drew his attention to the question of whether they, 'as Gloucestershire men', wished to act together. He recommended that a committee of trustees be formed at a further meeting. Whitcomb, however, objected to such meetings on the grounds that they tended to be occasions on which 'a certain number of persons came there with their friends'.

His line of argument was reinforced, and the separation of Gloucester underlined, by a public meeting called by the Mayor to consider steps to be taken 'for protecting the interests of the City in its several endowments'.[76] At that meeting J. P. Heane compared the Commissioners to Cromwell's Major-Generals; and while he thought there should be union between the City and the county, it ought not to be at the expense of the City.

Despite these emissions of discontent the County Committee

proceeded. Later in December Ducie chaired a meeting attended by all the county M.P.s, and by Lord Redesdale, Mr Stanton (who had inspected Gloucestershire for the S.I.C.), and the Mayor of Gloucester.[77] Ducie announced that it had been thought inadvisable to press Bristol to join with the Committee, 'having regard to the amount of Bristol endowments, and the large number of intelligent persons residing there'. This was probably interpreted by some prominent Gloucester citizens as a calculated slight to themselves; certainly it seems to reflect clearly the attitude of the leaders of the county towards urban middle-class men whom they considered to be their inferiors in matters as sophisticated as the organisation of middle-class education. The Bishop moved for an inquiry into the existing educational resources of the county, pointing to the valuable work done by the County Board in the diocese of Worcester.[78] He remarked upon the recent progress made by the Crypt School and hoped that a general scheme for the county might be put to the Commissioners. Lord Redesdale was evidently attending with some reluctance: probably reflecting on his unilateral reform of the Grammar School of which he was patron, at Chipping Campden, he said he would prefer the interference of the Endowed Schools Commissioners to the action of a local committee characterised by petty prejudices. But a committee of inquiry was appointed: it included Ducie, the Earl of Harrowby, Redesdale (who promised not to attend meetings), the Dean of Gloucester, Sir Michael Hicks-Beach, Sotherton-Estcourt, Canon Tinling (a former H.M.I.), Moseley (despite the secession of Bristol), the Mayors of Gloucester and Tewkesbury, and several headmasters of endowed schools.

The intensiveness of activity in the county, and his personal contact with Ducie, prompted Lyttelton, early in 1870, to intervene in Gloucestershire unofficially on two occasions. Both were attempts to undertake a rather hasty education of public opinion in order to smooth the way for official action by the Commission. They took the form of letters to Ducie and Winterbotham, another county M.P., and were printed in the *Gloucester Journal*.[79]

The County Committee had meanwhile further refined its plans by appointing sub-committees for dealing with three main departments of the county, the Gloucester district, the Cotswolds, and the Wooton district.[80] But the worst fears of those defenders of City interests must have been confirmed by an account of Fitch's proposals for Bristol charities which appeared in the *Journal* in April 1870. The editorial described this as 'a revolution' and 'a very alarming and monstrous innovation indeed'.[81]

While the County Committee was at work the Cathedral Chapter, led by Tinling, and the Town Council were proposing their own scheme for the City schools, which would have involved the amalgamation of the Crypt School, the Cathedral School, and Sir Thomas Rich's Bluecoat School.[82] Nothing came of this, however, until 1882 when, by a scheme of the Charity Commissioners, the schools of the City, excluding the Cathedral School, were put together under one trust.[83]

At a meeting of the County Committee with Fitch in December 1870, Ducie was most conciliatory towards Gloucester interests. Canon Tinling described the City's plan for uniting their schools and outlined the course of his discussion with the Commissioners in London. Fitch gave an account of the principles to be adopted in relation to the county.[84] Early in 1871 Ducie circulated a memorandum to members of the Committee which was a detailed list of suggestions relating to the precise place each endowed school would have in a county system. His first principle was that

if the Endowed Schools Act is to be carried on in Gloucestershire on the principles recommended by the Schools Inquiry Commission, and if it be true of the county as of the Kingdom in general, 'that at present each school is taking a line of its own, with little reference to the needs of the place in which the school stands . . .' (p. 577, Schools Inquiry Report); and if we agree with the Commissioners (p. 630) 'that it is essential to efficiency that the schools over a considerable district should be dealt with in relation to each other', we may be satisfied that a complete and systematic organisation of our Endowed Schools is necessary.[85]

It is impossible to know how much influence Fitch had brought to bear on Ducie; but in his memorandum the Lord Lietenant proposed that efforts should be made to bring Cheltenham College within the small circle of first-grade county schools under any scheme or schemes. In any case it seems that Curtis Hayward and Thomas Baker, members of both the County Committee and the Council of Cheltenham College, had known nothing of Ducie's proposal for the College before he announced it publicly.[86] The similarity between the Clifton scheme in relation to Bristol[87] and the Cheltenham College idea as part of the county plan would seem to suggest that Fitch's influence had been at work in the latter case also. Ducie was a member of the Clifton College Council. After a debate on Ducie's memorandum in which Cheltenham was eliminated from the plan, a copy of it was sent to the Commissioners and to each set of trustees in the county.

In fact nothing came of the Gloucestershire Committee's attempts to co-ordinate reform in the county. The Gloucester opposition, led by Heane, obstructed the smooth progress which might have been expected, by concentrating upon the issue of 'robbery of the poor' in other Endowed Schools Commissioners' schemes.[88] It is significant that the organisation of opposition on these grounds in Gloucester coincided, first of all, with the implementation of the Elementary Education Act, 1870, which provided for rate-aid, and secondly with the growing publicity afforded to the crucial Emanuel Hospital case in Westminster. The first notice of the progress of the Emanuel controversy was published in the *Gloucester Journal* on 29 April 1871.[89]

Nevertheless, until the implications of the 1870 Act began to be appreciated locally, it seemed that the County Committee provoked little opposition. It could be argued that opposition would have occurred in any case. But the most remarkable feature of local activity in both Devon and Gloucestershire was that co-operation outside the most important town in each case was proved possible, and that this co-operative activity was led by the gentry element in county society in much the same way as the Taunton Commission had autocratically determined the theoretical course of reform between 1864 and 1867.

The continuity of county activity is demonstrated most completely, however, in the work of the Northants Committee after 1869. In much the same manner as in Devon and Gloucestershire, leading members of the local community initially sought to educate local opinion on the subject of endowed schools reform by interpreting the recommendations of the S.I.C. and the terms of the 1869 Act.

The Middle Schools Committee of the Northants Society held its first important meeting after the passing of the Act in December 1870. In the chair was George Ward Hunt, recently Chancellor of the Exchequer under Disraeli, and a county M.P. The Secretary's report to the meeting took the form of a masterly summary of the S.I.C. Report and of the 1869 Act.[90] Cookson, the new Secretary, put two questions to the meeting:

Do we desire to anticipate the action of the new Commissioners? Can we hope, in any important respect, to do so?
In other words, are the general recommendations of the Commissioners on the one hand objectionable? or, on the other hand, are they inadequate? Or, lastly, is there any desirable remodelling or enlargement of the educational machinery of the county which we might expect to initiate more successfully than they?

He further asked whether they felt it their duty to create 'a voluntary "Provincial Authority" ' with a view to superintending the county's secondary education.

It was unanimously agreed that the Secretary should write to the Clerk of Trustees of each of the county's endowed schools asking them to call meetings of trustrees, and inviting them to send delegates to a meeting with the Middle Schools Committee in January 1871.[91] The subsequent general meeting was attended by representatives of the trusts of seven of the largest endowments in the county.[92] There was a unanimous expression of agreement to petition the High Sheriff to call a County Meeting to consider the operation of the Act and, 'if such a meeting see fit, to appoint a Committee to examine the requirements of the County in respect of Middle Class and Higher Education, and into the meeting of such requirements'.[93] Such County Meetings were uncommon. Their history is probably rooted in the mediaeval grand jury, and they seem to have been convened at moments of national, rather than local, emergency. One was held, for instance, to encourage military recruitment in Northants during the French Wars. The Sheriff summoned a meeting which was held in March 1871. It may fairly be called representative of the leading figures in the public life of the diocese of Peterborough and the county. Members of the great families were there, with a large collection of Anglican clergy and a sprinkling of businessmen.

Dr Magee, Bishop of Peterborough, spoke first, and made a measured defence of the Commissioners' declared intention of modifying endowments wherever necessary. His chief presupposition, shared by the six later speakers, was that the Commissioners, when they visited the county, should not be treated as interlopers, but should receive the benefit of the deep local experience of giving assistance to middle-class education. He thought that where a clear religious prescription was attached to an endowment, it should be respected. But he said that 'the living would be in a state of continual slavery to the departed' if certain due and just modifications were not made. He could not help thinking that such co-operation by trustees would make the application of the Act 'not only better and wiser, but smoother and happier'. The Revd Lord Alwyn Compton then moved the resolution that 'the Endowed Schools Act ... provides the machinery by which the secondary education of the county may be largely improved and extended'. He admitted that the county's schools were inefficient and that those who were supposed to use them sent their children to private schools. George Ward Hunt also argued for assisting the Commissioners, as did the Tory Lord Henley; Hunt thought some people's pride might be hurt by the final schemes but in the long run a greater amount of good might accrue to the whole county.

G. Stopford-Sackville, M.P., moved that a special committee be appointed to 'examine into the requirements of the county in respect of secondary education, and into the means of meeting such requirements'. Pickering Phipps, the brewer, said that this resolution was of the greatest importance, now that elementary education had been so improved, for an equal provision ought to be made for the classes immediately above the class for whom elementary education was intended.

This county gathering reached a surprising degree of unanimity. There was agreement on the need for revising the terms of endowments and, if necessary, for transferring or re-applying them; and, most important, for assisting, rather than blocking, the work of the Commissioners. Perhaps most remarkable of all, a Bishop who was a leading member of the Church Defence Institution had declared himself, with one significant exception, in favour of radical reform of endowments; and a leading member of a recent Conservative administration had warned that it would be necessary to accept the general reconstruction of endowments if county education were to prosper. The only member of the county's extensive Dissenting community who was noted as being present was Mr Toller, a leading Kettering Baptist, and he registered no objections. It should be remembered that the Middle Schools Committee had been generous in its attitude to Dissent since its inception in 1854.[94]

The special committee appointed at the meeting presented its report to an assembly at the George Hotel, Northampton, in September 1872. First they outlined the principles on which they had based their suggestions: 'That existing educational endowments or endowments convertible to educational purposes, ought to be so employed that every portion of the county should have within its reach sufficient efficient schools of such grades as it required; while at the same time endowments should, as far as possible, be retained in the localities to which they belong'. And they implied acceptance of the notion of the 'ladder' suggested by the S.I.C. in their recommendation that 'it should be possible for a scholar to rise through the whole gradation of schools, from the elementary to the highest grade'.

The Committee made specific proposals about the allocation of first- and second-grade status to particular schools, and suggested uses for the £5,000 of non-educational endowment which existed in Northampton. They also recommended that there should be large numbers of third-grade schools 'in reach of as many parents as possible, for those who send their children to them can seldom afford to pay boarding fees'. Entry to these schools should be according to merit, 'account being taken of conduct as well as educational accomplishment'. Competition for places would be confined to pupils in elementary schools. They concluded by stating that the schools indicated in their plan, together with schools outside the county boundary, 'would constitute, in addition to the elementary schools, an educational System for the county which would be fairly complete'.[95]

The impressive scheme was informed by twenty years' experience of dealing with matters of middle-class education. It showed, on the one hand, a close study of the main recommendations of the S.I.C. and the ways in which these had been reflected or diffused since 1869; on the other hand, an intimate knowledge of the financial and educational needs and resources of the county. Just as the county, through the Middle Schools Committee, had anticipated and attempted to meet the need for reform after 1854, so now in 1873 this newly constituted Committee was, in a far-seeing way, preparing to advance in conjunction with agents of the central government.

The bleak story of the abandonment of the scheme is recorded in a note scribbled by the Revd William Bury, the current Secretary, in the Middle Schools Minute Book. It is undated, and is the last entry: 'Subsequently an inquiry held at Northampton by an Assistant Commissioner with a view to applying the scheme to Northampton – Representations from Northampton strongly opposed – no further action taken – a reaction against the aims of the Commission set in.

Powers under the Endowed Schools Act transferred to the Charity
Commissioners – County scheme fell through – W.B.'

A similar county association was founded, albeit on an *ad hoc*
basis, in Leicestershire in 1871. Before the 1873 Select Committee on
the 1869 Act, the Revd J. H. Green, Master of Kibworth Grammar
School, said that he had been appointed Honorary Secretary of a
Leicestershire county committee in May, 1871. It had been intended
that the committee 'should look up all the Endowed Schools in the
county, and see how far (it) could become well acquainted with all
the affairs of our own neighbourhood, so that when the Commissioners came down, we should not be entirely ignorant of the
subject'. The spirit of the committee was friendly to the reception of
the Act.[96] Bishop Magee had written to the High Sheriff expressing
sympathy with the objects of the Act and of the Committee, saying
that the friends of education in the county should take the initiative
in promoting 'improvements in our middle-class system which in
some form or another are inevitable'.[97]

The most influential contributor to the first Leicestershire meeting
was Archdeacon Fearon of Loughborough who had given written
evidence about education in his region to the Newcastle Commission. He had been involved in the negotiations leading to the reform
of Loughborough Grammar School which T. H. Green had so
admired in his report to the S.I.C.,[98] and unlike many of his Anglican
colleagues he was a staunch supporter of the movement to found a
school board at Loughborough. He had been ever willing to co-
operate with Dissent, and his publications included a work on the
teaching of the science of common things in which he admitted a
heavy debt to Richard Dawes.[99] He expressed his sympathy with the
Endowed Schools Commissioners' schemes which had already been
published, and he suggested that, if Loughborough came under the
jurisdiction of the Commissioners, 'it ought to be quite possible to
pass pupils from the elementary schools to Loughborough Grammar
School, either through scholarships or in some other way'. He also
hoped that the Commissioners would use their powers to 'abrogate
all doctrinal distinctions', since, in no party sense, 'he was in favour
of 'comprehension rather than exclusion' in religion. The other
authoritative speaker at the meeting was the H.M.I., Blakiston, who
described 'an elaborate plan of organisation which had been adopted
in Yorkshire'.[100] J. M. Wallace, Headmaster of Loughborough, who
had given evidence to the S.I.C., also spoke encouragingly.

A committee of twenty-eight members was appointed and they published their report in February 1873. Their working principles had been, firstly, to see that all persons had a good school of appropriate grade within their reach; secondly, to make all local endowments useful to the whole county, while keeping them as far as possible in their original neighbourhoods; thirdly, to classify endowments according to local needs; and finally to encourage 'meritorious scholars' in elementary schools by means of a system of prizes and exhibitions.[101] The committee found that there was over £8,000 available in endowments and nearly £6,000 in convertible non-educational trusts. The smaller endowments, they thought, might be turned to scholarships for poor boys since this kind of encouragement came nearest to the original intentions of the founders. Their analysis of local needs was represented in a detailed table covering population, quality of buildings, and amounts of individual endowments. Their prescriptive grouping of schools into grades and boarding or day schools followed the pattern of the Northants scheme.

The Leicestershire scheme, particularly since it had been the work of men of apparently tolerant religious attitudes, like Fearon, seemed to be just and well balanced. But it did not specify the means by which the governing bodies of individual schools were to be appointed. In his evidence to the 1873 Select Committee J. H. Green was driven into a corner by a Liberal, Mr Powell, who drew from him the admission that he was in favour of the co-optative principle of selecting governors, and against the election of representative trustees by rate-payers.[102] After further questioning Green said that he wanted a Provincial Board which would include members nominated by Oxford, Cambridge and London Universities,[103] by the Lord Lietenant, by Quarter Sessions, and by the headmasters of the district. He was also unable to supply accurate information about the part played by Dissenters in making the county scheme.[104]

These county meetings and their context of continuing local activity in the field of middle-class education cannot be described as reflecting a national pattern of response to the work of the Endowed Schools Commission. But they do represent clear instances of collective endeavour by traditional rulers in each locality, and certain common features can be identified in each case. Indeed, in Devon, Leicestershire, Northants and Gloucestershire the prefixes to the committees' reports and schemes have much in common, even in their terminology. First of all the county committees were, in most cases, the inheritors of an earlier tradition of local endeavour in the supervision and management of endowed schools and of middle-class education of other kinds. With the exception of the West Riding they were expressions of interest in the rural, agricultural sector of middle-class provision, and were related to the Georgic tradition of concern for the structure and stability of county society. The committee comprised, in most cases, an ecclesiastical element – a hierarchy within a hierarchy – which had as its coping stone the Bishop of the diocese. The general management of their activity, however, seems to have lain in the hands of those among the traditional ruling class whose interest in education was of considerable standing. This element on each of the committees was reinforced by the participation of 'professional' educational administrators, sometimes headmasters, like Percival, but more often H.M.I.s, like Blakiston, Tinling, Norris, Moseley, and, most impressive of all, Temple.

Yet the traditional character of the committees, and their admitted weighting towards the Church, did not mean that their attitude to the Commissioners was obstructive or defensive; rather were they characterised by a middle-of-the-road tolerance which might be considered surprising in bodies of this kind. The leading figures – Ducie, Temple, Northcote and Compton, for instance – were 'liberals' in the sense that they can be identified as part of the general movement for gradual reform which found its chief extra-Parliamentary expression in the Social Science Association. But they were not radicals: their tendency was towards an autocratic notion of reform, particularly in relation to middle-class education, which, for the time being, necessitated playing down the representative element in the administration of county affairs and the maintenance of a tradition of local government by those who mattered on behalf of those who, as yet, were thought barely to understand their own needs in the field of middle-class schooling. In this they were performing a rôle which had been anticipated by the authors of the S.I.C. Report: they saw themselves as 'educating' middle-class parents.

It has been suggested that schemes and resolutions in four of the counties shared features which were of course derived fundamentally from the recommendations of the S.I.C. But it has not been possible to find other evidence for making substantial links between the activities of various counties. The Keighley scheme was unique. But even in the West Riding the work of local assistance was facilitated by Robinson's close links with the area. The Gloucester-shire Committee had been the first in the field, in 1869, stimulated, it seems, by the conference of the S.S.A., addressed by Fitch who later conveniently reappeared as an assistant commissioner. Gloucester-shire may have provided a model for other counties. The Devon Committee was formed in October 1870; the Middle Schools Com-mittee in Northants responded two months later; Leicestershire in May 1871. It is hard to avoid suggesting two possibilities: either a process of chain reaction; or the subtle motivation of local interests by the Commissioners themselves, or by former members of the S.I.C., in order to counteract anticipated local resistance by sectional interests. Whatever was the case, it cannot be denied that those who mattered in the counties responded in these cases with diligence and enthusiasm. It seems also that, even in contentious urban areas, the Commissioners were concerned to include a 'county' element among the new bodies of trustees. In Bristol and Bedford this was certainly the case.[105] They saw the county leavening as a means of stabilising the potentially mercurial fluctuations of urban representative poli-tics. Middle-class representative control of elementary education was acceptable; government of middle-class education by the middle classes was not.

Notes

1   See above, Chapter VIII, p. 201.
2   31 and 32 Victoria, cap 32; Hansard, Third Series, 31 and 32 Victoria, 1867–8, CXCII, p. 20.
3   Hansard, Third Series, 31 and 32 Victoria, CXCI, p. 1782.
4   Ibid, p. 1783.
5   See below, Chapter X, p. 254.
6   Hansard, Third Series, 32 Victoria, CXCIV, pp. 113–14.
7   This was one of Forster's miscalculations. He was later reminded that he had also promised Bristol Trustees that the Act would not interfere with the management of their schools.
8   Hasard, Third Series, CXCIV, p. 1362.
9   Ibid, p. 1371.
10 Ibid, p. 1373.
11 See above, Chapter II, 52. Report from Select Committee on County Financial Arrangements, 13 July 1868, p. iii.
12 BM, Gladstone Papers, BM Addl. MSS, 44608, written memorandum from Roby to Gladstone, 17 December 1868.
13 See above, Chapter II, p. 52.
14 *Times,* 4 August 1869.
15 Gladstone Papers, 44239, f. 336, letter from Lyttelton to Gladstone, 15

June 1869.

16   Report of the Endowed Schools Commissioners . . . , 1872, p. 7.

17   See below, Chapter X, p. 249.

18   Gladstone Papers, 44239, f. 336, letter of Lyttelton to Gladstone, 24
     October 1870.

19   Report of the Select Committee on the Endowed Schools Act (1869),
     1873; see evidence of Lyttelton, 28 February 1873.

20   Ibid, p. 45.

21   Ibid, loc. cit.

22   *Gloucester Journal,* 12 October 1869: extended report on the Social
     Science Congress which had ended 6 October.

23   Transactions of the National Association for the Promotion of Social
     Science, 1869 Bristol conference, London, 1870, p. 375.

24   O. F. Christie, *A History of Clifton College, Bristol,* 1935, pp. 23–6.

25   Transactions of the National Association for the Promotion of Social
     Science, Newcastle conference, 1870, London, 1871, pp. 310–17.

26   Ibid, p. 310.

27   Ibid, p. 315.

28   W. Temple, Life of Bishop Percival, London, 1921, p. 44.

29   These were, Canon Henry Moseley, Canon J. P. Norris, Canon Edward
     Girdlestone, and Matthew Davonport Hill.

30   Christie, *Clifton College,* p. 38.

31   PRO ED 27/1263, Clifton College File, letter of Percival to Fitch, 27
     March 1870.

32   *S.I.C.,* XIV, p. 237.

33   PRO ED 27/1263, Fitch to Hobhouse, 16 May 1870. The letter was
     addressed from 11, Baynton Park, Clifton.

34   Ibid, Fitch to Hobhouse, 18 November 1870.

35   *Western Daily Press,* 12 April 1875, public notice of official acceptance
     of the scheme.

36   See above, Ch. II, 44, for brief account of Robinson's career.

37   Report of the Select Committee on the Endowed Schools Act (1869),
     1873, evidence of Robinson, 11 March 1873.

38   *Times,* 19 January 1870, 'The Educational Movement, Leeds'.

39   See above, Chapter III, p. 74.

40   *Times,* 20 January 1870.

41   See above, Chapter VII, p. 172.

42   *Blackwood's Magazine,* III, February 1872, pp. 219–24.

43   Ibid, p. 219.

44   See, M.le Guillou, 'Technical Education 1850–1914', in G. Roderick
     and M. Stephens (eds.), *Where Did We Go Wrong?* Brighton, 1981–p.
     179.

45   *Blackwood's Magazine,* III, p. 220.

46   Ibid, p. 222.

47   PRO ED 27/5957., Keighley File, notes on Keighley for the direction of
     the Assistant Commissioner, undated.

48   Ibid, Conference Paper D, Fearon to Robinson, 22 February 1870. For
     Swire Smith, see G. W. Roderick and M. D. Stephens, *Education and*

Industry in the Nineteenth Century, London, 1978, p. 118.

49 PRO ED 27/5957, letter from Robinson to Fearon, 11 June 1870.

50 Fiftieth Annual Report of the Keighley Mechanics' Institute, Bradford, 1875, p. 24. (Copy in Keighley Reference Library.)

51 Ibid, p. 25.

52 PRO ED 27/1274, Colston's Hospital File, Interview Memorandum, 28 February 1871.

53 See above, Chapter III.

54 P. T. Marsh, *The Victorian Church in Decline: Archbishop Tait and the Church of England, 1868–82,* London, 1969, p. 69.

55 *Times,* 8 October 1870, 'Endowed Schools Act'.

56 *Plymouth and Exeter Gazette,* 3 February 1870, 'Exeter Grammar School'.

57 Ibid.

58 PRO ED 27/695, Exeter Charities File, Temple letter, 19 July 1870.

59 Ibid, Roby to Temple, 22 July 1870.

60 *Western Times,* 18 April 1871, 'The Endowed Schools Commission'.

61 *Plymouth and Exeter Gazette,* 4 May 1871.

62 PRO ED 27/695, Memorandum of Fitch, 15 January 1872.

63 Ibid, county scheme, 'July' (1871).

64 Homerton College, Fortescue–Brereton Letters, letter of Fortescue, 1 March 1871.

65 PRO ED 27/695, Memorandum of Fitch, 15 January 1872.

66 Quoted in E. G. Sandford (ed.), *The Exeter Episcopate of Archbishop Temple, 1869–85,* London, 1907, pp. 86–7.

67 See above, this chapter, p. 215.

68 For these Charity Commissioners (1849), see above, Chapter V, p. 109.

69 See above, Chapter III, p. 71.

70 *Gloucester Journal,* 16 October 1869, 'The Diocesan Conference'.

71 Ibid, 23 October 1869.

72 Ibid, 6 November 1869, 'The Endowed Grammar Schools'.

73 Ibid, 13 and 20 November 1869.

74 Ibid, 27 November 1869, 'The Endowed Schools of Gloucestershire: conference of trustees'.

75 See above, this Chapter, p. 221.

76 *Gloucester Journal,* 18 December 1869, 'Gloucester and the Endowed Schools Act'.

77 Ibid, 25 December 1869.

78 See above, Chapter III, p. 59.

79 *Gloucester Journal,* (i) 15 January 1870, letter from Lyttelton, dated Hagley, 10 January 1870; (ii) ibid, 5 February 1870.

80 Ibid, 15 January 1870.

81 Ibid, 9 April 1870.

82 For a discussion of the politics of the City scheme, see F. E. Balls, 'The Endowed Schools Act, 1869, and the Development of the English Grammar Schools in the Nineteenth Century', *Durham Research Review,* V, 20 April 1968, pp. 219–29. Also, Gloucester Chapter Minute Book, meeting at the Deanery, 31 March 1870; and PRO ED

27/1382, Gloucester United Charities, Interview Memorandum of Tinling, 2 December 1870.

83 A. Platts and G. Hainton, *Education in Gloucestershire, A Short History*, Gloucester, 1954, p. 16.

84 *Gloucester Journal*, 10 November 1870, 'Endowed Schools in the County'.

85 Ibid, 21 January 1871, 'Gloucestershire Endowed Schools'.

86 Ibid, 28 January 1871.

87 See above, this Chapter, p. 216.

88 The campaign began with a letter from Heane entitled, 'City Schools', in the *Gloucester Journal*, 4 March 1871.

89 See also below, Chapter X, p. 246.

90 Minutes of the Northants Middle Schools Committee, 3 December 1870.

91 For Cookson's letter, see Appendix.

92 These were, Daventry, Towcester, Northampton, Courteenhall, Wellingborough, Kettering, and Blakesley.

93 Minutes of the Northants Middle Schools Committee, 9 January 1871.

94 See above, Chapter VI, p. 147.

95 Printed copy of the scheme in the Middle Schools Minute Book, entitled, 'Recommendations to be submitted to Her Majesty's Endowed Schools Commissioners'.

96 Report of the Select Committee on the Endowed Schools Act (1869), 1873, evidence of Revd J. H. Green, 29 April 1873.

97 *Leicester Journal*, 12 May 1871, 'The Endowed Schools Act and the County of Leicester'. Mr Heygate, a local Tory MP, was not present, but may have been responsible for bringing Green as a witness to the Select Committee, of which Heygate was a member.

98 See above, Chapter VIII, p. 199.

99 B. H. Elliott, 'Leicestershire Worthies(3): Archdeacon Fearon', *Transactions of the Vaugham Archaeological and Historical Society*, XX, Leicester, 1972, p. 8.

100 Blakiston probably referred to the Keighley scheme, the work of Archdeacon Fearon's son; see above, this Chapter, p. 218.

101 Leicestershire County Record Office, DE 261/9. four-page printed document, undated, entitled, 'Leicestershire'. The provenance for the date is J. H. Green's statement to the Select Committee, in 1873.

102 Select Committee, 1873, p. 312.

103 Cf. the final Birmingham Scheme; see below, Chapter X, p. 254.

104 Select Committee, p. 310.

105 For Bedford, see ED 27/8a, Report of Mr Latham on Harpur's Charity, 13 January 1871, suggesting inclusion of 'foreign' trustees in the persons of the Lord Lieutenant, the County MPs, nominees of Oxford, Cambridge and London Universities, and a nominee of the masters. For Bristol, see leader in *Bristol Post*, 29 August 1871, regretting the representation of county elements in the draft scheme submitted by Fitch for Red Maids and Queen Elizabeth Hospitals.

CHAPTER X

Reaction

The Endowed Schools Commissioners have not come into possession of the entire educational endowments of the country, to refound them at their pleasure; but their authority is limited to the correction of abuses. There are none in Emanuel Hospital.

It was by tampering with the rights of property that M. Louis Blanc and his predecessors prepared the way for the Commune.

From a *Defence of the City of London Corporation against the Scheme of the Endowed Schools Commissioners* 1872

The difficulties confronting the Endowed Schools Commissioners have been summarised by a number of commentators; but it cannot be claimed that they have been analysed.[1] The Commissioners in their Report to the Privy Council in 1872 supplied their own interim description of the problems. These were: the appointment of new governing bodies, and in particular the question of co-opted governors; the grading of schools; indiscriminate gratuitous education, as distinct from selection for free education based on merit; the hospital schools; the operation of the 1870 Act in relation to endowed schools and other kinds of endowments, and the denominational character of many endowments.[2] All these problems were inextricably interlaced, though the difficulties were by no means all present in each of the cases with which they dealt. But in the most significant instances of opposition, where damaging publicity was reinforced by a considerable and varied battery of powerful interests, each of these problems played a part in marshalling the defences which confronted the Commissioners.

The focal points of opposition were the large endowments of the corporate towns and cities. In general the Commissioners had a relatively easy task when they came to deal with separate endowments in the rural counties: and these accounted for the majority of the cases which they handled. But the hospital schools of London and Bristol epitomised the condition of this general class of endowments, which had been so heavily criticised by the S.I.C.[3] It was, in the first instance, Hobhouse's obsession with the question of hospital schools, and consequently the disaster of the Emanuel Hospital case, which led to the co-ordination and orchestration of powerful opposition to the Commissioners. Indeed, if it were not unhistorical to do so, an attempt might be made to argue that, without the inhibition of the Emanuel case, the Endowed Schools Commissioners might have enjoyed a more extended term of activity.

The governors of Emanuel Hospital in Westminster, an Elizabethan foundation, were the members of the Court of Aldermen of the City of London. The school had been reported upon in a neutral way by Mr Skirrow for the Charity Commission in 1857.[4] D R Fearon paid a brief visit to the school for the S.I.C. in 1865, though, as a non-classical institution, it did not merit a separate report in his survey of London middle-class education. Of the hospital schools in the Metropolis he said that 'their sphere of usefulness might be extended so as to help towards forming a systematic education for the middle scholars of the third grade throughout London'. He wanted them to be converted from boarding to day education. Westminster, he found, was 'fuller of hospital schools than any other part of London'.[5] At two of the Westminster schools, Emanuel and Greycoat Hospitals, he noted that the curriculum was limited to elementary subjects, with no Latin or French. Yet the pupils remained until fourteen years of age.[6] The income of Emanuel, with only thirty boy-pupils, was £3,118; Greycoat, with 100 pupils, £2,736 p.a.[7] Later, at the height of the dispute over Emanuel Hospital in 1871, the Court of Aldermen denied having known of Fearson's visit; and on their examination of the Headmaster's minute book, they found that he had referred, on the date of the visit, to 'the examination by Her Majesty's Inspector'.[8]

Emanuel Hospital epitomised the waste in such schools, which the S.I.C. condemned on principle. The trustees were evidently aware of the interest which their type of school had attracted since the great inquiries into charities had begun, for they had been careful, in the 1840s and 1850s, to commission frequent reports of their own upon the condition of the school; though these had concentrated almost wholly on the financial state of the endowment.[9]

It seems likely that Hobhouse, with his marked antipathy towards what he considered to be moribund endowments, would have moved quickly in the matter of Emanuel Hospital on his own initiative in 1869. But Roby, long after the demise of the Commission, remembered that he had planted the idea in Hobhouse's mind: 'A number of wealthy endowments in Westminster, within a stone's throw of the Commissioners' office and of Parliament, seemed to me to invite large and early reform. Mr. Hobhouse readily took to the suggestion, and commenced proceedings'.[10] Roby's account did not go into detail about subsequent events, and he omitted to mention that the Court of Aldermen were among the first groups of trustees to take advantage of Clause 32 of the 1869 Act, which related to endowments with incomes over £1,000 p.a. and permitted trustees to prepare and submit their own schemes to the Commissioners. They made their first inquiry as early as 14 September, in the same month as the Commissioners began their work.[11] It is evident from the list of principles upon which they based their scheme, [12] and from the simple form of the document which they submitted in January 1870,[13] that the Court of Aldermen conceived of a bland scheme which barely altered the existing terms of government, and whose only novel feature was the proposal to erect new school buildings and a residence for the masters and other officers. In this they were consciously or unconsciously imitating the recent coup of the Haberdashers' Company by means of a Charity Commission scheme for their school at Monmouth.[14]

Roby acted as agent in the subsequent business, though Hobhouse was supervising the negotiations from Whitehall. In March 1870, Roby visited the school and met representatives of the governors.[15] He immediately produced a detailed report on the school's condition, saying that the Westminster pupils belonged to 'a class above the ordinary primary schools'. The parents were 'policemen, master artificers, etc.'. He had found that most of the pupils leaving the school recently had become clerks in the City of London. As with the schools of William Rogers, the Corporation saw their school as a useful training-ground for some of their future employees in City counting-houses.[16] The form of patronage operating at the school was of a kind to rouse the Commissioners to action; and it was clear that all the parents could well afford to pay £4 a year, instead of relying on the arbitrary selection of their children for free education. In the light of Roby's findings the Governors' scheme was rejected as a ground for negotiation by the Commissioners.

The blue touch-paper was lit when the Governors read the

Commissioners' draft scheme in August 1870.[17] The new Emanuel
Hospital, it was proposed, should be a third-grade boys' school
serving the immediate locality, and, with the girls' school at Greycoat Hospital, would constitute 'the United Westminster Schools'.
But the most inflammatory proposal was that the new governing
body should consist of the Dean of Westminster, the incumbent of a
Westminster parish, and the M.P.s for the borough, with only three
of the members nominated by the Corporation. There were also to be
two chosen by another public authority: for example, the Governors
of Christ's Hospital or of Westminster School, or the Universities.
These should then co-opt twelve others for a term of years to be
decided upon. This new constitution was the central issue as far as
the Corporation was concerned: their patronage and perquisites
would vanish for ever. But the feature of the scheme which they
chose to publicise in their own interests was the Commissioners'
proposal that their rights of nomination should be abolished; that
the fees of up to £25 p.a. were to be paid in most cases; and that
education should be made, for twenty per cent of the pupils, 'the
reward of merit', by means of scholarships most of which would be
attached to Westminster elementary schools. Thus the Commissioners delivered into the hands of the Corporation the motto
'Robbery of the poor on behalf of the middle classes', which was to
resound through the next three years of public turmoil. The fact that
under the scheme the Corporation would retain its trusteeship of the
almshouses was, by comparison, of little consequence.

The Court of Aldermen, or rather, Nelson, their solicitor, spent
the next three months preparing a very densely argued list of fifteen
objections to the draft scheme. In this their statements of self-interest
were surrounded and obscured by other debating points: for
instance, 'that no education is thereby provided for boys above the
age of fifteen'. Their main objectives were, '2. That it is not within the
scope of or made in conformity with the said Act inasmuch as the
schools proposed to be established may and probably will become
schools for the education of the rich';[18] '10. That it substitutes for
themselves a new governing body'. In defending the stewardship of
the Corporation, Nelson drew the Commissioners' attention to their
very successful promotion of the City of London School which, with
other similar institutions in London, was said to satisfy already the
educational needs of the middle classes. The Commissioners subsequently made concessions on minor points of detail, but the scheme

which they submitted for approval to the Education Department in February 1871, was in its main proposals essentially the original to which the Corporation had objected.[19]

The Governors now began to organise a compaign of obstruction. The Lord Mayor summoned interested parties to a meeting at the Mansion House in April 1871, at which the speakers included leading Conservative M.P.s. The Commissioners' maxim debated at the meeting was their refusal to incorporate gratuitous education. The Commissioners, on the other hand, were not lacking support in London. Roby received a letter, appropriately dated 1 May 1871, from one George Thomas of Westminster: 'Sir, Seeing your name in the Standard respecting Emanuel Hospital, I wish you as a working man *Success*. Our children have such difficulty in securing patronage from Guildhall, that we wish a local government for the Hospital. None of the present governors take any real interest in it, except for the patronage . . .' The *West Middlesex Advertiser* on 6 May carried a report of a meeting of the Vestry of Chelsea at which the case of Emanuel Hospital 'again came forward'. A Mr Cobb said that, while he excused 'the City weakness of feasting' on the ground that it was 'a failing of human nature', he knew that 'the City abounded in charities which they hardly knew what to do with'. Another vestryman quoted an article in the *Spectator* which contained a digest of the merits of the Commissioners' scheme, showing that 'instead of a few poor charity children, educated at a cost of £700, about one thousand children would receive a good education, including near five hundred girls'. A few days later the clerk to the Vestry received a reprimand from Nelson accusing speakers at the meeting of misrepresentation and calumny.[20]

At a meeting of the Court of Aldermen in April 1871, the Lord Mayor proposed laying before the public 'a simple statement of the facts of the Emanuel Hospital case'.[21] The result was the establishment by the Corporation of the School Trusts Defence Committee in the same month, with Nelson as its Secretary.[22] In a memorandum to the Court of Aldermen written at this time Nelson said that the Commissioners seemed determined 'to select Emanuel Hospital as the battleground upon which is to be decided the great question whether refuges for poor children are still to exist in this country', or whether 'all who cannot maintain their children and pay for their education are to cast them upon the rates'.[23] In mentioning the rates he was raising the most emotive spectre of all. He noted that the Commissioners had not yet published schemes for similar schools at Bristol, Exeter and Birmingham, 'whilst the purpose for which they were established, the reformation of abused or useless Grammar Schools, seems to be entirely neglected'. Nelson sent to every trust and town council in the Kingdom a *pro forma* petition which the trustees might submit to Parliament in support of the governors of Emanuel Hospital against the scheme of the Endowed Schools Commissioners. In June 1871, for instance, Roby received the following letter from the Town Clerk of Bridgnorth in Salop:

> In consequence of the large number of communications received requesting the Council of this borough to join in opposing the proposed extinction of Emanuel Hospital and other endowed school charities, and in the absence of any reliable information in favour of the same, I am directed by the Lord Mayor to request the favour of your supplying for the use of the Council a copy of the proposed scheme together with any other information you may consider necessary to enable them to arrive at a correct decision.[24]

And in a printed statement which the Commissioners submitted to the Privy Council in June 1871, Roby remarked that they had noted that the City Corporation had been circulating very widely, 'by sending to newspapers and in other ways', the Lord Mayor's remarks to the Commission of March 1871.[25]

Evidence of the Corporation's nationwide campaign took two forms. First of all there was the attention which provincial newspapers gave to the Emanuel case. In April 1871, for instance, the *Gloucester Journal* contained a long report headed, 'The Endowed Schools Commissioners and the London Corporation', with a verbatim account of all the resolutions passed at the Mansion House meeting; and another report a week later headed, 'Interference with Bequests to the Poor'.[26] In June the same newspaper carried a long summary of the petition to be sent to the Commons on behalf of the governors of Emanuel Hospital by the Town Council of Gloucester.[27] In the following month the *Leicester Journal* in a leader entitled 'Emanuel Hospital', and in spite of its earlier support for the principles of the 1869 Act, expressed satisfaction at the Endowed Schools Commissioners' receiving 'a salutory rap over the knuckles' for the 'theoretic perfection' of their scheme for Westminster.[28]

The second species of evidence took the form of the petitions which were presented, from London and many other parts of the country, to Parliament in June and July 1871. One hundred and eighty petitions were transmitted to the Lords alone.[29] In almost every case the form of words was: 'Petitions from the Corporation of Derby, and the governors of King James's Schools Sheffield; praying 'that the Funds of Educational and other Foundations in Westminster and elsewhere may not be diverted from the Objects of the Donors" '.[30]

The Court of Aldermen did not merely provoke a ground-swell of general resistance: they also chose a powerful spokesman for their cause. In June 1871, the Court requested the Sheriffs of the City to 'wait upon some Lord in Parliament and request His Lordship to present their Petition to the House of Lords', where they might expect more Conservative support than in the House of Commons.[31] This form of words obscured the fact that they had already chosen the Marquis of Salisbury as their parliamentary agent. He had perfect conservative credentials – as a staunch defender of the Church, in the 1860s, against militant Nonconformist agitation for disestablishment, and against pressure for the abolition of Church rates, for the reduction of the Anglican grip on the Universities, the endowed schools, and the voluntary system of elementary schooling.[32] He saw the Liberal party as an artificial amalgam of interests, held together by its leader's willingness to condone an attack upon the traditional rights of the Anglican establishment. The City of London Corporation hardly shared his high Toryism in politics and much less his traditional Churchmanship. But their choice of Salisbury unwittingly opened a further dimension of opposition to the Endowed Schools Commissioners.

Salisbury had been, from its origins, a leading member of the Church Defence Institution.[33] From 1872 onwards the *National Church* published detailed accounts of the work in progress of the Endowed Schools Commission. Its aim was not to obstruct completely the schemes of the Commissioners, but rather to make sure that in each case Church interests were protected in relation to the kind of religious education prescribed in new schemes and the composition of the governing bodies. In February 1872, a new Committee was set up 'to watch the proceedings of the Endowed Schools Commissioners respecting their proceedings affecting endowed Church schools throughout the country'.[34] In March 1873, a conference on the subject was organised, attended by a galaxy of clergy and laymen, including Salisbury, Lord Compton (of the Northants Society), Gregory, Heygate, Bishop Magee of Peterborough, Fagan of the Wells Diocesan Board, and numerous representatives of trusts, among them the disaffected Merchant Adventurers of Bristol, and others from Beaumaris, Bridgewater, Felsted and Kibworth (the latter represented by the Revd J H Green).[35]

In *Blackwood's Magazine* in July 1871, at the time of the Corporation's first offensive, George Hodgkinson fixed a broadside against the Endowed Schools Commission.[36] His main object seems to have been to defend the Corporation in the matter of Emanuel Hospital: he thought that the Commissioners' scheme was 'clearly against the spirit of the Endowed Schools Act',[37] and that, as well as removing the dead hand, they were tearing out the heart of the institution.[38] But the worth of Hodgkinson's attack upon the Commission should be measured against his professional reputation. A contemporary of Lyttelton at Cambridge, but his inferior as a scholar, he had become the first (and unsuccessful) Principal of the Royal Agricultural College, Cirencester, before he moved, with an equal lack of success, to the Normal Training College at York. In his 1871 article he said that he knew little of the third Commissioner, Robinson, except that he was 'a visionary in education . . . and an ardent votary of the "mother tongue" at the expense of Latin and Greek', and 'a strenuous political partisan'.[39] However, this 'little' knowledge was perhaps shaped by the fact that Robinson had successfully taken the place of Hodgkinson at York upon the latter's dismissal in 1854. On that occasion Hodgkinson had published 'The statement of G. C. Hodgkinson of the Training College, York, in his defence'.[40]

Another journal, at an opposite expreme from the *National Church,* expressed its opposition more guardedly. The *Nonconformist* in May 1871, in a long article on the Emanuel Hospital case, thought that the Commissioners' scheme, designed for taking endowments from the poor and devoting them to the 'higher and lower middle class' of the district, was 'unquestioningly a very surprising change, only to be justified in the case of necessity'. It was all the more surprising since the Court of Aldermen had not been charged with the maladministration of their trust.[41] The writer did not favour indiscriminate gratuitous education, but he thought that the Commissioners were applying their principle in a 'harsh and pedantic' manner. Rather extraordinarily he indicted them for defending Anglican foundations while, in this case, adopting a 'sternly radical' attitude to 'a comparatively popular and entirely unsectarian body' like the Corporation. By the proposed scheme Emanuel Hospital was seen as inevitably coming under the influence of the Dean and Chapter of Westminster. The *Nonconformist* evidently preferred control by a corrupt secular body to the influence of a local Anglican hierarchy.

The view expressed by that journal demonstrated the complexities of the Commissioners' task. The Emanuel case was treated by them as an instance of the application of equitable principle and rational reformist values to an institution which was managed by the worst kind of patronage in a manner both uneconomic and unsuited to the location of the school and the general needs of the time. Yet in 1871 the prickly conscience of the *Nonconformist* saw their work as a stalking horse to conceal the prejudices of three 'Anglican' agents of the central government. On the other hand the hidebound ruck of the Church Defence Institution equated the Commissioners' work in Westminster with the concurrent Liberal process of dismantling the Established Church in Ireland and the modification of the constitutions of the ancient Universities.

The Emanuel case provided the focal point for opposition to the work of the Commission. One element in the elimination of their difficulties in that instance was provided by the Elementary Education Act of 1870. Yet in their 1872 Report the Commissioners could legitimately claim that the 1870 Act had generally impeded the progress of their work. They said that a very large proportion of their time had lately been taken up with cases of elementary schools, mainly in rural parishes. This had arisen from the local efforts made to anticipate the compulsory provisions of the 1870 Act by supplying sufficient and suitable elementary schools in places where a deficiency was found to exist. The necessity for dealing with local applications from small trusts to the Education Department had interfered seriously with the Commissioners' work on larger endowments.[42] In August 1873, Parliament had passed an Act 'to continue and amend the Endowed Schools Act, 1869', which said that any school not defined as a Grammar School under the 1840 Act should, after September 1873, be treated as an elementary school. At a late date, therefore, one of the Commissioners' impediments was removed.

The 1870 Act introduced a new element into the politics of the Metropolis and of other towns by making possible the creation of school boards. The *Nonconformist* greeted the advent of the London School Board in July 1871, with the remark that it contained 'two of the most Liberal and justly-minded clergymen whom the National

Church can boast'. One of these was the Revd William Rogers.[43]
Among the topics considered early in its career by the London School
Board was City Charities, and this interest received considerable
notice in the press. Speaking at a School Board debate in May 1871,
T. H. Huxley referred to the Emanuel case, saying that what the
Commissioners intended doing with that charity was 'the very model
upon which he should desire to see legislation follow with regard to
other charities'.[44] At a meeting two months later Huxley unsuccess-
fully proposed that the Endowed Schools Commissioners should
consider the claims of the children in elementary schools who would
benefit from the endowments which were under consideration.[45] He
saw the co-operation of the Commissioners with the London School
Board as 'the first practical step in the national organisation of
English education'. It is notable that Huxley's candidature at the first
School Board election had been supported by Hobhouse, who was
treasurer of his sponsorship committee.[46]

It is hardly surprising, therefore, that when the Commissioners,
having seen their first Emanuel scheme turned down by the Lords in
1871, prepared a second, they should have included in it the proposal to give the London School Board the power to elect six governors
of Emanuel Hospital, with the Chairman of the Board as *ex officio*
governor.[47] Throughout the controversy the *Times* remained
staunchly on the side of the Commission: immediately after the
defeat of the first scheme a leading article commented, 'the very
existence of these feeble institutions is a scandal at a time when so
much is promised for education'.[48] The article considered that under
the scheme the poor 'have as much chance of sharing the revenues of
Emanuel Hospital as ever they had', and noted that 900 children
would be admitted in the place of the previous 150.

Hobhouse was a casualty of the Emanuel battle. In March 1872,
he was appointed a legal member of the Council at Calcutta, and
departed, to be replaced by Roby.[49] In another direction the continuing activity of the Commissioners produced a more positive reaction.
In May 1872, the *Times* noted that the Grocers' Company had
shown 'a good and wise example to other wealthy guilds in the City'
by asking the Commissioners to aid them in establishing a middle-
class school in north London out of the surplus revenues of the
Company. This became the Grocers' Company School which was
built at Hackney Downs and eventually became an L.C.C. school in
1905 as soon as the Company could rid itself of the responsibility.[50]

The *Times* reporter hoped that, if other companies were to imitate the Grocers, 'they might delay, if not altogether arrest, the inroads which are already contemplated upon their rich spoils'. The Grocers' Company had undoubtedly been wise: their cunning in 1872 prompted no less a City figure than Alderman Lawrence, M.P., to ask Lyttelton, before the 1873 Select Committee, whether the Commissioners had been 'bought off' by the Company.[51]

At the second attempt the Emanuel Hospital scheme passed through Parliament in May 1873. Replying to opponents of the scheme, Gladstone constructed a masterly defence of the Commissioners' work, but concentrated heavily upon indicting the Corporation.[52]

He began by narrowing the field of debate, which he thought an essential presupposition in a case where 'the points are so numerous and the details so intricate that it is difficult to bring the House to a close and accurate view of what the subject at issue really is.[53] He emphasised that the scheme involved no new principle – 150 schemes had already passed through the Commons – 'but it happened to deal with a governing body which is of a very formidale character'. He mentioned that the governing body of Eton had been completely refashioned under the 1868 Public Schools Act, without demur; though this was hardly an apposite comparison. The Corporation, on the other hand, required that 'there shall be one law for the world at large, and another for the Corporation of London'. And this was a body which for thirty years had enjoyed the proud distinction of being the only unreformed corporation in the country.[54] The motion was defeated by a majority of forty-eight,[55] and the scheme for Emanuel Hospital, as part of the United Westminster Schools, later received the Royal Assent.

The Nonconformist protest against the work of the Commissioners emanated largely from Birmingham. In July 1871, 'Watchman' wrote a letter to the *Nonconformist* recommending that an interested body – either the Liberation Society or the Central Nonconformist Committee of Birmingham – should take on the task of scrutinising the draft schemes of the Commissioners on behalf of the Nonconformists, and of communicating to the localities action which might be thought necessary.[56] This brought an immediate reply from Frank Schnadhorst, the Liberal secretary of the Central Nonconformist Committee, in which he said that the matter had recently been taken in hand.[57]

The chief complaint of the Nonconformists was that in some of their schemes the Commissioners were permitting the appointment of too many co-optative governors – often members of the Church of England – in mainly dissenting areas.[58] In November 1871, a leader in the *Nonconformist* acknowledged the enthusiasm with which that journal had initially greeted the 1869 Act. But it noted that 'you can infuse into such measures almost any spirit you please, religious or political'. The chief anxiety, the writer asserted, came from the fact that all three Commissioners were Anglicans; that they were also men of 'liberality' should not lead dissenters to ignore Winterbotham's eloquent demand for an attitude of 'watchful jealousy' towards their activities.[59]

The Central Nonconformist Committee sent a general deputation to meet the Commissioners in April 1872. It included dissenting political figures, like Miall and Leatham, a large delegation from Birmingham led by Dale, J. S. Wright of the Grammar School Association, and Chamberlain; and a Manchester contingent led by James Heywood.[60] Miall expressed their general appreciation of the educational merits of the 1869 Act and of many of the Commissioners' schemes. But Dale pointed out that, in twenty schemes which they had investigated, there were to be 111 Anglican governors and only eighteen Nonconformists. Specific objections were then made to schemes for Chelmsford and Gillingham. Lyttelton was able to reply that these had been changed. It seems that the outcome of the meeting pleased both parties, since in the following month the *Nonconformist* appealed for the prolongation of the Commission, with the important proviso that there should be official representation of dissenters upon it.[61] In January 1873, the same journal noted with approval the 'final' composition of the proposed governing body of King Edward's School, Birmingham, under the revised scheme.[62]

It might have been anticipated that the reform of the School at Birmingham would entangle the Commissioners in a variety of problems. The political jockeyings which accompanied the creation of the School Board helped to produce tensions which must have influenced the negotiations of Lyttelton and his colleagues. The politics of Birmingham elementary education caused Lyttelton some despair, for he wrote to his former Cambridge friend (and distant relative), Fortescue, in December 1870, that, although 'my Endowed Schools Commission gets on fairly well, but slow', his neighbours' School

Board at Birmingham, 'or almost any Board they could have elected, will quarrel horribly.'[63]

But Birmingham politicians had behaved with remarkable tolerance and harmony during the S.I.C.'s investigation of the Grammar School and through the various educational associations which had preceded the National League.[64] Moreover, Lyttelton, as the Commissioner responsible for dealing with King Edward's foundation, knew his men and was intimately acquainted with the area and its recent development. As the author of the S.I.C. chapter on the eight great endowments he must have been aware that Birmingham would be high on his list of priorities in 1869. In fact he had referred to Birmingham as 'the leading case' among the eight.[65]

Like the City of London Corporation, the Governors of King Edward's School took advantage of Clause 32 of the 1869 Act[66] and submitted their own scheme to the Commissioners in July 1870.[67] But, as has already been seen, there were other interested groups to be considered, notably the Free Grammar School Association and the Town Council. The 1870 Act proved its relevance to this case at an early stage: J. S. Wright, for the Association, told the Commissioners that 'if a School Board for Birmingham is elected . . . it will have to be the governing body for the Free Grammar School'.[68]

But Lyttelton seems not to have taken the embryo School Board seriously into account when preparing a detailed memorandum for his assistant, J. L. Hammond, in August 1870.[69] His first plan, based upon local knowledge, was to have a large body of appointed governors balanced by *ex officio* trustees, like the Mayor and some Anglican clergy, and nominees of the Town Council who would be largely Dissenters. It is clear that he thought that the shifting political composition of a School Board would make such a body unsuitable for the long-term control of a large endowment. Early in 1871 Hammond published a resumé of the Commissioners' intentions in Birmingham, and a Liberal local paper was critical of them, expressing particular disapproval of the inclusion of the Bishop of Worcester as an *ex officio* trustee.[70] At a meeting between the Grammar School Association and the Town Council in March 1871, it became clear that both bodies had moved away from their emphasis on the School Board towards the idea of having the Town Council as the representative element among the governors.[71] However, Dixon hoped that the School Board would soon become 'a truly representative body'.

In January 1872, the Commissioners announced that a scheme was ready for publication.[72] As has been seen, this was eventually accepted by Dissenters, but was blocked nevertheless by the more conservative of the existing governors.[73] The spokesman in Parliament for the governors was Salisbury.[74] In the case of the great endowment in Birmingham, then, a scheme which had received general approval in the town was vetoed through the work of agents of the closed corporation of twenty governors. The final scheme for the School, engineered by the Charity Commission, did not become law till 1878, and it was at two retrograde removes from the original proposals of the S.I.C. for the School. The Taunton Report had recommended the creation of twenty-one new governors, ten of whom would have been members of the Town Council.[75] The 1873 scheme of the Endowed Schools Commissioners included the same number of governors, but with eight from the Town Council and four from the School Board. The 1878 scheme retained eight councillors, but added three representatives from the Universities of Oxford, Cambridge and London. It was to these three proposed members that Bright and Chamberlain made their objection in Parliament in 1878. It was therefore ironic that the 1873 scheme should have foundered over the question of removing Church instruction from the School, rather than on account of the composition of the governing body.

The sequence of events which led to the downfall of the Edward Schools Commission is well known. Despite Forster's attempt to save the Commission and Part II of the Bill in the Select Committee of 1873, the Conservatives committed themselves before the 1874 Election to removing the three Commissioners.[76] The amending Bill was introduced by the new Government in July 1874.[77] It removed the triumvirate. Henceforward there were to be five Charity Commissioners, including two Commissioners for endowed schools.[78]

P. H. J. H. Gosden has said that the 1874 Act did less than the Conservatives had promised.[79] The reason for their apparent moderation has not been dealt with in recent studies; but it was revealed by Disraeli's biographers. The new Prime Minister saw that the Liberals would incite violent feelings if the 1874 amendment went as far as Salisbury wished: that is, if it protected all endowed schools from secularisation. Therefore Disraeli tried to make a compromise in order to mollify the Liberals. Aided by Gathorne Hardy he persuaded Salisbury to accept a modification of the Bill which he considered to be 'first in importance' among the measures which his Government proposed. When Salisbury capitulated before Disraeli's proposal, Lord Derby, formerly Stanley of the S.I.C., exclaimed, 'Thank God we have got rid of the only rock ahead'.[80]

On 19 April 1876, Lyttelton took his own life. For several years he had been suffering from bouts of intense depression which had less and less frequently been balanced by his great excesses of energy. Among a number of factors which contributed to his final collapse were the death of a dearly loved daughter in 1875 and the intensity of the opprobrium he had suffered as Chief Commissioner. Lyttelton was the epitome of the type of country gentleman, devoted to public affairs, which Hobhouse had remembered in the person of his own father.[81] Gladstone published a brief memorial to Lyttelton in which he wrote that 'his mastery, and his energetic handling of the subject of public endowments will, it is probable, greatly redound to his reputation in future times'.[82] He had only very briefly held political office early in his career, and there can be little doubt but that his *forte* had been the forthright prosecution of his own views and the views of others in relation to the inquiries with which he had been associated in the 1850s and 1860s. He had trimmed his opinions on Church matters considerably and controversially during the period of his service on the S.I.C., and perhaps his own best interests would have been served by his declining the Commissionship offered to him in 1869. Certainly his experience of county affairs, and the deference which had earlier been his due in Birmingham did not equip him satisfactory for the arduous tasks of diplomacy and conciliation of local interests which he had undertaken in his dealings with endowments after 1869.

Lyttelton had been subjected to a perpetual battering by opponents during his tenure of office after 1869. He might have expected more favourable treatment from the Revd J. L. Brereton; but in 1874 Brereton published his 'County Education' which, while being primarily an exposition of his general 'county' principles and containing plans for county colleges, included also some gratuitous criticisms of the Endowed Schools Commission.[83] In his final pages he blandly proposed that a system of four 'provinces', based largely upon the Universities, should replace Part II of the 1869 Bill; and that endowments within these provinces should be combined and redistributed, the schools so created being guaranteed by the possibility of a local rate of one half-penny.[84] Brereton evidently grafted what he had assimilated from the S.I.C. Report on to the principles he had formerly enunciated with Fortescue, which had excluded both rate-aid and the use of endowments.

Brereton sent copies of 'County Education' to a wide circle of men, including Matthew Arnold, the Dukes of Bedford and Devonshire, Temple, Forster, Harrowby, Ducie, Redesdale, Northcote, Acland, Kerrison, and the Marquis of Salisbury.[85] Arnold wrote a courteous acknowledgement; but the only reply to survive came from Lyttelton who wrote impatiently from the Commission office in June 1874. After suggesting tht Brereton had underestimated the expense of his new scheme, he continued, frustrated and at the end of his tether:

> . . . when you attack us as mischievous because we do not in practice bring about what you so glibly spin off on paper, I can only say that I believe if you were a week in this office, you would find the impossibility of it. It is not local *jealousies* precisely; it is *simply the desire to keep what we have,* which prevents us from throwing all sorts of endowments into a hotch-pot, and distributing them as we see best. . . . Nor do I believe that it could be done even with the aid of Provincial Councils, which as you well know, we of the old Commission (the S.I.C.) always assumed as indispensable coadjutors in such difficult and drastic work.[86]

The sole surviving member of the original triumvirate maintained his interest in endowments and secondary schooling in a remarkable and ultimately successful way. H. G. Robinson became in 1880 a member of Lord Aberdare's Departmental Committee on Intermediate and Higher Education in Wales. Aberdare was the H. A. Bruce who had served as Vice-president at the time the S.I.C. was constituted.

In an updated memorandum, written presumably before the Disraeli Government had begun to dismantle the Commission in 1874, Robinson had noted that the complicated Bristol schemes were awaiting approval – if approval could be expected – 'from a (Conservative) minister of whose views on the subject we know nothing, and whose policy has yet to be declared, and very possibly shaped'.[87] His glee at having deposited the parcel of Bristol schemes in the lap of a Conservative politician was scarcely concealed.

Conclusions

The Endowed Schools Commission was the victim of political and religious forces whose magnitude and close direction had not been anticipated accurately by Forster and Ripon in 1869. The abuse and criticism which the original three-man Commission suffered were the products of the way in which they interpreted the Act, and of the atmosphere created by the discussions at the Social Science Association meeting in 1869. The Act itself had been accepted, and continued to be accepted in some quarters, with relative equanimity, and the problems of the period from 1869 to 1874 were in almost every case circumvented by the Commission. Their task was dealt with slowly, but it came remarkably close to accomplishment, in so far as it had always been admitted that the time at their disposal would be too short. The S.I.C. Report had clearly revealed the weaknesses of many endowed schools; Parliament had acknowledged the urgent need to do something to remedy abuses. On the other hand Lyttelton was accurate in his analysis of the Commissioners' task in 1872: 'Our experience in attempting to work the Act has shown that the country was hardly prepared for its reception'.[88] Few persons denied, in principle, the need for general reform; but in practice, when confronted by assistant commissioners, there was usually a retreat into conservative guardianship of the *status quo*. In fact, much of the Commissioners' valuable time was taken up with the process of educating the public about the application of the Act to local endowments. In this task they were assisted by unofficial agents like Temple and Northcote in Devonshire, Ducie in Gloucestershire, by Canon Mosely in Bristol, the Revd H. J. Barton and Christopher Cookson in Northants, and Archeadcon Fearon in Leicestershire.

The Commissioners might have anticipated the working of prejudice and self-interest in individual cases; but they could not have expected the organised opposition, which took three forms. The first Emanuel Hospital scheme invoked the defensive conservatism of the City of London. Resistance was inevitable: but the national campaign which followed was not, and the buttressing provided by the campaign not only protected Emanuel Hospital for the time being, but also represented the obverse of the Commissioners' own attempts to educate the public. After the publicity stage-managed by Nelson, trustees throughout the country were prepared for their own resistance and had their own prejudices reinforced by more powerful authority. They had been 'Saatchied'. The Church Defence Institution represented only one section of opinion in the Established Church, but, like the City Corporation, it provided a focal point and could command valuable Parliamentary action against the Commissioners' schemes; and it ultimately prepared the ground upon which the policy of the 1874 Tory Government was constructed. The Central Nonconformist Committee was the least important among the three groups since, while it criticised the Commission and some of its decisions, its members were able to accept compromises in the knowledge that Liberal policy was flowing in the general direction of their own aims after 1868. Its rôle was that of prompter rather than destroyer.

The extremes of bitterness among the anticipatory obituaries for the Commission are best exemplified in the harangues of the *National Church* and by the anonymous author of 'The Endowed Schools Commission: Shall It Be Continued?' The *National Church* issued a proclamation: 'As it was remarked by a contemporary, "It is impossible to exaggerate the gain to the friends of religious education, in having got rid of gentlemen who, while we desire to do full justice to their conscientious and painstaking activity, proceeded on principles so mischievous as to make any improvement under their auspices unpopular".[89] It was an implicit feature of the 1869 Act that it had gaps through which the Commissioners would be permitted to apply the recommendations of the S.I.C. It was practically impossible that the draftsmen of the Bill should have prescribed a solution for every situation which arose in the process of reform. Yet the combination of the Commissioners' power of subjective interpretation of the Act, and the publicly declared views of two of them in 1869, provided a scaffolding for any fabric of opposition which might be erected by conservative interests. Lyttelton was Chief Commissioner by precedence. But the spirit of the Commission's work emanated from the firm views of Hobhouse, the equity lawyer.

After Hobhouse's death Lord Davey wrote of his 'logical and fearless adherence to principle' and of the tenacity and thoroughness of his work.[90] Roby, however, came closer to the mark when he spoke of his colleague's tendency to see the Commissioners' rôle 'too much as judges . . . and too little as administrators'. Hobhouse was, he said, 'much more of the lawyer than of the diplomat'; opposition to his work by trustees was apt to appear to him as faithlessness rather than fidelity to their trust. He was 'hardly able to understand the ignorant complacency and blind adherence with which the founder's will and ancient rules were regarded by some of the local administrators'.[91]

Hobhouse's attitude, and the problem it helped to create, highlight the complexities of the dilemma in which the Commissioners found themselves. The aim of the Act, on which all seem to have been agreed, was the improvement of the existing provision of education for the middle classes. But from Hobhouse's point of view one of the important consequent functions of the Commission would be to remove some of the abuses and anomalies attached to ancient trusts: this nurtured a thicket of local conservative resistance. As a corollary to this he believed that what may be called 'legal charity' did 'far more harm than good to the poor'.[92] His statement of this severe economic principle before the Social Science Association identified him as wishing to destroy 'the rights of the poor'. In concert with Roby he decided to tackle the big corporations and unfortunately took on an undefeated champion in his first contest. He had been asked to work a law which was sound in principle but widely distasteful in character. He compared the operation of the 1869 Act to that of the 1834 Poor Law Amendment Act which, he said, 'was more discussed, but was very imperfectly understood or accepted by the country'.[93]

Unwise appointments had been made; the public had been inadequately prepared for the 1869 Act. But the fact remains that the Act was passed in a blaze of complacency. The contexts of the Act and of the Commission provide a clue to the failure of the latter and the successful reception of the former. The Act and the S.I.C. matched the periods in which they were created. The S.I.C. was part of a great series of educational inquiries, and its labours seemed even more strenuous than those of the Commissions preceding it. It has already been shown that it was related to similar inquiries into Endowed Schools in Scotland and Ireland; it was close cousin to the 1863 Inquiry into the Courts of Common Law and Chancery. Two of its members, Acland and Forster, sat on the Select Committee on the Oxford and Cambridge Universities Bill in 1867; Roby gave evidence to the same Committee.[94] In relation to professional education, it preceded the Royal Commission on Miltary Education, 1868, which reported in 1870 and was chaired by Lord de Grey and Ripon,[95] joint architect of the 1869 Bill. Temple, Benson and Moseley all gave evidence to this 1868–70 inquiry; and while the S.I.C. was sitting, some of its witnesses gave evidence also to Pakington's 1865 Select Committee. These various inquiries provide for the S.I.C. a framework within which it can be placed in perspective.

On the other hand, the implementation of the main recommendations of the other inquiries proved to be unpopular: reform of the Commission system in the Army and changes at the Universities were companions of the reform of endowed schools, and helped to create a climate in which all might be similarly indicted. The 1869 Act enjoyed the temporary privilege of being smuggled in under the shadow of the Irish Church Bill. But in the long term it was more vulnerable than any of the other measures because its implementation was by comparison painfully slow. Over all hung Gladstone's continuing threat to tax charities, the fact of the Irish Church's disestablishment, and the prospect of a similar fate for the Church of England. In 1873, after his 'promotion' to India, Hobhouse wrote that, though the Commission had been much more successful than he had anticipated, he had aways believed that the triumvirate were 'missionaries sent to lighten the heathen, and to be persecuted and perish at their hands',[96] though this was surely a sour retrospective judgement, for it hardly accounted for the industry and enthusiasm of the Commissioners' early work.

The achievements of the Endowed Schools Commission were but a pale reflection of the vision created by the S.I.C. It is true to say that the vision was spun from a relatively innocent conception of the problems associated with the reform of middle-class schooling, against a background of political compromise at national level; while the Commissioners were confronted by the emergence of a new kind of attitude in local affairs after 1869.

The Report of the S.I.C. was the culmination of a debate which was characterised by an Arnoldian chain-reaction. One major source of ideology about middle-class education emanated from the letters which Thomas Arnold had published in 1832. There was no other coherent analysis of the middle-class problem at that time or throughout the 1840s. Hence there was frequent quotation from the Sheffield letters which were used to flavour the debate as it developed in the 1850s. The exodus of the Tractarians from Oxford in the 1840s left the field of College tuition open to young liberals like Charles Lake, a Newcastle Commissioner, and Benjamin Jowett; and it was in the mid-1840s that the Arnold legend was promoted most strongly by Stanley's 'Life', published in 1844.[97] From the new liberal spirit of the Universities came the generation of young men intensely interested in public affairs and in the removal of current social abuses. Temple, Green and Bryce led this cohort.

The expression of a wider concern for the solution of social problems, anticipated by the Central Society of Education in the 1830s, was embodied in the discussions of the Social Science Association after 1857. Here, participants like Acland, Lyttelton, Fitch, Norris and Robinson began to re-formulate the ideas of Arnold in a context which had been changed by the creation of the executive Charity Commission in 1853. There was henceforward the possibility of using existing endowments as the nuclei of a reformed system of secondary education. The optimism engendered by the new opportunity for more effective legal reform was the foundation on which Temple was able to construct, in 'National Education', a programme of practical suggestions which were to form the agenda for the labours of the S.I.C. in the 1860s.

But Arnold's philosophy had contained conservative as well as liberal elements, and this characteristic was echoed in the attempts at apolitical consensus which were a feature of the meetings of the Social Science Association. And just as the mature Thomas Arnold was a theoretical reformer, but never an iconoclast, so the Association tried to harmonise Utilitarian demands for radical reform with respect for established institutions. Running parallel to the S.S.A. discussions about what should be done there was the practical activity of the Charity Commission which, implicity obeying the precepts of economy and efficiency, sought to make the most of sources of revenue from ancient endowments. Endowments in themselves embodied the paradoxical notion of reviving the institutions of the past so that they might be made more appropriate for satisfying current needs.

However, the work of the S.S.A. was discursive and largely theoretical. What has been largely overlooked in the discussion of middle-class education as it evolved before the 1860s is the practical activity undertaken within the ancient institutions of the county and the diocese. In England and Ireland the county and the diocese were treated as the only practical bases upon which a reformed system of secondary schooling might be created. It was from rural communities that the impulse for change – supported by real experimentation – came. The traditional paternalism of the government of county communities was applied to provision or improvement of middle-class schools. This took a variety of forms: the practical stimulus supplied by the agricultural societies, with plans for farms and schools, later to be capped by the system of Universities' Local

Examinations which had their roots in the pioneering work of the Bath and West Society; the central stimulus to local effort which came from the National Society after 1838; and the County School movement begun by Brereton and Fortescue.

There is no integumental connection, in terms of hard evidence, between Brereton's work in the English provinces, and the educational experience which his colleagues may have brought from Ireland. But it is hard to resist attempting to establish connections between the colonial paternalism of the efforts to reform Irish middle-class schooling, within a county framework, presided over by liberal Anglican clergy and laymen, and the network of middle-class schemes initiated by the traditional leaders of county communities in England. In addition, for English chancery lawyers, and for the mid-century commissions of inquiry, Irish experience of an earlier period suggested models for future endeavour and experience of failure in the face of prejudice.

It is far easier to identify a rural county party at work on the S.I.C. than it is to perceive any profound appreciation by its members of the needs of developing urban communities in relation to middle-class education. The academic liberals who had emerged from their Oxford and Cambridge colleges in the 1840s and 1850s were united on the S.I.C. with sympathetic figures from county society; and so the Arnoldian prescription, which had been adapted by Temple, became linked with the experience which Acland, Northcote and Lyttelton possessed: experience of providing appropriate forms of elementary and secondary education from above in their localities. The radical tone of the S.I.C. proposals has to some extent prevented historians from seeing some of the Commissioners as representatives of a traditional, pre-democratic community. The proposed Provincial Boards might seem to have been a radical innovation; but they were more closely related to the diocesan and county committees of the period before 1864 than to representative town councils and municipal corporations, and to the county councils created after 1888. The S.I.C. based its recommendations more clearly upon the concept of a stable rural community with its theoretically harmonious, interdependent social hierarchy, than upon the practical working of a kind of democracy among the bourgeoisie of urban communities. This is hardly surprising, since there had been no co-ordinated urban attempts to present plans for the organisation of middle-class schooling before the 1860s.

The recommendations of the S.I.C. can be seen as an attempt to introduce a civilising element into what was felt to be an inevitable surge towards democratisation in the 1860s. Most of the members of the Commission could have sympathised with the object of a memorial presented to Palmerston in 1857: the petitioners favoured the adoption of an educational franchise, that is, giving the vote to those who had received a liberal education.[98] Among the signatories were Archbishop Sumner, Fortescue, Brougham, Shaftesbury, Viscount Sandon, James Booth, J. T. Coleridge, M. D. Hill, the Marquis of Kildare, Professor H. W. Acland, and A. P. Stanley, as well as 'many barristers'. But the S.I.C.'s belief that a paternalistic kind of reform, based upon sound equity principles, would be acceptable to a wide range of interested parties after 1867 was mistaken. The Endowed Schools Commission, led by Lyttelton, triggered generally favourable responses among the various county committees which emerged. In the towns, however, the principle of representation, as in Birmingham, and a tradition of corrupt conservatism, as at Bristol and in the City of London, disturbed the Commissioners' work.

The mistaken paternalism of the S.I.C. persisted after 1875 as a factor in the pattern of secondary-school reform. In 1878, in the debate on the final scheme for King Edward's School, Birmingham, Acland, who had stood as Liberal candidate for the town in 1860, asked 'all who valued culture in their municipal institutions in England to pause before they adopted a principle (the representative principle) which would compel them to give way to every petty local influence in the boroughs'.[99]

As one of the leading participants in the mid-century debate on middle-class education, Acland can here be seen as continuing to epitomise the S.I.C.'s position as the most significant agency in a period of political transition. His was the kind of paternalism which was rooted in the gradualist soil of the rural counties, accepting organic, rather than radical change; patronising the increasing political consciousness of the towns by seeming to respond to the 'needs' of the urban middle class, whether through the meetings of the Social Science Association, or by means of the 1869 Act; accepting the application of democratic principles to the provision and administration of some elementary schooling, but withholding representative control from the crucial stabilising agencies of middle-class education; bringing in the reformed Universities to hold the pass against the onslaught of the surging democracy of the towns; and

introducing a modicum of rational competition as a counterpoise to
the privileges of middle-class fee-payers.

When the Royal Commision on Secondary Education reported in
1895 it respectfully prefaced its review and recommendations with
an acknowledgement of the frustrated promise of the Taunton Commission and the 1869 Act. What had been accomplished in two-and-
a-half decades since the early Commission was considered to have
been largely the result of the energy and ideas it had released in
England. Frederick Temple, giving evidence to the 1895 Commission as Bishop of London, could point with muted satisfaction to the
manner in which the Higher Grade elementary schools promoted by
the larger school boards had to some extent begun to serve the
purposes which the Taunton Commission had envisaged for its
third-grade schools.[100] The 1895 Commission was chaired by James
Bryce who, like many of his contemporaries expressing strong interest in the future of secondary schooling, wished to see it resist the
current onslaught of science and technical subjects in the curriculum.
Michael Sadler, performing a kind of 'Temple' role on the Bryce
Commission, tried to strike a balance between the claims of science
and the humanities in the curriculum, and asserted the coincidence,
in principle, of technical and secondary education: for him, the
Technical Institution Acts of 1889 and 1891 heralded a compromise
in the curriculum between the ancient classical model and the
modern scientific experiments of the Higher Grade schools and some
of the grammar shools.[101] But the balance of forces was against
Sadler's point of view. After the Board of Education Act, 1899,
traditional influences carried greater weight in official places, and,
under Robert Morant, the Board's Secondary Regulations led the
grammar-school curriculum into grooves which were conven-
tionally biased towards literary studies.

In other words, the Taunton model of secondary education held
sway well into this century: the Utilitarian, urban model of
schooling, which had experienced a brief, energetic revival under the
school boards, generally receded in influence after 1900. It would
not be extactly true to say that the Georgic model of Taunton took its
place, but it has been the case in the twentieth century that the
S.I.C.'s conception of the dominance of a gentlemanly, liberal tradition in secondary schooling long eclipsed the claims of practical and
useful forms of secondary education. Even in Wales, which began to
create a new system of intermediate schooling after 1889, the

Taunton tradition ultimately prevailed, as Gareth Elwyn Jones has recently shown;[102] and what had started as a system intentionally with a broadly based curriculum developed in narrowly academic forms. Martin Wiener has recently, by means of a brilliant blending of imaginative literature, contemporary social comment, and reflective journalism, constructed a persuasive depiction of a declining industrial dynamic over the past 150 years. In doing so, he made one of the pivots of his argument the paradox of a depression in the agriculture sector of the British economy in the late nineteeth century, and of the parallel diffusion of rural, anti-urban values throughout an increasingly urban, industrial community.[103] The rural depression of the last quarter of the nineteenth century has obscured the positive attempts which were made in the period from the 1830s through to the 1860s to use educational engineering as a means of preserving the integrity of the landed interest in British society and the national economy. The form of middle-class schooling evisaged by the Taunton Commissioners and their predecessors in the shires contributed substantially to the kinds of educational institutions which were to evolve after 1900. The apparent 'failure' of the Edowed Schools Act, and therefore of the Taunton Commission, conceals its ultimate success as one of the key determinants of the nature of schooling in the twentieth century.

Notes

1   E.g. (i) P. H. J. H. Gosden, *The Development of Educational Administration in England and Wales,* Oxford, 1966, p. 65–71; (ii) P. T. Marsh, *The Victorian Church in Decline, Archbishop Tait and the Church of England,* London, 1969, pp. 69–71.
2   Report of the Endowed Schools Commissioners to Her Majesty's Privy Council, 1872, pp. 12–36.
3   For the Taunton Commission's indictment of Hospital Schools, see *S.I.C.,* I, p. 211.
4   A copy of Skirrow's Report is in PRO ED 27/3359, Emanuel Hospital File, 23 June 1857.
5   *S.I.C.,* VII, Report on the Metropolitan District, p. 335.
6   Ibid, p. 338.
7   *S.I.C.,* X, London Division, Report of Assistant Commissioners, pp. 184–5.
8   PRO ED 27/3359.
9   Ibid contains governors' reports of 1844, 1846, 1855, and 1856. The 1855 Report, for example, is 111 pages long.
10   Hobhouse and Hammond, op cit., p. 49.
11   City of London R.O., Guildhall, Minutes of Court of Aldermen, 14

September 1869, p. 50; document headed, 'Report of Committee for giving notice of . . . the intention of the Governors to prepare their own Scheme . . . approved and sealed accordingly'.

12 Ibid, 16 November 1869, p. 61.

13 PRO ED 27/3363, Emanuel Hospital File, 'Scheme for the Regulation of (Emanuel Hospital) Charity, prepared by the Lord Mayor and Aldermen of the City of London . . . pursuant to the Provisions of the Endowed Schools Act of 1869'.

14 See above, Chapter VIII, p. 196.

15 PRO ED 27/3363, letters (i) from Roby to Nelson (City Solicitor), 26 February 1870; (ii) from Nelson to Roby, 1 March 1870. Roby's report is in the same file.

16 See above, Chapter VIII, p. 195.

17 PRO ED 27/3363, the Draft Scheme; see also, City of London R.O., Emanuel Hospital, Box 5/7, Roby's summary of the Scheme.

18 PRO ED 27/3363 letter from Nelson to Roby, 29 November 1870.

19 Ibid, letter from Lord Lyttelton to Cumin at the Education Department, accompanied by printed scheme and objections.

20 *West Middlesex Advertiser,* 13 May 1871.

21 *Times,* 6 April 1871, 'Court of Common Council'.

22 Ibid, advertisement, 27 April 1871.

23 City of London R.O., Court of Aldermen, Box 5/12, undated memorandum.

24 PRO ED 27/3364, letter of June 1871.

25 Ibid, 22 June 1871.

26 *Gloucester Journal,* 22 and 29 April 1871.

27 Ibid, 17 June 1871.

28 *Leicester Journal,* 5 May 1871.

29 Journal of the House of Lords, CIII, pp. 302–618.

30 Ibid, p. 343 (12 June 1871).

31 City of London R.O., Minutes of Court of Aldermen, 27 June 1871.

32 P. Smith (ed.), *Lord Salisbury on Politics,* Cambridge, 1972, p. 66.

33 See above, Chapter VIII, p. 194.

34 *The National Church,* New Series, III, May 1873, 'The Endowed Schools Commission', p. 106. In this article the establishment of the committee is recorded.

35 Ibid, March 1873, 'Church of England Endowed Schools Trust Conference', p. 62.

36 *Blackwood's Magazine,* DCLXIX, Vol. CX, July 1871, 'Education, Endowments and Competition', 81–99.

37 Ibid, p. 92.

38 Ibid, p. 94.

39 Ibid, p. 89.

40 For Hodgkinson's biographical details, see Boase, op. cit.

41 *Nonconformist,* 17 May 1871, p. 489.

42 Report of the Endowed Schools Commissioners to the Privy Council, 1872, pp. 27–8.

43 *Nonconformist,* 19 July 1871, p. 701.

44 *Times,* 11 May 1871, 'Charities: the London School Board'.
45 Ibid, 13 July 1871, 'The Endowed Schools Commission and the London School Board'.
46 Hobhouse and Hammond, op. cit., p. 54. On his return from India Hobhouse was elected a member of the London School Board.
47 *Times,* 28 September 1871, 'London School Board: Emanuel Hospital'.
48 Ibid, 11 June 1871.
49 Ibid, 27 March 1871.
50 Ibid, 20 May 1872, 'A Good Example'.
51 Select Committee on the Endowed Schools Act (1869), 1873, p. 433.
52 Hansard, Third Series, CCXV, May–June 1873, pp. 1875–1960.
53 Ibid, p. 1892.
54 Ibid, p. 1896.
55 Ibid, p. 1956.
56 *Nonconformist,* 5 July 1871, p. 660.
57 For Schnadhorst's later work as founder of the National Liberal Association, see Boase, op. cit.
58 *Nonconformist,* 22 November 1871. For Winterbottom, see above, Chapter IX, p. 213. He had been Forster's front-bench colleague at the First Reading of the 1869 Bill.
60 *Nonconformist,* 17 April 1872, p. 395.
61 Ibid, 22 May 1872, p. 530. See also Schnadhorst's evidence to the 1873 Select Committee, 6 May 1873, p. 350. Mr Leatham was a member of that Committee.
62 *Nonconformist,* 1 January 1873, p. 5. But see below, this Chapter, p. 237, for the later disputes over the Birmingham Scheme.
63 Devon County R.O., Fortescue Papers, 1262m/FC97, letter of Lord Lyttelton to Earl Fortescue (then Lord Ebrington), London, 2 December 1870.
64 See above, (i) Chapter VI, p. 146; (ii) Chapter VIII, p. 197.
65 PRO ED 27/4891, Birmingham King Edward's School File, memorandum of Lyttelton to Assistant Commissioner J. L. Hammond, 26 August 1870.
66 For Clause 32 and Emanuel Hospital, see above, this Chapter, p. 243.
67 PRO Ed 27/4891, (i) letter from Whateley, secretary to the Governors, informing the Commission of their decision to prepare a scheme, 19 August 1869; (ii) seventeen-page draft scheme of Governors, 29 July 1870.
68 Ibid, interview memorandum, J. S. Wright of the Association, 15 July 1870.
69 Ibid, Lyttelton's memorandum on Birmingham, 26 August 1870.
70 *Birmingham and Midland News,* 19 January 1871.
71 *Birmingham Daily Gazette,* 2 March 1871.
72 Report of the Endowed Schools Commissioners, 1872, p. 8.
73 PRO ED 27/4893, 'Case of the Governors against the Scheme of the Commissioners', 1873 (otherwise undated).
74 Hansard, Third Series, May–July 1873, CCXVI, p. 1156.
78 Ibid, CCXI, p. 87.

79   Gosden, op. cit., p. 69.

80   G. E. Buckle and W. F. Moneypenny, *Life of Benjamin Disraeli, Earl of Beaconsfield, V, 1868–76,* London, 1920, pp. 333–4; pp. 360–1.

81   See above, Chapter I, quotation at head of chapter.

82   ——, *Brief Memorials of Lord Lyttelton, London, 1876:* biographical sketch by W. E. Gladstone, p. 46.

83   J. L. Brereton, *County Education: a Contribution of Experiments, Estimates, and Suggestions,* London, 1874.

84   Ibid, pp. 127–8.

85   A list of recipients is included in the Brereton Papers at Homerton College, Cambridge.

86   Fortescue–Brereton Papers, letter of Lyttelton to Brereton, 16 June 1874.

87   PRO ED 27/1291, Bristol Grammar School File, undated memorandum in H. G. Robinson's hand. The memorandum makes it clear that he was positively hoping for a stay of execution, even after the Election.

88   Report of the Endowed Schools Commissioners, 1872, p. 37.

89   *The National Church,* August 1874, 'The Endowed Schools Bill', p. 180.

90   Hobhouse and Hammond, op. cit., p. 51.

91   Ibid, p. 50.

92   Ibid, loc. cit.

93   Ibid, p. 52.

94   Special Report from the Select Committee on the Oxford and Cambridge Universities Bill . . . , 31 July 1867, p. ii.

95   Royal Commission appointed to Inquire into the Present State of Military Education and into the Training of Candidates for Commissions in the Army, 1870, p. 46.

96   Hobhouse and Hammond, op. cit., p. 46.

97   C. Harvie, *The Light of Liberalism,* London, 1976, p. 34.

98   *Times,* 19 December 1857.

99   Hansard, Third Series, February–March 1878, p. 795.

100   Royal Commission on Secondary Education (the Bryce Commission), 1895, II, p. 358.

101   Ibid, I, p. 136.

102   Gareth Elwyn Jones, Controls and Conflicts in Welsh Secondary Education, 1889–1944, Cardiff, 1982.

103   M. J. Wiener, *English Culture and the Decline of the Industrial Spirit,* Cambridge, 1981.

Appendix

Letter from the Revd Christopher Cookson, secretary of the Middle Schools Committee, Northants Education Society, to the Trustees of Northants Endowed Schools

Dallington Vicarage,
Northampton
December 8th, 1870

Sir, You are probably aware that in the year 1864 a Royal Commission was appointed for examining into the condition of the Endowed Schools of England. This Commission made a report to Her Majesty in 1868. In this Report certain general principles were recommended with a view to providing, as far as might be possible, sufficient and efficient Grammar Schools of various grades for the whole country; and, in connection with this, the character and condition of every Endowed Grammar School were described in accordance with reports made to the Commission by Inspectors appointed under their authority. And further, specific recommendations as to the remodelling of many of these schools were made, involving in many cases a redistribution of funds.

There is no doubt that ultimately the Commission will visit each of the Districts into which they divided the country, and will, with the assistance of Parliament, make many changes of great importance to the Schools and to the community. In these circumstances, the Northants Educational Society thought at their last Annual Meeting that it was desirable that something should be done with a view to meeting, and, if possible, guiding the future action of the Commissioners in this County; and they requested the Middle Class Schools Committee of that Society to take the matter in hand.

That Committee met last week (the Rt Hon. G. Ward Hunt being in the chair), and after taking into consideration the Report of Her Majesty's Commissioners, they came to the conclusion that it was desirable in the first instance to invite the co-operation of the trustees of the several Schools, and that (as the matter is of great interest to the whole County) to call a Public Meeting, at which some action more or less authoritative might be originated.

I am requested, therefore, to ask you (if you see no objection) to be so good as to summon a meeting of the Trustees of . . . . School, at your earliest convenience, and to lay this letter before them, asking them whether they would be willing to send some Representative or Representatives of their Body to hold a Conference with the Committee of the Educational Society, on Monday, 9th January, 1871, at Noon, in the Rooms of the Religious and Useful Knowledge Society, Gold Street, Northampton.

I shall feel particularly obliged by your communicating to me the decision of your Trustees as soon as possible, in order that I may know whether to summon the Committee of which I am Secretary.

I am, etc.,

Source: Minute Book of the Middle Schools Committee of the Northants Education Society. See main text, Chapter IX.

Bibliography

A   **Primary source materials**

I   *Record offices and repositories*

Henry Austin Bruce Papers, Glamorgan County Record Office, Cathays Park, Cardiff.

James Bryce Papers, Bodleian Library, University of Oxford.

Fortescue–Brereton Correspondence, Homerton College Library, Cambridge.

Fortescue Papers, Devon County Record Office, Exeter.

Gladstone Papers, British Library.

Granville Papers, Public Record Office.

Thomas Hill Green Papers and Letters, Balliol College Library, Oxford.

Kay-Shuttleworth Papers, John Rylands Library, Manchester.

Bath and Wells Diocesan Board of Education, Minute Books, 1838–47; 1847–57; 1857–74; Deanery Office, Wells.

Prospectus of an Agricultural College and Farm, Proposed to be Founded under the Auspices of the Bath and West of England Society. Copy in Bath City Reference Library, catalogued as B.630.

Proceedings of the Bristol Town Council, 14 May 1867, to 18 June 1872. Bristol Civic Record Office.

Bristol Charities Minute Books. In the keeping of the Bristol Municipal Charities Trustees, Union Street, Bristol.

Bristol School Board Minutes, I, March 1871, to March 1873. Bristol Civic Record Office.

Letters concerning the Proposed Dorset County School, national system of education and parish schools, 1863. Dorset County Record Office, Dorchester, catalogued as P97/SC1.

Gloucester Cathedral Chapter Minute Book, January 1865, to January 1891, Gloucester Cathedral Library.

'Leicestershire': a document describing the scheme of a county committee appointed to reform and re-organize county endowed schools, c. 1873, Leicestershire Record Office, Leicester.

Minutes of the Court of Aldermen, Corporation Record Office, Guildhall, City of London.

Annual Reports of the Manchester Church Education Society, Local Room,

Manchester Central Library.

Monmouth Borough Records, 1847–1866, Gwent County Record Office, Cwmbran, Gwent.

Annual Reports (i) of the Winchester Diocesan Board of Education, 1839–59; (ii) of the Basingstoke Mechanics' Institute, 1855–9. Hampshire County Record Office, Winchester.

Minute Books of the Worcester Diocesan Board of Education. Worcester Diocesan Library.

At Church House, Westminster: (i) Annual Reports of the National Society for 1839, 1840, 1851 and 1866; (ii) Minute Book of the Middle Schools Committee of the National Society, November 1865, to May 1880.

Public Record Office: Endowed Schools files

Abergavenny, ED 27/6588.

Beford, Harpur Trust, ED 27/8a, 8b.

Bristol Grammar School, ED 27/1284, 1291, 1312–16.

Birmingham, King Edward's School, ED 27/4891–3.

Bromsgrove School, ED 27/5325.

Campden (Gloucestershire) Grammar School, ED 27/1340.

Clifton College, ED 27/1263.

Colston's Hospital, Bristol, ED 27/1274.

Emanuel Hospital, Westminster, ED 27/3359, 3363, 3364.

Exeter Grammar School, ED 27/695, 697.

Gloucester United Charities, ED 27/1382–96.

Guilsborough (Northants) Grammar School, ED 27/3661.

Keighley Grammar School, ED 27/5957.

Kidderminster Grammer School, ED 27/5407.

Monmouth School, ED 27/6609, 6612, 6671, 6660.

Newport (Salop), Adam's School, ED 27/3977.

Northampton Grammar School, ED 27/3672.

Oundle School, ED 27/3684, 44933.

Peterborough Cathedral School, ED 27/3686.

Towcester Grammar School, ED 27/3703.

II *Government and parliamentary papers*

Journal of the House of Lords, 1871–4, CIII–CVI.

Reports of the Commissioners of the Board of Education in Ireland, 1809–12, reprinted, December 1813.

Report of the Commissioners of Education in Ireland, to His Excellency the Lord Lieutenant, of the Proceedings of their Board from the 18th of November 1813, to the 25th of March 1814.

Reports from Commissioners (Brougham Inquiry), II: Charities; various volumes, 1818–37.

Report from the Select Committee to whom the several petitions complaining of the Depressed State of Agriculture of the United Kingdom were Referred, June 1821.

Report from the Select Committee on Education in Ireland, May 1838.

Report made to His Majesty by a Royal Commission of Inquiry into the State of the Universities of Scotland, October 1831.

Report from the Select Committee on Agriculture, August 1833.

A Return of the Charitable Funds and other Property in the Possession, Order, or Disposition of each Municipal Corporation in England and Wales, July 1834.

Report of the Committee appointed to Inquire into the Municipal Corporations in England and Wales: London and Southwark, London Companies, April 1837.

Report of the Select Committee of the House of Lords appointed to Inquire into the State of Agriculture in England and Wales, June 1837.

Fourth Report of the Commissioners of National Education in Ireland, for the Year 1837.

Report from the Select Committee on Foundation Schools and Education in Ireland, August 1838.

Committee of Council for Education, Minutes, 1839 onwards.

Seventh Report of the Commissioners of National Education in Ireland, for the Year 1840.

Ninth Report, ibid., 1842.

Reports from Commissioners, XX: Commission on Charities, 1849.

Report of Her Majesty's Commissioners appointed to Inquire into the Staff, Discipline, Studies, and Revenues of the University and Colleges of Oxford, 1852.

Report of the Commissioners appointed to Inquire into the existing State of the Corporation of the City of London, 1854.

First Report of the Charity Commissioners for England and Wales, 1854.

Second Report, ibid., 1855.

Third Report, ibid., 1856.

Fourth Report, ibid., 1857.

Fifth Report, ibid., 1858.

Papers on the Re-organization of the Civil Service Presented to both Houses of Parliament, 1855.

Report of Her Majesty's Commissioners appointed to Inquire into the Endowments, Funds, and actual Condition of all Schools endowed for the purpose of education in Ireland (Kildare Report), 1858.

Report from the Select Committee on Civil Service Appointments, July 1860.

Report of Her Majesty's Commissioners appointed to Inquire into the State of Popular Education in England (Newcastle Report), 1861.

Reports from Commissioners, XVII: Part I, 1863. National Education (Ireland): 29th Report of the Commissioners of National Education for the Year 1862.

First Report of Her Majesty's Commissioners appointed to Inquire into the Superior Courts of Common Law, and Courts of Chancery in England and Ireland, 1863.

Report of the Children's Employment Commission (1862): Third Report, 1864.

Charities, Return to an Order of the House of Commons, dated from 1865,

Copies of Correspondence between the Treasury and the Board of Inland Revenue, in August and September 1863.

Report of the Commissioners appointed to Inquire into the Revenues and Management of Certain Colleges and Schools, and the Studies pursued and Instruction given therein (Clarendon Report), 1864.

Report from the Select Committee on Education, April 1865.

First Report from the Select Committee on Metropolitan Local Government, April 1866.

Special Report from the Select Committee on the Oxford and Cambridge Universities Education Bill, July 1867.

Report of the Commissioners on the Employment of Children, Young Persons, and Women, in Agriculture, 1868.

Report of Her Majesty's Commissioners appointed to Inquire into the Education given in Schools not comprised within Her Majesty's Two Former Commissions, bearing date respectively 30th June in the twenty-second year, and 18th July in the twenty-fifth year of Her Majesty's reign (Taunton Report), 1867–9.

Report from the Select Committee on County Financial Arrangements, July 1868.

Report of the Royal Commission appointed to Inquire into the Present State of Military Education and into the Training of Candidates for Commissions in the Army, 1870.

Report of the Endowed Schools Commissioners to Her Majesty's Privy Council, 1872.

First Report of the Royal Commissioners appointed to Inquire into the Endowed Schools and Hospitals (Scotland), 1873.

Third Report, ibid., 1875.

Report from the Select Committee on the Endowed Schools Act (1869), 1873.

Report from the Select Committee on the Charitable Trusts Acts, July 1884.

Second Report of the Royal Commission on Technical Instruction, I, III, 1884.

Report from the Select Committee on the Endowed Schools Acts, 1886.

Report from the Departmental Committee on Agriculture and Dairy Schools, I, 1887.

Final Report of a Departmental Committee on Agriculture and Dairy Schools, 1888.

Board of Education: Special Reports on Education Subjects, VIII, 1902.

Report of the Departmental Committee appointed by the Board of Agriculture to Inquire into the Report upon the subject of Agricultural Education, 1908.

III   *Newspapers, periodicals and journals*

Times
Daily News
Bath Chronicle
Birmingham Daily Post

Bradford Observer
Bristol Gazette
Bristol Post
Bristol Times and Mirror
Exeter and Plymouth Gazette
Gloucester Journal
Hereford Times
Leicester Journal
Monmouthshire Beacon
Monmouthshire Merlin
Northampton Herald
Northampton Mercury
Usk Observer
West Middlesex Advertiser
Western Daily Press
Western Times.
The Agricultural Magazine, XIV, 1806.
The Annual Register, 1868–74.
Blackwood's Magazine
The Edinburgh Review
Gardener's Chronicle and Agricultural Gazette, 1846.
Macmillan's Magazine
The National Church, 1870–4.
The Nonconformist, 1841–74.
The Quarterly Journal of Education, I to IX.
The Westminster Review.
Transactions of the Royal Agricultural Society, 1840–68.
Journal of the Bath and West of England Society for the Encouragement of
    Agriculture, Arts, Manufactures, and Commerce, I to VIII, 1853–60.
The Annals of Agriculture
Annuals Reports of the British Association for the Advancement of Science,
    1853–70.
Letters and Papers on Agriculture (Bath and West of England Society),
    1785–1802.
Journal of the Society of Arts
Transactions of the National Association for the Promotion of Social
    Science, 1857–86.

B   Unpublished theses and dissertations

Bartrip, P. W. J., *The Career of Matthew Davenport Hill, with special
    reference to his place in penal and educational reform movements in
    mid-nineteenth-century England.* Ph.D., University of Wales, 1975.
Clayton, J. D., *Mr Gladstone's Leadership of the Parliamentary Liberal
    Party, 1868–74.* Ph.D., University of Oxford, 1959.
Hey, Colin G., *The History of Hazelwood School, Birmingham, and its
    influence on educational developments in the nineteenth century.* M.A.
    (Ed.), University of Wales, 1954.

Johnson, J. R. B., *The Education Department, 1839–64: a study in social policy and the growth of government*. Ph.D., University of Cambridge, 1968.

Johnson, W. B., *The Development of English Education, 1856–82, with special reference to the work of Robert Lowe*. M.Ed., University of Durham, 1956.

Mylward, R. C., *A quantitative study of the growth of science teaching in the endowed grammar schools of England and Wales, 1800–1900*. M.Ed., University of Wales, 1975.

Sheen, I. D., *The development of elementary and secondary education in Abergavenny, 1869–1902*. M.Ed., University of Wales, 1977.

Taylor, A. F., *Birmingham and the Movement for National Education, 1867–77*. Ph.D., University of Leicester, 1964.

Williamson, J. M., *A study of the public schools for the education of the lower-middle classes in the nineteenth century*. M.Ed., University of Wales, 1975.

C Other works

Acland, A. H. D. (ed.), *Memoir and Letters of the Rt Hon. Sir T. D. Acland*, privately printed, London, 1902.

Acland, Thomas Dyke, 'Elementary Introduction to the Chemistry of Practical Farming', *Bath and West Society Journal*, 1855.

Acland, Thomas Dyke, *The Education of the Farmer*, London, 1858.

Acland, Thomas Dyke, *Some Account of the Origin and Objects of the New Oxford Examinations*, London, 1858.

Adamson, J. W., *English Education, 1789–1902*, London, 1930.

Addy, S. O., *Middle-class Education in Sheffield, by an Oxonian* (reprinted from the *Sheffield Daily Telegraph*), Sheffield, 1883.

Akenson, Donald H., *The Irish Education Experiment: the National System of Education in the Nineteenth Century*, London, 1970.

—— , Albert Middle-class College in Suffolk (prospectus, May, 1865). (Copy in the D.E.S. Reference Library.)

Allsobrook, David Ian, 'The Reform of the Endowed Schools: the work of the Northants Education Society, 1854–1874', *History of Education*, II, No. 1, January 1973.

Anderson, Olive, *A Liberal State at War: English Politics and Economic History during the Crimean War*, New York, 1967.

Anderson Olive, 'The Political Uses of History in Mid-nineteenth-century England', *Past and Present*, XXXVI, April 1967.

Anderson, Olive, 'The Janus-face of Nineteenth-century English Radicalism: the Administrative Reform Association', *Victorian Studies*, VIII, 3, March 1965.

Anderson, Robert, 'Secondary Education in Mid-Nineteenth-century France: some social aspects', *Past and Present*, LIII, November 1971.

Armytage, W. H. G., 'Augustan Academic Honeycombs: Some Eighteenth-century conventicles of science', in *The Changing Curriculum*, London, 1971, pp. 37–50.

Armytage, W. H. G., A. J. Mundella, 1825–1897: the Liberal background to the Labour Movement, London, 1951.

Armytage, W. H. G., 'Secondary Education', in Crick, Bernard (ed.), Essays on Reform 1967, a Centenary Tribute, Oxford, 1967.

Armytage, W. H. G., Civic Universities, London, 1955.

Armytage, W. H. G., 'Education in Sheffield', in Linton, D.(ed.), Sheffield and its Region, British Association, Sheffield, 1956.

Archer, R. L., Secondary Education in the Nineteenth Century, Cambridge, 1921.

Arnold, Matthew, A French Eton, London, 1864.

Arnold, Matthew, 'Porro Unum et Necessarium', in Mixed Essays, London, 1880.

Arnold, Matthew, Culture and Anarchy, London, 1909 edition.

Arnold, Matthew, 'Endowments', in Super, R.H.(ed.), Dissent and Dogma, Michigan, 1968.

Arnold, Thomas, The Miscellaneous Works, Collected and Republished, London, 1845.

Askwith, Betty, The Lytteltons: a family chronicle of the Nineteenth century, London, 1845.

Atkinson, Norman, Irish Education: a history of educational institutions, Dublin, 1969.

Auchmuty, J. J., Irish Education: a historical survey, Dublin and London, 1937.

Austin, Roland, The Crypt School, Gloucester . . . 1539–1939, Gloucester, 1939.

Aydelotte, William O., 'The Country Gentleman and the Repeal of the Corn Laws', English Historical Review, LXXXII, No. CCCXII, January 1967.

——— , Middle-class Education and Class Instruction in the Mechanics' Institutions, considered in two reports of the Society of Arts, London, 1857.

Baines, Edward, Education Best Promoted by Perfect Freedom, London, 1854.

Balls, F. E., 'The Endowed Schools Act, 1869, and the Development of the English Grammar Schools in the Nineteenth Century, I: The Origins of the Act', Durham Research Review, 19, September 1967.

Balls, F. E., 'The Endowed Schools Act, 1869, and the Development of the English Grammar Schools in the Nineteenth Century, II: The Operation of the Act', Durham Research Review, 20, April 1968.

Balls, F. E., 'The Endowment of Education in the Nineteenth Century: the case of the Bedford Harpur Trust', History of Education, VI, No. 2, June 1977.

Bamford, T. W., The Rise of the Public Schools, London, 1967.

Bamford, T. W., Thomas Arnold, London, 1960.

Bamford, T. W., Thomas Arnold on Education, Cambridge, 1970.

Banks, J. A., Prosperity and Parenthood: a study of family planning among the Victorian Middle Classes, London, 1954.

Banks, Olive, Parity and Prestige in English Secondary Education, London, 1955.

Bassett, Arthur Tilney (ed.), *Gladstone's Speeches, Descriptive Index and Bibliography*, London, 1916.

Baxter, R. Dudley, *The New Reform Bill: the Franchise Returns Critically Examined*, London, 1866.

Bennett, W. J., *Crime and Education: the Duty of the State Therein*, London, 1846.

Birmingham Church of England Defence Association, *Lectures delivered in the Town Hall, Birmingham*, Birmingham, 1861.

Bowen, Desmond, *The Idea of the Victorian Church: a study of the Church of England, 1833–1889*, Montreal, 1968.

Boyd, A. K., *Radley College, 1847–1947*, Oxford, 1948.

Brereton, J. L., *Principles and Plan of a Farm and County School*, Exeter and London, 1858.

Brereton, J. L., *County Education, a letter addressed to the Rt Hon. the Earl of Devon*, London, 1861.

Brereton, J. L., 'On Education as Connected with Agriculture', *Journal of the Royal Agricultural Society of England*, XXV, 1864.

Brereton, J. L., *The County College, an Educational Proposal*, addressed to the University of Cambridge, London and Cambridge, 1872.

Brereton, J. L., *County Education, a Contribution of Experiments, Estimates and Suggestions*, London, 1874.

Brereton, J. L., *County Education, Accounts of the Devon and Norfolk County School Associations for 1875 . . .* , London, 1876.

Briggs, Asa, 'Thomas Attwood and the Economic Background of the Birmingham Political Union', *Cambridge Historical Journal*, no. 2, 1948.

Briggs, Asa, 'The Background to Parliamentary Reform in Three English Cities, 1930–32', *Cambridge Historical Journal*, X, No. 3, 1952.

Briggs, Asa, *Victorian People: some reassessment of people, institutions, ideas, and events, 1857–67*, London, 1954.

Briggs, Asa, *The Age of Improvement*, London, 1959.

Briggs, Asa, and Saville, J., (eds.), *Essays in Labour History*, London, 1960.

Briggs, Asa, 'Middle-class Consciousness in English Politics, 1780–1846', *Past and Present*, April 1956.

Briggs, Asa, *Victorian Cities*, London, 1963.

Brook, Ray, *The Story of Huddersfield*, London, 1968.

Brose, Oliver J., *Church and Parliament: the Re-shaping of the Church of England, 1828–60*, London and Stanford, 1959.

Brougham, Henry, Lord, 'Observations on the Judges of the Court of Chancery and the Practices and Delays Complained of in that Court', *Edinburgh Review*, XXXIX, October 1823.

Bruce, H. A., *Letters of the Rt Hon. Henry Austin Bruce, GCB, Lord Aberdare of Duffryn*, 2 volumes, privately printed, 1902.

Bryans, E., *A History of St. Peter's College, Radley, 1847–1924*, Oxford, 1926.

Bryce, James, 'The Work of Educational Endowments', *Macmillan's Magazine*, XIX, April 1869.

Burn, W. L., *The Age of Equipoise*, London, 1964.

—— , *Rejoinder of the Free Grammar School Association to the*

Memorandum of the Governors in answer to the Proposals for Reform, Birmingham, 1865.

—— , Bath and West and Southern Counties Society: *Catalogue of the Library,* Bath, 1964.

Caird, James, *English Agriculture in 1850–1,* London, 1852.

Campbell, John, Lord, *Lives of the Lord Chancellors . . . ,* VIII, London, 1869.

Cannadine, David, 'The Calthorpe Family and Birmingham, 1810–1910: a Conservative Interest Examined', *The Historical Journal,* XVIII, No. 4, 1975.

Capel, Revd H. M., and Temple, Revd F., *Addresses Delivered before a Private Meeting at the Mayor of Birmingham's Residence, 13 February 1867,* Birmingham, 1867.

Carlile, Nicholas, *A Concise Description of the Endowed Grammar Schools of England and Wales,* I and II, London, 1818.

Cavanagh, F. A., 'Lord Brougham and the Society for the Diffusion of Useful Knowledge', *Journal of Adult Education,* IV, No. 1, October 1929.

Chadwick, Owen, *The Victorian Church,* 2 volumes, London, 1966.

Checkland, S. G., *The Rise of Industrial Society in England, 1815–85,* London, 1964.

Christie, O. F., *The Transition from Aristocracy, 1832–67,* London, 1927.

Christie, O. F., *A History of Clifton College, 1860–1934,* Bristol, 1935.

—— , *The History of the Royal Agricultural College, Cirencester, with a description . . . ,* Cirencester, c. 1860.

Clapham, Sir John, *An Economic History of Modern Britain,* Cambridge, 1938.

Clark, George Kitson, 'The Electorate and the Repeal of the Corn Laws', *Transactions of the Royal Historical Society,* Series V, 1, 1951.

Clark, George Kitson, *The Making of Victorian England,* London, 1963.

Clark, George Kitson, *Churchmen and the Condition of England,* London, 1973.

Cole, G. D. H., *Studies in Class Structure,* London, 1955.

Cole, H. W., *The Middle Classes and the Borough Franchise,* London, 1866.

Collins, William Lucas, 'County Grammar Schools', *Blackwood's Magazine,* CIII, No. DCXXVII, January 1868.

Compton, J. M., 'Open Competition and the Indian Civil Service, 1854–76', *English Historical Review,* LXXXIII, No. CCCXVII, April 1968.

Connell, K. H., *The Population of Ireland, 1750–1845,* Oxford, 1950.

Connell, W. F., *The Educational Thought and Influence of Matthew Arnold,* London, 1950.

Constable, Revd John, *An Address to the Students of the Royal Agricultural College, Cirencester,* London, 1865.

Cowherd, R. G., *The Politics of English Dissent: the Religious Aspects of Liberal and Humanitarian Reform Movements from 1815 to 1848,* London, 1959.

Cowley, Abraham, *The Second and Third Parts of the Works of Mr Abraham Cowley . . .*, London, 1689.

Cowling, Maurice, *1867: Disraeli, Gladstone and Revolution,* Cambridge, 1967.

Cromwell, Valerie, 'Interpretations of Nineteenth-century Administration —— an Analysis', *Victorian Studies,* IX, 1966.

Cullen, L. M., *An Economic History of Ireland since 1660,* London, 1972.

Dawes, Richard, *Hints on an Improved and Self-paying System of National Education . . .*, second edition, 1847.

Douglas Smith, A. E., *The City of London School,* second edition, Oxford, 1965.

Dowling, P. J., *A History of Irish Education, a study in conflicting loyalties,* Cork, 1971.

Dunbabin, J. P. D., 'British Local Government Reform: the Nineteenth Century and After', *English Historical Review,* XCII, No. 365, October 1977.

Duppa, Baldwin Francis, *The Education of the Peasantry in England, What It Is and What It Ought to Be, with a somewhat detailed account of the Establishment of M. de Fellenberg at Hofwyl . . .*, London, 1834.

Duppa, Baldwin Francis, 'County Colleges of Agriculture', Central Society of Education, Third Publication, London, 1839.

Durcan, T. J., *History of Irish Education from 1800, with special reference to manual instruction,* Bala, 1972.

Dyos, H. (ed.), *The Study of Urban History,* London, 1968.

Dyson, A. E., and Lovelock, J. (eds.), *Education and Democracy,* London, 1975.

Edmonds, E. L., and O. P. (eds.), *"I Was There": the Memoirs of H. S. Tremenheere,* Eton, 1965.

Edmunds, E., 'Middle-class Education', *Journal of the Farmers' Club,* February 1865.

Edwards, R. D., and Williams, T. D. (eds.), *The Great Famine,* Dublin, 1956.

——, *The Endowed Schools Commission: Shall It Be Continued?'* London, 1873.

Ernle, Lord, *English Farming, Past and Present,* London, 1961.

Evelyn, John, *Sylva, or a Discourse of Forest-trees and the propagation of timber,* London, 1664.

Faber, Geoffrey, *Jowett,* Oxford, 1957.

Fearon, J. P., *The Endowed Charities: with some suggestions for further legislation regarding them,* London, 1855.

Feuchtwanger, E., *Disraeli, Democracy and the Tory Party,* London, 1968.

Findlay, J. J. (ed.), *Arnold of Rugby, His School Life and Contributions to Education,* London, 1925.

Finer, S. E., 'The Transmission of Benthamite Ideas, 1820–50', in G. Sutherland (ed.), *Studies in the Growth of Nineteenth-century Government,* London, 1972.

Finer, S. E., *Life and Times of Sir Edwin Chadwick,* London, 1952.

Fink, D. P. J., *Queen Mary's Grammar School, Walsall,* Walsall, 1954.

Fitch, J. G., 'Educational Endowments', *Fraser's Magazine,* January 1869.

Fitzmaurice, Lord Edmond, *Life of Granville George Leveson-Gower, Second Earl Granville, K.G.,* 2 volumes, London, 1905.

Fletcher, Joseph, *The Farm-school System of the Continent,* London, 1851.

Fletcher, Sheila, *Feminists and Bureaucrats,* Cambridge, 1980.

Fortescue, Hugh, Earl, *The Devon County School: Its Objects, Costs and Studies,* Exeter, 1862.

Fortescue, Hugh, Earl, *Public Schools for the Middle Classes,* London, 1864.

Foster, John, *Class Struggle and the Industrial Revolution: Early Industrial Capitalism in Three English Towns,* London, 1974.

Fraser, Derek, 'Education and Urban Politics, c. 1832–85', in Reeder D. (ed.), *Urban Education in the Nineteenth Century,* London, 1977.

Fraser, Derek, *Urban Politics in Victorian England: the structure of politics in Victorian Cities,* Leicester, 1976.

Freeman, A. B., *Bristol Worthies,* second series, Bristol, 1909.

Gash, Norman, *Politics in the Age of Peel: a Study in the Techniques of Parliamentary Representation, 1830–50,* London, 1953.

Gash, Norman, *Reaction and Reconstruction in English Politics, 1932–52,* Oxford, 1955.

Gash, Norman, *Mr Secretary Peel,* Cambridge, Mass., 1961.

Gill, Conrad, 'Birmingham under the Street Commissioners, 1769–1851', *University of Birmingham Historical Journal,* II, 1947–8.

Girdlestone, Edward, 'The Improved Administration of Existing Charitable Funds, by their Application to the Endowment of Parochial Schools', *Transactions of the National Association for the Promotion of Social Science,* London, 1859.

——, Report of the Proceedings at the Ceremony of Laying the Foundation Stone of St Thomas Charterhouse New School Building —— by the Rt Hon. W. E. Gladstone, M.P. . . . , London, 1856. (Copy in the D.E.S. Library.)

—— , Victoria History of the Counties of England: Gloucestershire, II, London, 1907.

Gomez, G., 'The Endowed Schools Act, 1869 —— a Middle-class Conspiracy? The South-west Lancashire Evidence', *Journal of Educational Administration and History,* University of Leeds, VI, No. 1, January 1974.

Gordon, Peter, 'The Endowed Schools and the Education of the Poor', *Durham Research Review,* No. 17, September 1966.

Gosden, P. H. J. H., *The Development of Educational Administration in England and Wales,* Oxford, 1966.

Green, T. H., *Works* (ed. Nettleship, R. L.), 3 volumes, London, 1888.

Gregory, Robert, *Do Our National Schools Provide for All Whom They Ought to Train?* Letter to the Archbishop of Canterbury, London, 1865.

Griffith, George, *The Endowed Schools of Worcestershire and Their Fulfilment,* London, 1852.

Griffith, George, *History of the Free Schools, Colleges, Hospitals and Asylums of Birmingham, and Their Fulfilment,* London, 1861.

Griffith, George, *The Endowed Schools of England and Ireland, Their Past, Present and Future,* London and Stourbridge, 1864.

Griffith, George, *Going to Markets and Grammar Schools,* 2 volumes, London, 1870.

Griffiths, A. R. G., 'The Irish Board of Works and the Famine Years', *Historical Journal,* XIII, No. 4, 1970.

Grounds, A. D., *A History of King Edward VI Grammar School,* Retford, Workshop, 1970.

Guttsman, W. L. (ed.), *A Plea for Democracy: an edited selection from the 1867 Essays on Reform, and Questions for a Reformed Parliament,* London, 1967.

Hadden, R. H., *Reminiscences of William Rogers,* London, 1880.

Halévy, Elie, *The Liberal Awakening,* London, 1961.

Halévy, Elie, *The Triumph of Reform,* London, 1961.

Halévy, Elie, *The Victorian Years, 1841–95,* London, 1961.

Hamer, D. A., *Morley, Chamberlain and National Education,* London, 1968.

Hare, Thomas, *Treatise on the Election of Representative,* London, 1859.

Hanham, H. J., *Elections and Party Management: Politics in the Time of Gladstone and Disraeli,* London, 1959.

Harrison, Brian, 'Philanthropy and the Victorians', *Victorian Studies,* IX, No. 4, June 1966.

Hart, Jenifer, 'Nineteenth-century Social Reform: a Tory Interpretation of History', *Past and Present,* XXXI, 1965.

Hart, Jenifer, 'The Genesis of the Northcote-Trevelyan Report', in G. Sutherland (ed.), *Studies in the Growth of Nineteenth-century Government,* London, 1972.

Harvie, Christopher, *The Lights of Liberalism, University Liberals and the Challenge of Democracy, 1860–86,* London, 1976.

Hans, Nicholas, *New Trends in English Education in the Eighteenth Century,* London, 1951.

Heeney, Brian, *Mission to the Middle Classes,* London, 1969.

Hennock, E. P., *Fit and Proper Persons,* London, 1973.

Henriques, U. R. O., *Religious Toleration in England, 1787–1833,* London, 1961.

Higginson, J. H., 'The Evolution of "Secondary Education" ', *British Journal of Education Studies,* XX, No. 2, 1972.

Hill, Alfred (ed), *Essays upon Educational Subjects, read at the Educational Conference of June 1857,* London, 1857.

Hill, C. P., *The History of Bristol Grammar School,* London, 1959.

Hobhouse, Arthur, *The Dead Hand,* London, 1880.

Hobsbawm, E. J., and Rudé, G., *Captain Swing,* London, 1969.

Hobsbawm, E. J., *Industry and Empire,* London, 1974.

Hodgkinson, George G., 'Education, Endowments and Competition', *Blackwood's Magazine,* CX, No. DCLXIX, July 1871.

Honey, J. de S., *Tom Brown's Universe: the development of the Victorian Public School,* London, 1977.

Hook, Walter Farquar, *On the Means of Rendering More Efficient the*

Education of the People, London, 1846.

Horn, Pamela, *Education in Rural England, 1800–1914*, London, 1978.

Hudson, K., *Patriotism with Profit: British Agricultural Societies in the Eighteenth and Nineteenth Centuries*, London, 1972.

Hughes, Edward, 'Civil Service Reform', *History*, XXVII June 1942.

Hughes, K. M., 'A Political Party and Education: Reflections on the Liberal Party's Educational Policy, 1867–1902', *British Journal of Educational Studies*, VIII, May 1960.

Hurt, John, *Education in Evolution*, London, 1971.

Hussey, R. A., *Letter to Thomas Dyke Acland: Diocensan Schools for the Middle Classes*, London, 1839.

Icely, H. E. M., *Bromsgrove School through Four Centuries*, Oxford, 1953.

Jameson, John, *The History of the Royal Belfast Academical Institution, 1810–1960*, Belfast, 1959.

Johnson, J. R. B., 'Administration in Education before 1870: patronage, social position and rôle', in Sutherland, G. (ed.), *Studies in the Growth of Nineteenth-century Government*, London, 1972.

Jones, D. K., 'The Educational Legacy of the Anti-Corn Law League', *History of Education*, III, No. 1, Janaury 1974.

Jones, E. L., *Agriculture and the Industrial Revolution*, Oxford, 1974.

Jones, Ernest, *Notes to the People*, London, 1851.

Jones, Gareth Elwyn, *Controls and Conflicts in Welsh Secondary Education, 1889–1944*, Cardiff, 1982.

Jordan, W. K., *The Charities of London, 1480–1660*, London, 1960.

Jordan, W. K., *The Charities of Rural England, 1480–1660*, London, 1961.

Jordan, W. K., *Philanthropy in England, 1480–1660*, London, 1959.

Kay-Shuttleworth, Sir James P., *Education Essential to the Success of Trade and Commerce*, Manchester, 1854. (Copy in John Rylands Library, Manchester.)

Kay-Shuttleworth, Sir James P., *Medical and Middle-class Education: an address . . .* , Manchester, 1856.

Kay-Shuttleworth, Sir James P., *Public Education as Affected by the Minutes of the Committee of Privy Council, from 1846 to 1852*, London, 1853.

Kay-Shuttleworth, Sir James P., *Four Periods of Public Education*, London, 1862.

Keeton, George W., *The Modern Law of Charities*, London, 1962.

Kirk, K. E., *The History of the Woodard Schools*, London, 1937.

Kissack, Keith, *Monmouth: The Making of a County Town*, London, and Chichester, 1975.

Kitchener, F. E., *Rugby Memoirs of Archbishop Temple, 1857–69*, London, 1907.

Lambert, Royston, *Sir John Simon, 1816–1904, and English Administration*, London, 1963.

Lambert, Royston, 'Central and Local Relations in mid-Victorian England: the Local Government Act Office', *Victorian Studies*, VI, No. 2, December 1962.

Lamport, Revd William, 'Proposals for the Further Improvement of

Agriculture', in, *Letters and Papers on Agriculture, etc., Selected from the Correspondence of the Bath and West of England Society . . . ,* Bath, 1802.

Lang, Andrew, *Life, Letters and Diaries of Sir Stafford Northcote, First Earl of Iddesleigh,* London, 1899.

Latimer, John, *The History of the Society of Merchant Venturers of the City of Bristol, . . . ,* Bristol, 1903.

Lawson, John, *A Town Grammar School through Three Centuries,* Oxford, 1963.

Layton, David, *Science for the People: the origins of the school science curriculum in England,* London, 1973.

Lee, J. B., *Middle-class Education and the Working of the Endowed Schools Act,* with an introductory note by the Rt Revd the Lord Bishop of London (F. Temple), London, 1885.

Leese, John, *Personalities and Power in English Education,* London, 1950.

Lewis, R. A., 'Edwin Chadwick and the Administrative Reform Association, 1854–6, *University of Birmingham Historical Journal,* II, 1949–50.

Lewis, William, *A Century of Agricultural Progress, 1777–1877,* Bath, 1879.

Levi, Leone, *Wages and Earnings of the Working Classes,* London, 1867.

Loudon, J. C., *The Utility of Agricultural Knowledge to the Sons of the Landed Proprietors of England,* London, 1809.

Lowe, Robert, *Middle-class and Primary Education,* two speeches delivered at the Annual Dinner of the Liverpool Philomathic Society, and at the conference on Education at the Town Hall, 22 and 23 January, London, 1868.

Lowe, Robert, *Speeches and Letters on Reform,* London, 1868.

Lubenow, William C., *The Politics of Government Growth: Early Victorian Attitudes to State Intervention, 1833–48,* Devon, 1971.

Lynch, P., and Vaizey, J., *Guinness's Brewery in the Irish Economy, 1759–1876,* Cambridge, 1960.

—— , *Brief Memorials of Lord Lyttelton . . .* with a biographical sketch contributed by the Rt Hon. W. E. Gladstone, London, 1876.

Lyttelton, George, Baron, *Ephemera,* London, 1865.

Maccoby, S., *English Radicalism, 1832–52,* London, 1935.

Maccoby, S., *English Radicalism, 1853–86,* London, 1938.

McCord, Norman, *The Anti-Corn Law League,* London, 1958.

MacDonagh, Oliver, *Early Victorian Government, 1830–70,* London, 1977.

MacDowell, R. B., *Public Opinion and Government Policy in Ireland, 1801–46,* London, 1952.

MacDowell, R. B., *British Conservatism, 1832–1914,* London, 1959.

Machin, G. I. T., 'Gladstone and Nonconformity in the 1860s: the Foundation of an Alliance', *Historical Journal,* XVII, No. 2, 1974.

McElligott, T. J., *Education in Ireland,* Dublin, 1968.

Mack, E. C., *Public Schools and British Opinion, 1789–1860,* London, 1938.

Mack, E. C., *Public Schools and British Opinion, since 1860,* New York,

1941.

Magnus, Philip, *Gladstone: a biography,* London, 1954.

Marcham, A. J., 'The Birmingham Education Society and the 1870 Education Act', *Journal of Educational Administration and History,* VIII, 1, 1976.

Martin, A. P., *Life and Letters of the Rt Hon. Robert Lowe, Viscount Sherbrooke,* two volumes, London, 1893.

Martineau, Harriet, *The Endowed Schools of Ireland,* London, 1859.

Martineau, Harriet, 'Middle-class Education: I. Boys; II. Girls', *Cornhill Magazine,* X, July–December 1864.

Marsh, P. T., *The Victorian Church in Decline: Archbishop Tait and the Church of England,* London, 1969.

Marsh, P. T., 'The Primate and the Prime Minister: Archbishop Tait, Gladstone and the National Church', *Victorian Studies,* IX, No. 2, December 1965.

Meacham, Standish, 'The Church in the Victorian City', *Victorian Studies,* XI, No. 3, March 1968.

Miall, Arthur, *Life of Edward Miall,* London, 1884.

Mill, J. S., 'The Middle Class: a review of "Democracy in America" (de Tocqueville)', *Edinburgh Review,* October 1840.

Mill, J. S., *Representative Government,* Everyman edition, with an introduction by A. D. Lindsay, London, 1910.

Miller, Dr J. C., *The Church of England in Birmingham: a letter to the Hon and Revd G. M. Yorke,* Birmingham, 1864.

Milton, John, *Prose Writings,* with an introduction by K. M. Burton, Everyman edition, London, 1927.

Mingay, G. E., *Landed Society in the Eighteenth Century,* London, 1963.

Mingay, G. E. (ed.), *The Victorian Countryside,* two volumes, London, 1981.

Mitchell, Duncan, 'Social Mobility in Nineteenth-century Devon', *Agricultural History Review,* VII, 1959.

Moneypenny, F., and Buckle, G. E., *Life of Benjamin Disraeli, First Earl of Beaconsfield,* six volumes, London, 1910–20.

Morley, John, *Life of William Ewart Gladstone,* three volumes, London, 1903.

Morley, John, *Life of Richard Cobden,* London, 1906.

Mortimer, James, 'A plea for a great Agricultural School', *Special Reports on Educational Subjects,* VIII, Board of Education, 1902.

Morell, J. D., *On the Progress of Society in England, as Affected by the Advancement of National Education,* London, 1859.

Mowat, Charles Loch, *The Charitable Organization Society, 1869–1913,* London, 1961.

Mumford, Alfred A., *The Manchester Grammar School, 1515–1915: A Regional Study of the Advancement of Learning in Manchester since the Reformation,* London, 1919.

Mumford, W. A., *William Ewart, M.P.: a Portrait of a Radical,* London, 1960.

Murphy, James, *The Religious Problem in English Education: the Crucial*

Experiment, London, 1959.

Musgrove, Frank, 'Middle-class Education and Development in the Nineteenth Century', *Economic History Review,* XII, 1959.

Musgrove, Frank, 'Middle-class Schools and Families, 1800–1880', in Musgrove, P. W. (ed.), *Society, History and Education, a Reader,* London, 1970.

Namier, Lewis, *England on the Eve of the American Revolution,* London, 1931.

Neale, R. S., 'Class and Class-consciousness in early Nineteenth-century England: three classes or five?' *Victorian Studies,* X, No. 2, 1968.

Neale, W. G., *At the Port of Bristol, I, Members and Problems, 1848–99,* Bristol, 1968.

Neate, Charles, 'Endowments', *Macmillan's Magazine,* XXII, September 1870.

Nettleship, R. L., *Thomas Hill Green: a Memoir,* London, 1906.

New, Chester, *The Life of Lord Brougham to 1830,* Oxford, 1961.

Newsome, David, *History of Wellington College,* London, 1959.

Newsome, David, *Godliness and Good Learning,* London, 1961.

Northcote, Sir Stafford, 'A Few Words on Water', *Bath and West Society Journal,* 1855.

Orwin, C. S., and Whetham, E. H., *A History of British Agriculture, 1846–1914,* London, 1964.

Owen, David, *English Philanthropy, 1660–1960,* Oxford, 1965.

Parkin, G. R., *Life and Letters of Edward Thring,* London, 1898.

Parkin, R., 'The Central Society of Education, 1836–40', Educational Administration and History Monographs, No. 3, Leeds, 1975.

Patterson, H. Temple, *Radical Leicester: a History of Leicester, 1780–1850,* Leicester, 1954.

Pawson, H. Cecil, 'A Plan of an Agricultural and Experimental Farm in Northumberland', *Agricultural History Review,* VIII, 1960.

Peacock, Thomas Love, *Crotchet Castle,* London, 1831.

Percival, Alicia, *Very Superior Men: some early nineteenth-century headmasters and their achievements,* London, 1973.

Percival, J. (Bishop of Hereford), Introduction to J. J. Findlay (ed.), *Arnold of Rugby* (q.v.), London, 1925.

Perkin, Harold J., 'Middle-class Education and Employment in the Nineteenth Century: a Critical Note', *Economic History Review,* XIV, 1961.

Perkin, Harold J., *The Origins of Modern English Society, 1780–1880,* London, 1972.

Petty, Sir William, *The Advice of W. P. to Mr Samuel Hartlib for the advancement of some particular parts of learning,* London, 1647.

Pillips, J. Rowland, 'The Municipal Government of London', *Edinburgh Review,* CXLII, October 1875.

Platts, A., and Hainton, G. H., *Education in Gloucestershire: a Short History,* Gloucester, 1954.

Pollard, Hugh M., *Pioneers of Popular Education, 1760–1850,* London, 1956.

Powles, John Endell (J.E.P.), *The Free Grammar School of William Jones at*

Monmouth: Statement and Suggestions, Newport (no date). (Copy in Newport (Gwent) Reference Library.)

'A Practical Man', *Public and Middle-class School Education: What It Is and What it Should Be*, London, 1865. (Copy in D.E.S. Library.)

Pratt, A. T. C., *People of the Period*, two volumes, London, 1897.

Reader, W. J., *Professional Men*, London, 1966.

Reardon, Bernard M. G., *From Coleridge to Gore: a Century of Religious Thought in Britain*, London, 1971.

Redlich, Josef, and Hurst, Francis W.,*The History of Local Government in England*, London, 1958.

Reeder, David (ed.), *Urban Education in the Nineteenth Century*, London, 1977.

Reid, T. Wemyss, *Life of the Rt Hon. W. E. Forster*, two volumes, London, 1888.

Richards, Eric, 'The Leviathan of Wealth: West Midlands Agriculture, 1800–1850', *Agricultural History Review*, XXII, Part II, 1974.

Richter, Melvin, *The Politics of Conscience: T. H. Green and his Age*, London, 1964.

Roach, J. P. C., 'Victorian Universities and the National Intelligentsia', *Victorian Studies*, III, No. 2, December 1959.

Roach, J. P. C., *Public Examinations in England, 1850–1900*, Cambridge, 1971.

Roach, J. P. C., 'Middle-class Education and Examinations: Some Early Victorian Problems', *British Journal of Educational Studies*, X, No. 2, May 1962.

Roberts, David, *Victorian Origins of the British Welfare State*, New Haven, 1960.

Robinson, H. G., *A Sketch of the Reasons for Establishing Training Colleges for Teachers of Schools above the Elementary . . .*, London, 1875. (Copy in Kay-Shuttleworth Papers, John Rylands Library, Manchester.)

Roderick, Gordon W., and Stephens, Michael D., *Education and Industry in the Nineteenth Century*, London and New York, 1978.

Robson, William A., Jennings, W. Ivor, and Laski, Harold, J. (eds.), *A Century of Municipal Progress, 1835–1935*, London, 1935.

Rodgers, Brian, 'The Social Science Association, 1857–86', *The Manchester School*, XX, No. 3, 1952.

Rogers, P. W., *A History of Ripon Grammar School*, Ripon, 1954.

Rubinstein, W. D., 'Wealth, Élites and the Class Structure of Modern Britain', *Past and Present*, No. 76, August 1977.

Russell, Sir E. John, *A History of Agricultural Science in Great Britain, 1620–1954*, London, 1966.

Russell, George W. E., *Letters of Matthew Arnold, 1848–88*, two volumes, London, 1895.

St John, J. A., *The Education of the People*, London, 1858.

Sanderson, Michael, 'The Grammar Schools and the Education of the Poor, 1786–1840', *British Journal of Educational Studies*, Vol. XI, No. 1, November 1962.

Sanderson, Michael (ed.), *The Universities in the Nineteenth Century*, London, 1975.

Sanderson, Sir T. H., and Roscoe, E. S., *Speeches and Addresses of Edward Henry, XVIth Earl of Derby, K. G., with a Prefatory Memoir by W. E. H. Leckey*, two volumes, London, 1894.

Sandford, E. G. (ed.), *Memoir of Archbishop Temple by Several Friends*, two volumes, London, 1906.

Sandford, E. G., *Frederick Temple, an Appreciation, with a biographical introduction by William Temple*, London, 1907.

Sandford, E. G., *The Exeter Episcopate of Archbishop Temple, 1869–85*, London, 1907.

Sargant, William Lucas, *Lord Lyttelton and Mr William Lucas Sargant on the Education of Birmingham and on Commissions of Inquiry*, Birmingham, 1865.

Seaborne, Malcolm, 'Early Theories of Teacher Education', *British Journal of Educational Studies*, XII, No. 3, October 1974.

Searby, Peter (ed.), *Educating the Victorian Middle Class*, London, 1982.

Sellman, R. R., Devonshire Village Schools in the Nineteenth Century, Devon, 1967.

Sheppard, Francis, *London 1808–70: the Infernal Wen*, London, 1971.

Simon, Brian, *Studies in the History of Education, 1780–1870*, London, 1960.

Simon, Brian, *Education and the Labour Movement, 1870–1920*, London, 1965.

Simon, Brian, and Bradley, Ian, *The Victorian Public School*, London, 1975.

Smith, Frank, *The Life and Work of Sir James Kay-Shuttleworth*, London, 1923.

Smith, J. W. Ashley, *The Birth of Modern Education: the contribution of the Dissenting Academies, 1660–1800*, London, 1954.

Smith, Paul, *Disraelian Conservatism and Social Reform*, London, 1976.

Spring, David, 'The English Landed Interest in the Age of Iron and Coal, 1830–80', *Journal of Economic History*, XI, No. 1, Winter 1951.

Stanley, A. P., *Life and Correspondence of Thomas Arnold*, London, 1844.

Stansky, Peter, 'Lyttelton and Thring: a study in nineteenth-century education', *Victorian Studies*, V, No. 3, March 1962.

Staunton, Harold, *The Great Schools of England*, London, 1869.

Stenton, M., *Who's Who of British Members of Parliament, 1832–85*, London, 1976.

Stephens, W. B. (ed.), *A History of the County of Warwick, VIII, The City of Birmingham*, London, 1964.

Stewart, W. A. C., *Progressives and Radicals in English Education, 1750–1970*, London, 1972.

Stone, Lawrence, 'Literacy and Education in England, 1640–1900', *Past and Present*, No. 42, February 1969.

Sturt, Mary, *The Education of the People*, London, 1967.

Sutherland, Gilliam (ed.), *Arnold on Education*, London, 1974.

Sutherland, Gillian (ed.), *Studies in the Growth of Nineteenth-century Government*, London, 1972.

Sutherland, Gillian, 'Secondary Education: the Education of the Middle Classes', in Sutherland, Gillian (ed.), *Government of Society in Nineteenth-century Britain: Commentaries on British Parliamentary papers: Education,* Dublin, 1977.

Sutherland, James, 'Our Grammar Schools: 1. As They Were; 2. As They Are; 3. As They Ought To Be, *Gentleman's Magazine,* I, New Series, June–November 1868.

Sylvester, David, *Robert Lowe and Education,* Cambridge, 1974.

Temple, Frederick, 'National Education', in *Oxford Essays,* Oxford, 1856.

Temple, William, *Life of Bishop Percival,* London, 1921.

Tholfsen, Trygve R., 'The Artisan and the Culture of Early Victorian Birmingham', *University of Birmingham Historical Journal,* IV, 1953–4.

Tillyard, A. I., *A History of University Reform, from 1800 A.D. to the present time,* Cambridge, 1913.

Thompson, David M., 'The 1851 Religious Census: Problems and Possibilities', *Victorian Studies,* XI, No. 1, September 1967.

Thompson, David M. (ed.), *Nonconformity in the Nineteenth Century,* London, 1972.

Thompson, E. P., *The Making of the English Working Class,* London, 1963.

Thompson, F. M. L., *English Landed Society in the Nineteenth Century,* London, 1963.

Thompson, Harry S., *Agricultural Progress and the Royal Agricultural Society,* London, 1864.

Thornton, F. V., *The Education of the Middle Classes in England,* London, 1862.

Tompson, Richard, *The Charity Commission in the Age of Reform,* London, 1979.

Trevor, Meriel, *The Arnolds: Thomas Arnold and his Family,* London, 1973.

Tusser, Thomas, *A Hundreth good pointes of Husbandrie,* London, 1557.

Vincent, J. R. (ed.), *Disraeli, Derby and the Conservative Party: the Political Journals of Lord Stanley, 1849–69,* London, 1978.

Vincent, J. R., *The Formation of the Liberal Party, 1857–68,* London, 1972.

Walker, W. G., *A History of the Oundle Schools,* London, 1956.

Wainwright, David, *Liverpool Gentlemen: A History of Liverpool College . . . , from 1840,* London, 1960.

——, *Proceedings at the Opening of the West Riding Proprietary School, August 6 1834,* Wakefield, 1834.

Ward, W. R., *Victorian Oxford,* Oxford, 1965.

Warlow, William Meyler, *A History of the Charities of William Jones . . . at Monmouth and Newland,* Bristol, 1899.

Waterhouse, Rachel E., *The Birmingham and Midland Institute, 1854–1954,* Brimingham, 1954.

Watkins, D. J., *The History of Sir Thomas Rich's School, Gloucester,* privately printed, 1966. (Copy in the Gloucester County Record Office, Shire Hall, Gloucester.)

Webb, Sidney and Beatrice, *English Poor Law History,* London, 1929.

Webb, Sidney and Beatrice, *English Local Government from the Revolution* to the Municipal Corporations Act: the Manor and the Borough, Part II, 1908.

Wiener, M. J., *English Culture and the Decline of the Industrial Spirit*, Cambridge, 1981.

Williams, G. L. (ed.), *John Stuart Mill on Politics and Society*, Brighton, 1976.

Williams, Raymond, *The Country and the City*, London, 1973.

Woodard, Nathaniel, *A Plea for the Middle Classes*, London, 1848.

Woodard, E. L., The Age of Reform, 1815–70, Oxford, 1962.

Wyse, Thomas, *Speech of Thomas Wyse, Esq., M.P., on the Extension and Improvement of Academical, Collegiate and University Education in Ireland . . . delivered at Cork, November 13 1844*, London, 1845.

Wyse, Thomas, 'Education in the United Kingdom. Its Progress and Prospects', *Central Society of Education*, first publication of 1837.

Wyse, Thomas, *Education Reform; or the Necessity for a National System of Education*, 1, (there was no Volume II), London, 1836.

Index